KW-222-037

Contents

Preface

This book is the product of the friendship enjoyed for many years by the authors, and their meetings in London and Lagos. The book has benefited from the international travels of both authors who between them have visited some forty countries, mostly for educational reasons. The book itself has been written in Kuala Lumpur, Lagos, London and Nairobi.

It expresses the authors' observations of the communication problems, systems and solutions in many developing countries, contrasting them with the very different ones in the industrialised world.

It deals with the impact – either ineffective or harmful – of Western-style communication methods, and also brings out the inadequacies of communication in developing countries between the urban and rural sectors.

We hope the book will be enlightening and thought provoking, and may suggest solutions to the communication puzzle which confronts communicators in the countries which comprise the diversified industrialising world, so loosely termed the Third World.

D
2.6
JEF

Communication in Industrialising Countries

Frank Jefkins and Frank Ugboajah

WITHDRAWN
from
STIRLING UNIVERSITY LIBRARY

140763
7/87

MACMILLAN
PUBLISHERS

© F. Jefkins and F. Ugboajah, 1986

All rights reserved. No reproduction, copy or transmission
of this publication may be made without written permission.
No paragraph of this publication may be reproduced, copied
or transmitted save with written permission or in accordance
with the provisions of the Copyright Act 1956 (as amended).
Any person who does any unauthorised act in relation to
this publication may be liable to criminal prosecution and
civil claims for damages.

First published 1986

Published by *Macmillan Publishers Ltd*
London and Basingstoke
*Associated companies and representatives in Accra,
Auckland, Delhi, Dublin, Gaborone, Hamburg, Harare,
Hong Kong, Kuala Lumpur, Lagos, Manzini, Melbourne,
Mexico City, Nairobi, New York, Singapore, Tokyo*

ISBN 0-333-39330-9

Printed in Hong Kong

British Library Cataloguing in Publication Data
Jefkins, Frank
  Communication in industrialising countries.
  1. Mass media — Developing countries
  I. Title   II. Ugboajah, Frank Okwu
  302.2′34′091724   P92.2

ISBN 0-333-39330-9

Dedicated to our wives Frances and Junie.

1
Introduction

The South consists of scores of countries, mostly ones which have gained independence from colonialism since the Second World War. Some of the Asiatic ones also gained freedom from wartime occupation so that they have experienced domination from a second imperialist power. In some cases, economic associations have continued with former colonial powers, but others have shifted their relations to different nations of the North. For instance, Indonesia has favoured English-speaking nations rather than the former colonial Dutch.

Moreover, there are considerable differences between the economic stature of different 'developing' countries, largely because of the extent or lack of industrialisation. The more successful economies depend on the export of primary products: extractive and agricultural; industrial manufacturers; and tourism.

The South is also divided into Third and Fourth Worlds. (The First World consists of the democratic 'West' and the Second World of the communist 'East'). In the Third World are the developing countries (e.g. Nigeria), plus the more developed or newly industrialised countries (NICS such as Korea, Taiwan, Singapore), and the Fourth World is made up of the impoverished nations such as Bangladesh.

Even among the developing countries there are big differences and inequalities as can be seen among the countries of West Africa and the Caribbean.

It is not possible, therefore, to regard the South as a world of similarly developing countries. All the fifty countries of Africa, for instance, are quite individual.

A major problem is the complexity of races, ethnic groups, religions and languages within single countries. There are various reasons for these divisions, and many of them stem from the unfortunate effects of colonialism.

For instance, the frontiers created by colonists were ones which suited the conflicting interests of rival powers such as British, Dutch,

French, German, Spanish and Portuguese. The colonial map was drawn in contradiction of existing kingdoms. In West Africa, vertical lines were drawn through the horizontal formations of existing tribal lands so that today we find unnatural countries like Nigeria and Ghana which consist of ethnic groups which are split between neighbouring countries.

Populations are also infused with non-local people whose ancestors, such as Indians and Chinese, were introduced as indented labour to work on colonial enterprises. In the Caribbean the African slave was freed and the Indian was brought in to grow sugar. In southern and central Africa, the Indian was brought in to build railroads, in Fiji and Mauritius to grow sugar, while the Chinese have migrated all over the Far East and South East Asia, and even to the Caribbean. Developing countries are often populated not only by indigenous people but by migrants. The story of Africa is itself one of black migration. Some countries such as Kenya, Zambia and Zimbabwe are relatively new, peopled by ethnic groups which moved into these territories only shortly before or during colonial occupation. The Kenyan peoples were mostly nomadic. East and Central Africa did not have the long established kingdoms of West Africa which preceded the links with Europe which go back 700 years.

While the Arab nations have long cultural histories their industrial development has largely come with the discovery of oil, and the Gulf states saw a meteoric rise in economic status in the mid to late 20th century, particularly since the British pulled out of the Trucial States and the United Arab Emirates were formed. These petroeconomies have attracted numerous nationals to develop both the industries and the social and commercial infrastructure. In Kuwait, for instance, some 141 nationalities are represented, and a large international hotel may have staff drawn from as many as 120 countries. In addition to people from Arab countries (including Palestinians), populations are made up of Europeans, Americans, Indians, Pakistanis, Bangladeshi, Thais, Koreans, Filipinos, Chinese, Japanese and many others.

The main languages spoken are Arabic and English although neither may be widely read, and visual media such as television and video are popular. The communication problems in Arab countries are therefore great, although there has been a remarkable growth in the press, whether produced inside or outside the Middle East, but the Arabs have created communication problems since there are comparatively few Arabs but large numbers of immigrant workers.

Another situation is more recent, and is built upon the historical one. Colonial powers were mostly concerned with supplying their home countries with the natural products and the produce of colonies. They built harbours, warehouses, roads and railways to transport this wealth to Europe. Their towns were mostly for trading purposes. Very little infrastructure was created for the inhabitants of the colonies, although missionaries did develop schools and certain health services.

When Independence came, the new governments had to create new towns, roads, social and public services. Today we have cities like Nairobi and Jakarta which bear little resemblance to the former colonial capitals. All the modern internal infrastructure of roads, domestic airways, electricity, gas, telephones, postal services, schools, hospitals plus the administration by central, state and local government has been developed. Urbanisation and population explosions, the migration from rural areas to the city, and in some cases the breakdown of traditional village farming, have all created huge social and economic changes.

On top of all this, changes have been rapid and abrupt, and have not evolved over a century or more as in Europe. Whereas Britain had its Education Act in 1870, Nigeria introduced Universal Primary Education only a few years ago. The pace of change therefore imposes great strains on the communication processes. In certain cases there has been undue copying of the methods of the North, in others it has been necessary to take advantage of indigenous techniques.

All in all, communication in the developing world has been an untidy process of dealing with two levels of people, the literate and the illiterate, the rich or privileged and the poor who are often very poor.

In this book we shall dispense with all the convenient labels bestowed on the developing world by the people of the industrialised nations. They are mainly the convenient tags of politicians and economists, and are seldom used or even known by the people of these categorised countries. In these countries there is a remarkable range of development from simple pottery and weaving to the high technology of electronics and computers.

We shall therefore refer to the *industrialised countries* of the old world and the *industrialising countries* of the new world. And even some of that so-called new world is very old when we remember the thousands of years of Arab and Asiatic civilisations.

THE COMMUNICATION NEED

Throughout the industrialising world, inspired by independence, there has been need for communication to explain new ideas, new life styles, new industries, new products or services. There has been tremendous scope for public relations although this has sometimes been limited to government departments conscious of the need to educate people about social services or how to improve agricultural production. This official information work has been separate from government propaganda.

Moreover, the opportunity to use public relations has been blunted in two ways. The multi-nationals have either survived independence, or moved in as nations become more sophisticated, and they have tended to confine their public relations efforts to corporate and public affairs rather than to distributor and consumer relations. Some of it has been solely to maintain good relations with the authorities, and whether it was true public relations is another matter. Even British firms operate slush funds. Indigenous companies have often been confused by the recommendations of foreign management consultants who have listed public relations among desirable appointments without providing a job specification. Sometimes public relations has been lumped together with personnel management, so ignorant have management consultants been about public relations.

The result of this mis-advice led to uncertainty over the necessary skills and qualifications of applicants. Indigenous companies, including parastatals, in Africa have played safe by requiring applicants either to hold a degree (any degree!) or to have had journalistic experience. Few people in the countries concerned had experience or qualifications in public relations. Most training became on-the-job self-training.

Lack of understanding about the function of public relations, and absence of any job specification, led to appointments to fit the list of appointees recommended by the management consultants. Thus, public relations officers were appointed — to do what? It happened in African states in the '60s and '70s, and it is happening in the Gulf states in the '80s. So-called public relations officers are well-educated adult office boys who buy airline tickets for their bosses, meet company guests at the airport, and maybe write the odd news release. It has only been a clear management need to communicate, as when communication problems have arisen, e.g. with Arab banking, that the true role of the public relations officer has been discovered and allowed to develop.

FACTORS IN COMMUNICATION

There are major factors in communication which affect successful communications. They are not just local ones but concern international communications, for many ethnic groups are spread throughout the world and have to be reckoned with. Christian, Islamic, Buddhist, Hindu and other communities are often intermixed, and their members attach different meanings and values to certain words, colours and behaviour. Behaviour, for instance, may relate to dress, foods, festival days and alcoholic beverages, together with special attitudes towards children, marriage, the place of women in society and respect for and care of elders. There are today many Arab banks, but the Islamic attitude to interest as unearned money introduces a dimension into banking which was largely of Jewish origin. There was even a time when Christianity frowned on usury, but no doubt the Rothschild family ended that when they financed the various parties embroiled in the Napoleonic wars.

Riots were sparked off in Indonesia in 1984 by anti-government sermons in Muslim mosques, accusing General Suharto of ranging himself too closely with the wealthy Chinese and Christian minorities when new draft laws appeared to be anti-Islamic. Although Muslims form the majority of Indonesians, the government has long tried to resist Islamic pressures. The new legislation was aimed to harmonise ethnic relations in a country where the Chinese are not allowed to display signs in Chinese character signs, and have to adopt European names, this resulting from the attempt by Chinese Communists to take over the country some years ago. The five draft Bills aimed at creating a framework for an open society but provoked riots in Jakarta's poor dockland area, leaving 18 dead. The government's enlightened 'Pancasila' policy, in spite of the ruling Golkar party having four-fifths of its support from Muslims, had to fight accusations of being anti-Islamic. Even well-meaning attempts to establish racial harmony can be resisted.

Another example of the sensitive and volatile nature of race relations was seen in Malaysia when 120 members of the Sungei Buloh Indian Association met outside the famous Batu caves near Kuala Lumpur on October 16, 1984, to protest at a slur on their community.

The caves house a Hindu temple. The alleged insult had occurred in a locally published guide book *Kesusasteraan Melaya Klasik* which speculated on the origins of Indians. The reference was said to harm racial unity. Three hundred copies of the book were burned on a bonfire at the caves. This followed earlier criticism of the book and its author by the University of Malaya Tamil Language Society.

It is also curious how certain ideas are repeated in different societies, possibly because they had a common origin in the mists of time, or because they were either transmitted by voyagers and colonialists or adopted by foreigners. One such idea which could be significant in communication is the reaction to the number 'three'. In Britain it is idiomatic to say 'Two's company, three's none', while the superstitious Chinese believe it is unlucky to have three people in a picture. Very similar to these beliefs is the Arab saying that your neighbour is your enemy but your neighbour's neighbour is your friend!

LANGUAGE, LITERACY AND VOCABULARY

We have to be careful what we mean by literacy, and not be too quick to condemn illiteracy as if illiterates have little means of communication. As we shall see, 'illiterates' can often communicate very well indeed and in ways superior to those of conventional literates in the industrialised world. There is, in fact, oral and visual literacy as well as that associated with reading and writing. However, let us first consider the problems of dual and multi-language societies coupled with conventional literacy.

Literacy tends to be higher in Asiatic and Caribbean countries than in African and Arabic countries, but for different reasons. Wherever they may be found, the Chinese are great readers. After all, they did invent paper and some of the earliest forms of printing, and maybe they are right in regarding the rest of us as barbarians! In Hong Kong, for instance, there are 100 daily newspapers, and the wall newspapers of Beijing (Peking) have had a significant communication effect in modern China.

In the Caribbean it helps that there is usually a single European language such as English, Dutch, French or Spanish and the people have mostly lost the languages of their African or Asiatic ancestral homelands, although there may be local patois. Also, if a country is an island, it is easy for newspapers to be distributed quickly compared with Nigeria where hundreds of miles separate major cities. An interesting feature of newspapers like the Trinidad *Guardian* is their wealth of international news, and the interest Trinidadians (who have often travelled abroad or have relatives overseas) take in the outside world. The single language results in the black West Indian of West African descent having advantages over his modern-day cousins in West Africa who still speak tribal languages as well as European ones. The West Indian's standard of English and range of vocabulary is usually higher than that of even the reasonably well-educated West

African. In fact, the standard of education of the black West Indian is generally superior to that of black Americans, and if they emigrate to North America, 'the cold' as they call it, they are industrious and occupy skilled jobs.

The Speak Mandarin campaign launched in Singapore around 1980 seeks to promote Mandarin as the single Chinese language, in addition to English which is the national language. According to Chen Hung[1], principal of Ngee Ann Polytechnic, using Mandarin instead of the dozen or so dialects is 'an energy conservation exercise'.

Neighbouring Malaysia makes English the second language to Bahasa Malaysia. In this much larger country, where it is the government's ambition to quadruple the population to seventy million, the people are mostly Malay, Indian or Chinese, and whereas the majority of Singaporeans are Chinese, the Malays predominate numerically in Malaysia. Thus it is understandable that, while English continues to be the business language, with the majority of newspapers being printed in English (e.g. *New Straits Times,* the *Star,* and the *Malay Mail*) the government urges all people to learn the national Bahasa (language) Malaysia. The English language newspapers print 'know your Bahasa Malaysia' features with words in the two languages. There is therefore an inevitable confusion of business and private languages (including Chinese), which resembles the situation of the Irish, Scots and Welsh who have their own languages as well as English. The duality of languages is also emerging in the USA where immigrant languages like German, Italian and Polish had given way to English, but the arrival of so many Mexicans and Puerto Ricans has introduced Spanish as a second language in many parts of the country. Public notices can be seen in both languages.

From the above remarks it can be seem that language can be both an aid to literacy and a communication barrier between different ethnic groups. In many parts of the world English has become the leading link language, and in the late 20th century there have been interesting developments. The spreading influence of Amercian multi-nationals has been one reason for the adoption of English in other countries, and so has the EEC in Europe, while Japanese exporters have found it necessary to learn English. The Arabs, having to deal especially with the British and the Americans, have found it expedient to learn English. Throughout the world, English language newspapers are published and not merely for the benefit of English speaking expatriates and visitors. And perhaps remarkably, in a Moscow hotel the signs are in Russian and English. This may be very flattering to people from Britain, the Commonwealth and the USA, but it does mean that people all over the world have access to the language with the richest vocabulary. It is a far cry from the days when one had to know German in order to study economics!

One of the problems in countries where there are two or more languages, and especially where English is a second language, is the limited number of words in personal vocabularies. It is easier to extend one's vocabulary if only one language is used. Another problem occurs with translations when it is essential to give the translator the meanings of words which may be either technical jargon or which have no counterpart in the foreign language. This can happen even when translating from English into European languages.

Some languages, like Bahasa Malaysia as spoken in Malaysia and Indonesia or Yoruba in Nigeria, have a small number of words compared with an extensive and versatile language like English. In the Malay language there is even a lack of plurals so that it is necessary to say man-man instead of two men, and emphasis is achieved by similar reduplication.

From the media point of view the presence of many languages creates the weakness of small circulation vernacular newspapers in contrast to the big circulations attracted by a newspaper in a single language. Nevertheless, it is interesting to note that the continual increase in the number of newspapers is Nigeria now includes a number printed in Hausa or Yoruba. The same problem occurs on radio and television because if programmes from the same station are broadcast in various languages listeners have only limited air-time allotted to their particular language. With television it is possible to have sub-titles in another language.

Multi-language societies require notices, instructions and labels on products printed in, say, three different languages. This has presented marketing difficulties with products sold to villagers in large countries like Nigeria where people may be either illiterate or unable to read any of the languages printed on the label or package. With foods like milk powder or medicines this can lead to dangerous misuse of a product.

LANGUAGE OF COLOUR

In different parts of the world colours are of especial significance. Chinese restaurants the world over are characterised by their exuberant use of red. Green was the favourite colour of Prophet Muhammed and is therefore popular in Arab countries. Likewise, green is the house colour of Nigeria Airways, Nigerian shipping and of banks and business houses, doubtless because the Moslem Hausas are the largest ethnic group in Nigeria.

The Chinese have an interesting language of colours which has to be observed if one is to communicate with them. The Japanese have made mistakes in trying to sell products to the Chinese without first considering which colours would be acceptable. Pale blue sewing machines were not popular in Singapore! For the Chinese yellow or gold represents money and prosperity, red health and happiness, green long life and blue sadness.

The significance of colours is apparent in multi-racial societies, and an interesting study of this topic was made by undergraduates at the Institute Teknologi Mara, and the following is extracted from their report *The Role of Colours in the Malaysian Community*. While black symbolises courage for the Malays, it means evil for Indians and death for Chinese. Black generally has bad connotations such as Black Death, black magic, black market and blacklist. White, however, usually means peace and purity and is worn by both Muslim and Hindu religious elders although it is not favoured by the Chinese. Blue is liked by Malays as a colour representing beauty and liberty, but for the Chinese and Indians it means grief. Red is popular with all three races, symbolising prosperity and happiness for the Chinese, valour and might for the Malays, and being generally liked by the Indians. Yellow is the Malay royal colour and is used in talismen and amulets. To the Chinese yellow is the colour of joy and wealth (resembling gold), while for the Indians it is the colour likely to appease the gods. Green is liked by all three races, but especially by Muslims as already noted. It is happily the colour of the well-known Holiday Inn logo, usually written high on the building and in lights at night!

Certain colour combinations, such as black on yellow or orange, are popular in industrialised countries because they achieve maximum attention, but they may not appeal in other parts of the world even if they are borrowed from nature. A slightly different and successful combination in industrialising countries is the red on yellow used for the caps and labels of Maggi sauces.

An example of the failure of colours to communicate occurred in Botswana in 1984 when traffic signals were installed in Gaborone. They had to remain hooded until the authorities felt confident that motorists understood the meaning of red, amber and green. It is not obvious that red means stop. To the Western mind red means danger, while to the Chinese it means almost the opposite. It could have quite different meanings to rural Africans in Botswana, a country with no colour television, unless received from South Africa.

LANGUAGE OF SYMBOLS

A picture speaks louder than words, it is said, and a symbol is a kind of shorthand picture. Symbols communicate quickly and effectively, and they can be important in identifying companies and products. Those who travel will be familiar with the international symbols in hotels, shops, restaurants, airports and on highways. The simple English word STOP is often found in countries where another language is normally spoken, but generally a sign or symbol will be used, such as an arrow pointing in a certain direction.

Animals are popular symbols. National birds like the scarlet ibis of Trinidad, the mouflon of Cyprus, the falcon of Saudi Arabia, the garuda of Indonesia or the mythical bird from the ruins of Great Zimbabwe may be displayed. Sometimes they form part of company identity schemes and may feature in logos or, in the case of airlines, be painted on the tail-fins of aircraft.

The lion has been adopted as a powerful symbol for thousands of years, for example the Lion of Judaea and the one depicted on the famous gate at Micinea in Greece. MGM's roaring lion is a Hollywood legend. The Bank of China has its seated lions by the front

Fig. 1.1

entrances of its branches, and outside the Chinese emporiums in Hong Kong. It is also the symbol, in a different stance, of the Hong Kong and Shanghai Banking Corporation, and in Malaysia there is a Lion stout. At festival time the Chinese like to prance along the streets inside fierce lion-like costumes, rather like the traditional circus horse. For years a large figure of a lion stood outside Waterloo Station, and it now graces Westminster Bridge near County Hall.

In Britain a black cat is considered lucky, but a black cat is unlucky in Nigeria. Order a bottle of Guinness in Indonesia and the waiter is more likely to understand if you say 'a black cat beer' because in that country a black cat is featured on the label.

Similarly, an extra symbol used by Guinness Malaysia is a bulldog, and in Singapore it is a wolf. When Guinness tried to standardise the labelling in the two countries Singaporeans thought the new bulldog inferred an inferior product. Unfortunately a change from the familiar is often regarded as a change for the worse. Guinness had to revert to the acceptable wolf symbol for Singapore.

Together with the bulldog symbol on the Malaysian label is Chinese wording which describes the stout as Black Dog, and in China the slogan reads *Black Dog Beer Good For You.* In Chinese dialect the customer will ask for the Black Dog since there is no translatable equivalent of Guinness. The typical Guinness label (with the local company name) is extended at the top to include the bulldog label and the Chinese slogan.

The Red Cross symbolises the famous international voluntary aid organisation, except in Muslim countries where it is represented by the more acceptable green crescent. This makes use of the crescent adopted on many other symbols, including national flags in Muslim countries. With independence, the Malaysian Red Cross became the Red Crescent, the red being retained although the Malays are Moslems, but perhaps in deference to the Chinese and Indians.

The Christian cross symbol can be offensive to Arabs to the extent that the original typographical logo of Saudia (Saudi Arabian Airlines) had to be changed because inadvertently the design incorporated the optical illusion of a cross as shown here if the reader looks closely at the white space between the 's' and the 'a'.

Fig. 1.2

Once this was spotted a new logo was designed!

Fig. 1.3
This is the current logo of Saudi Arabian Airlines.

ABBREVIATIONS

In the press and in speech, abbreviations are very common, from the Caribbean to the Far East. They are different from those in industrialised countries where abbreviations are frequently used for the names of the companies and organisations, e.g. IBM, KLM, TUC and NUM. Place names and people's names are often reduced to initials. In the West Indies there is the habit of shortening words like T'dad for Trinidad, which allows a narrow column width in a newspaper to carry larger size headlines. In South East Asia and the Far East there are many familiar initials such as HK for Hong Kong, KL (very common) for Kuala Lumpur, and PNG for Papua New Guinea. Singapore is shortened to S'pore. Personal names may be reduced to the initials of forenames, for instance 'C.K'. The Asean press will also reduce the long names of countries as in the case of Indon for Indonesia.

Sometimes initials can be embarrassing and a company name may have to be changed to permit one which is more acceptable. MAL for Malaysian Airlines was inappropriate in Europe where mal is French for sickness as in mal-de-mer meaning sea sickness. Consequently, the airline changed its name to Malaysian Airline System with the initials MAS. On the other hand, whereas the Mass Transit Railway of Hong Kong sounded like a cattle truck service, MTR has become acceptable. In Singapore, construction of the underground railway system began with the bold use of MRT, for Mass Rapid Transit.

OTHER KINDS OF LITERACY

Mention was made earlier of kinds of literacy other than the ability to read and write. These are *visual* and *oral* literacy. These open up very interesting areas of communication, especially in Africa. They are rather like the blind man's heightened sense of hearing.

Visual literacy is the ability to remember things as mental pictures, a skill often lacking in Westerners. It applies, for instance, to remembering descriptions of people. A Western witness is often unable to give an accurate description of a person, whereas an African can be precise. The author has had many experiences of being recognised a long time after a previous encounter, even by hotel staff who meet thousands of guests in the course of a year.

Oral literacy is the ability to remember detailed information and be able to repeat it accurately. In Ghana, for instance, a street trader will act as a postman when he returns to his village to replenish his stocks. He will convey messages between villagers and their friends or relatives in the city, often very complicated ones about marriages or business deals. Yet this clearly very intelligent person can neither read nor write.

These two forms of communication confound the notion that illiterate people are unintelligent or unable to communicate and comprehend. An interesting example of this realisation is that 'illiterates' have been found capable of operating computers, and this opens up fascinating new possibilities in industrialising countries where computers can now be used quite easily when written communication was more difficult. Moreover, the computer uses universal languages and sophisticated programmes can be run without elaborate use of conventional literacy.

References

1 *Straits Times*, Singapore, October 13, 1984.

2
The Role of
Public Relations

In the opening chapter we have discussed some of the communication problems that exist in many parts of the industrialising South, and shown how they are often more complex or of ethnic origin compared to the industrialised North. These difficulties are often compounded by the presence of multi-ethnic, multi-language, multi-religion societies with varying levels of literacy. Nevertheless the principles of public relations remain identical, although the need, role and practice may differ from that in the industrialised world, and even from country to country and continent to continent. This makes the study of public relations even more fascinating and valuable, but first it is essential to establish a clear understanding of the nature of public relations, and to challenge some fallacies. Then we shall consider a comprehensive definition of public relations which can be applied internationally.

THE WORD 'FAVOURABLE'

An over-simplification commonly adopted in industrialising countries is that public relations is to do with 'favourable images', 'favourable climates of opinion' and with publishing and broadcasting information which is 'favourable' to an organisation. If that was what public relations was all about we would be in the propaganda business, and there would be no place for public relations. Of course it is nice to be liked and well thought of. Even a government prefers to be loved. But that has to be earned. A good reputation could be thrust upon people for it is what people believe it to be, not what we tell them it is, and there is a difference between the two.

Moreover, public relations has to deal with the real world in which things are not always favourable. Consequently, unfavourable situations have to be accepted, faced up to, and dealt with frankly and

14

honestly. A hotel can have a fire, an airline may have an air crash, the chairman may die, the train may be late, and power failures and water shortages are common occurrences in some countries. We cannot pretend that disasters have not happened. The important thing is that they are explained so that false stories do not appear in the media and that rumours do not spread. Sometimes, even disasters can be turned to good account if the organisation is seen to handle them honestly and efficiently.

So we cannot expect all news to be good news and in public relations we are not only concerned with good news. We are not apologists or pretenders that things are better than they are or have never happened. We do not put a gloss on things, act as trouble-shooters or try to throw up a defensive smoke-screen. To do so, as some unprofessional public relations officers do and some managements expect them to do, is to be counter-effective. Public relations is a powerful communication tool, but if it is to work successfully it must be credible. Unless our messages are believed they will fail to achieve their primary objective which is *understanding*.

UNDERSTANDING

Now we have arrived at the purpose of public relations. As will be explained further on, public relations is not selling, sales promotion, advertising and propaganda, and it may have nothing to do with marketing. It is a separate subject. Its aim is to achieve understanding through knowledge, and few things are more difficult to achieve than understanding. But selling, sales promotion, advertising and even propaganda can fail through lack of understanding, and understanding can be a necessary part of many aspects of the marketing strategy. In addition, there are many non-commercial organisations which do not engage in promotional activities, but still need to be understood.

Why is it necessary for an organisation to be understood, and how does public relations contribute to this? Understanding usually depends on overcoming the four negative states of *hostility, prejudice, apathy* and *ignorance*. Let us examine each of these in turn, and then the true nature of public relations should be apparent.

Hostility

People tend to be conservative, and to stick to the things they know best. In countries where life is simple and unsophisticated and where the majority of the people live on the land and exist in small village communities, they feel secure with traditions that may have persisted for centuries. Oil tankers, lorries, buses and cars may pass by on a modern highway, yet the villages do not change. One sees this all over Africa and Asia. Even when the young people of the village become educated and are attracted to the cities, many of their life styles remain even though they adopt Western values, dress differently and eat different food. Deep down the old traditions often remain, and they may have to live abroad to change their attitudes fundamentally. This is not to say that many of the old values are not good ones, such as respect for elders or healthy habits. However, some of the old ways are not so good, such as carrying water long distances when today it can be piped to communities, employing children on farms instead of sending them to school, working small plots of land when the cities need food and large-scale farming is necessary, or producing inferior crops or livestock when better strains and breeds are available.

Countries which have built new infrastructures since independence and can serve their people with roads, water, gas, electricity, hospitals, schools and other services can seldom do so without upsetting traditions and revolutionising life styles. Hostility towards some changes is inevitable.

Public relations techniques can be used and are, in fact, used to overcome hostility to new concepts. That is why public relations is such a necessary part of communication in industrialising countries. People in other parts of the world are often surprised that public relations exist in the developing South, forgetting that they take for granted life styles and public services which have been evolved gradually over the past 200 years compared to a mere 20 or 30 years in many ex-colonial states. The colonials seldom bothered beyond satisfying their own needs. Cities like Nairobi, Singapore and Jakarta are very different from those of the past. The hinterlands are now resembling those European countries with urbanisation catching up with that of Europe in the 19th century. But people have to understand the benefits of these changes, and they may well resent them. The sheer pace of change can be bewildering. A country like Nigeria now has domestic air services when it never had stage coaches. This leap into the 20th century occurs when the North is already beckoning the 21st.

Prejudice

People everywhere suffer from prejudices derived from upbringing and environment. Again, prejudice is a form of security, protecting people from the unknown, different and possibly dangerous. It is very difficult to overcome prejudices because they are deeply instilled in attitudes to life and to other people. In the industrialising countries they are not helped by legacies left by colonisation which often acted with disregard for conquered people. The artificial geographical borders of colonies created prejudices between tribes and nations, and these have been perpetuated by tragic ethnic disputes, jealousies, riots and sometimes civil war in ex-colonial countries. Public relations is one of the means of uniting people and reducing bitter prejudices to acceptable differences. We see evidence of the success of government information services in doing so in many countries. But it takes time. It took centuries in Britain, a century in Germany and Italy, while new problems with Hispanic people are now erupting in the USA and Britain has its problems with post-Second World War immigrants. The saying, 'prejudice dies hard', is sadly very true.

Thus prejudice is mostly based on fear, but as the American president Franklyn D. Roosevelt said in the '30s when combatting the American depression of that time, the American people had only to fear 'fear itself'. Public relations can destroy fear by familiarising people with new ideas, public services, products and commercial services. This is the information and educational role of public relations.

Apathy

Not only are people hostile and prejudiced but they can be apathetic to change. They are content with things as they are. They are fully occupied with their own affairs which are important things like their families, friends, homes, jobs and other personal interests. In rural areas, they care little about what goes on in the next village, and even less about the affairs of the distant town and city. This apathy is understandable, but it is the biggest obstacle to effective communication.

The nature of public relations is that it should be methodical, that is, planned and repetitive. It is therefore a powerful weapon for defeating apathy. Both government and commercial information services adopt persistent programmes, whether through the mass media, or through travelling cinemas and other mobile units. Entertainment can be coupled with this dissemination of information, thus attracting attention, interest and participation. Whether it is the government information service in Malaysia, or Whitehead's demonstrating their textiles in Malawi, a blend of showmanship and education can break down apathy.

Ignorance

Nobody knows it all, and few people know our particular subject better than we do. Ignorance about many things is inevitable, no matter how well educated or experienced we are. Most people are ignorant of the fact that there are fifty countries in Africa. Foreigners regard Britain as England when Britain actually comprises England, Scotland, Wales and Northern Ireland. How many people know the difference between southern and South Africa? Or the geographical location of the Arab states? Most people's ignorance is profound, and the public relations officer has to learn never to assume anyone knows anything about anything with which he has to deal. He must take nothing for granted, and must be a master of simple explanations.

The peoples of the industrialising nations are inevitably ignorant of a great many things outside their normal experience. This is not their fault. It does not mean they are unintelligent, or even uneducated. Perhaps the best meaning of being educated is that one is aware of one's ignorance and humbly one realises how much more there is to learn.

Public relations therefore faces a battle where ignorance is concerned, and it is true that a little knowledge is dangerous. We now come full circle for the purpose of our public relations process is to effect a transfer from the negative states of hostility, prejudice, apathy and ignorance to the positive states of sympathy, acceptance, interest and knowledge which leads to the ultimate aim of *understanding*.

DEFINITIONS

In the light of the discussion so far let us consider three definitions which are popular in the public relations world, and have been adopted universally.

> *Public relations practice is the deliberate, planned and sustained effort to establish and maintain mutual understanding between an organisation and its public.*

This definition of the (British) Institute of Public Relations emphasises that the purpose of public relations is not only the establishment of *understanding*, as we have said already, but of *mutual* understanding. We are not only concerned with transmitting messages, but of receiving them. Public relations is the intelligence service of an organisation, its ears and eyes as well as its voice. It is necessary to understand what people think and know, how well informed or misinformed they are about the organisation. We can monitor the media and note what is being published or broadcast about the organisation. We can collect suggestions and complaints. And we can use research techniques to discover opinions, attitudes and the extent or otherwise of awareness. All this means that we have to listen as well as speak. Public relations is two-way communication, unlike advertising or propaganda which tell people what we want them to read, hear or see. The response is the kind we seek, whereas in public relations other people may be conveying messages to us, some of which may be surprising, unexpected or possibly unfavourable.

However, the really significant words in the Institute of Public Relations definition are 'deliberate, planned and sustained effort'. Public relations activities should not be haphazard, but should be planned as a forward programme, and that means planned in advance for a period of time and usually for not less than a year. Of course, the plan can be flexible so that changes can be made if necessary, but time and money needs to be carefully planned and budgeted. This effort needs to be sustained as a continuous campaign. The author's own definition takes this a step further.

Public relations consist of all forms of planned communication outwards and inwards, between an organisation and its publics, for the purpose of achieving specific objectives concerning mutual understanding.

This is a slightly more businesslike definition on the management-by-objectives principle. The planned programme aims to achieve defined objectives. If there are precise objectives the success or otherwise in achieving these objectives can be assessed, either by observation and evidence, or by conducting a research survey. There is little point in spending time and money, effort and resources, on a public relations programme if it has no objectives and the results cannot be measured. Practical public relations is tangible. In the past public relations has been criticised for being intangible, but it is intangible only if no objectives have been set. Intangible public relations is a waste of time and money.

An even better definition is the Mexican statement which resulted from a World Assembly of Public Relations Associations which was held in Mexico City in August 1978. This states:

> *Public relations practice is the art and social science of*
> *analysing trends, predicting their consequences, counselling*
> *organisation leaders, and implementing planned programmes*
> *which will serve both the organisation's and the public interest.*

Not only does this very practical definition stress the need for *planning*, but it emphasises the need for initial research, clearly defines the advisory role of public relations, and points out that public relations activities should be *socially responsible*. Workmanlike, positive statements about the nature of public relations are contained in this definition. This shows a distinct move away from simplistic concepts about concentrating on favourable images. It was noticeable that, in his speeches during his year of office as president of the Institute of Public Relations, Peter Smith repeatedly quoted this definition in preference to the one normally attributed to the Institute of Public Relations. The four most significant aspects of the Mexican statement will now be discussed, but a more detailed study of marketing research will be found in Chapter 7.

PLANNING

Forward planning is not always understood in countries where the market or merchant mind is more used to immediate bargaining, dealing and selling, and when both the risk and the profit is more personal. The idea of investing, forecasting and planning to achieve future objectives, can be alien. This is found especially in regard to advertising, which is seen to be unnecessary and a challenge to personal selling ability. Linked with this is an attitude, often found in African communities, which contrasts with that of the industrial capitalist world. This attitude is one which accepts the past (although is little concerned with history beyond handed down traditions), lives absolutely in the present, and is unwilling to consider the future except with a certain fatalism. This is not utterly confined to the developing world: one finds a similar attitude in Greece where centuries of Turkish occupation, followed by war-time occupation and dictatorial government, has left the Greeks unwilling to contemplate the future very hopefully.

So what is the approach to public relations, having already commented on the naive devotion to achieving favourable this or that? It has to adopt the following six-point formula if it is to obey the process of transferring negative attitudes to positive ones. To do this the planning formula follows six logical stages which are similar to the steps outlined in the Mexican statement. The definition is virtually an international acceptance of the Six Point Public Relations Planning Model.

SIX POINT PLANNING MODEL

1 Appreciation of the *situation* or the communication audit.
2 Listing and determining the *objectives* which shall be given priority.
3 Defining the groups of *people* or *publics* to whom the public relations message must be communicated.
4 The *media* and *methods* which are best used to communicate the message to the defined publics in order to achieve the selected objectives.
5 The *budget*. What will it cost in time (staff salaries or consultancy fees), cost of materials (from news release headings to films, videos or mobile units plus expenses in transport, accommodation, hospitality and so on).
6 The assessment of *results*, as apparent from experience or observation, or as revealed by the use of research techniques. If there were set objectives the public relations should produce recognisable or measurable results. Thus we have tangible public relations.

Let us examine each of these in turn.

Appreciation of the Situation

Before a public relations campaign can be put into operation it is necessary to determine the extent of hostility, prejudice, apathy and ignorance. It is no use assuming that we know the answers. To do so is to accept the *mirror* image of the situation, that is what we (or our superiors) think is the image of the organisation which people outside the organisation have of it. We need to discover the current or actual perceived image, that is what others know or do not know, like or dislike about the organisation. Neither is likely to be a perfect image, and one of the aims of public relations is to create a correct image. That correct idea or impression depends on knowledge and experience, and an organisation can possess only the image it deserves. As we said at the beginning of this chapter we cannot invent a favourable image, but we can make sure that it is as good as it should be.

If the image is poor there can be two very different reasons for this bad situation. Either, people are misinformed, or the organisation has itself behaved badly and so created a bad image. In the latter case, the research will provide valuable feedback, and the public relations manager can report complaints and criticisms to management. When these faults have been corrected the public relations manager can make known the changes or improvements, and so earn for the organisation the image it deserves.

He cannot ignore the faults and pretend they do not exist. It is not his job to be an apologist. However, there may be cases when there are unfortunate experiences which have to be dealt with frankly. Faults may be temporary or unavoidable, and the task of the public relations officer will be to issue honest explanations. Members of the public may not like what has gone wrong, and an atmosphere of genuine hostility may exist, but when proper explanations are given — admitting responsibility — the hostility can be converted into acceptance, understanding, perhaps even sympathy, and possibly respect. It pays to take people into your confidence, not run away and go on the defensive. There is a saying that honesty pays, and this applies very much to the handling of difficult and often very *unfavourable* situations.

Sometimes people simply do not know how good the organisation is, and a true image has been lost by default. This is where the public relations programme can concentrate on telling the story of the organisation in order to gain credit for its achievements. It is foolish not to do this, or to assume that everyone already knows. Understanding is built on knowledge.

The research may produce surprising revelations about negative attitudes. There may, for instance, be something wrong with the corporate identity as was shown with the example in the previous chapter of the original Saudia logo. It could be that the company name is confusing or misleading, and a new name should be adopted. In some countries a British or American-sounding name may suggest greater efficiency than a local one, while in others a national name will be respected more than a foreign one. For instance, a better image has resulted from changing Barclays Bank in Nigeria to Union Bank, and in Trinidad to Republic Bank. Because of its operations in Asia, the United Africa Company was renamed UAC. But when Omo was changed to Daisy in Zambia people thought it was an inferior detergent.

On the other hand, the research may reveal unexpected strengths which can be developed further. An hotel owner may have thought his hotel had a good reputation for the food, only to find that guests found the car-parking facilities better than at other hotels. The store may be preferred because of its air-conditioning rather than its prices, the airline for the days of the week when it flies certain routes, or a product may be preferred because of the secondary use to which its container may be put.

Methods of Appreciating the Situation

The following are some of the methods which can be adopted. The marketing research methods are explained in Chapter 7.

1 By conducting opinion, attitude or image studies.

2 By monitoring the media to check what is being said about the organisation in the press or on television, press cuttings and monitored scripts being collected for this purpose.

3 By conducting personal interviews with employees, customers, clients, or distributors.

4 By asking customers to complete questionaires requesting opinions, appraisals or comments, as sometimes used by hotels and transportation companies.

5 By studying company results, sales and stock figures.

6 By studying general feedback such as complaints or suggestions received from customers or other members of the public.

Defining Objectives

Having analysed the situation it is now necessary to predict or consider the consequences of the situation as revealed, and to plan an objective campaign which will deal with the organisation's communication needs. A great many objectives may now present themselves, and at this stage they should all be listed even though for various reasons, such as the budget, they cannnot all be included in the final campaign plan. As the plan develops, priorities will emerge and certain objectives can be discarded. Let us now consider hypothetical objectives which might be set according to the results of our survey, or communications audit as it is sometimes called.

1 To change the image of the organisation   It may be that a company once famous for one product or service has now changed to providing something quite different. The old image may still linger and it is necessary to be literally 'off with the old and on with the new'. A typical example might be a firm which once made clocks but now makes computers.

2 To make politicians more aware of an organisation's activities This has been an essential public relations operation in countries like Zimbabwe where the entire economic political situation has changed with independence. During the past few years it has been necessary for companies to invite ministers and senior civil servants to visit them and to learn what they do. Conversely, it has been necessary for company managements to understand the plans, policies and requirements of government departments. This can also apply as indigenous industry develops in many countries, like Nigeria, where the economic thrust is towards national industries in place of imported foreign goods.

3 To create better management-employee relations This is a major communication problem which varies from country to country according to the kind of society. For instance, there is closer worker-management liaison in Germany than in master and servant class-oriented Britain, while Japan has great respect for elders and guaranteed lifetime jobs. The situation is very different in Third World countries. Right across and up and down Africa the management-employee relationship can be very different.

Take Zimbabwe and Nigeria as two very different examples. The one has a post-colonial situation in the sense that management, even ownership, continues to be white, and multi-racial attitudes prevail. This exists in a different way in Nigeria where white expatriates may conduct management, but a very different and fairly distant post-colonial history is replaced by largely indigenous industry, trade and commerce. Attitudes by and to management differ. But in both cases there is need to bring management and employees closer together, and increasingly this is recognised as being beneficial to the success of the enterprise.

4 To educate the market about new products As societies develop, and the cash economy grows, increased buying power makes it possible for more people to buy more goods. This is aided by the spread of public services such as electricity, liquid gas, water, telecommunications, transport and urbanisation with its stores and supermarkets. More people can absorb more goods and trade flourishes. There is progress from the economic necessities of life, from food, clothes and shelter to more sophisticated goods. Many of these new products may be strange. Their novelty may appeal to some, they may represent better standards of living, but advertising alone may not sell them. They may have to be explained, and market education — a primary purpose of public relations — will be necessary. Sometimes it may be very important to create confidence in an indigenous product when previously people had confidence only in imported foreign products.

An enigma exists here. The foreign product may be considered superior to the home produced one. This may have been true once, but the industrialising countries can often nowadays produce goods of equal quality, and usually more cheaply. For instance, the economic situation in Nigeria has encouraged the manufacture of products like detergents which are identical to expensive imports.

In Malaysia, which is rich in raw materials, HICOM has set up a motor-car plant to produce the Proton Saga. The name of the car resulted from a public competition. Although there has been some Japanese assistance, the new car is not a foreign one assembled in Malaysia but one specially designed as a Malaysian vehicle. Before the car appeared there was much speculation about the price, and whether the arrival of the Proton Saga would mean that imported cars would cost more. There was need for market education, but the speculation in the press and in conversation (and the author was in Malaysia at the time) showed that the new enterprise had yet to adopt public relations techniques.

Throughout the industrialising world there must be hundreds of instances where the educational skills of public relations can be applied with great success to the introduction, establishment and business success of new home-produced goods. Their acceptance can contribute to the economic growth of the countries concerned. We are back to those four negative states of hostility, prejudice, apathy and ignorance which public relations can combat and convert into positive states. Here, too, is some justification for the use of the so often misused term 'favourable', for a favourable market situation is desirable. But it must be truly earned by the merits of the product, and this can be supported by national pride in ability to compete efficiently with imports.

This is not easy, and from the older industrialised countries can be quoted the story of the watch. Watch and clock making was historically a British craft. The old craftsmen resisted mechanisation and lost the trade to the Swiss, Germans and Americans who were prepared to adopt mass-production methods. The Swiss dominated the market. When imports were impossible, watch-making returned to Britain where watch factories were established. Fine watches were made. Some earned fame, as when Hillary used a British watch when he climbed Mount Everest. Then the whole watch industry changed, first with the digital and then the quartz. Today, the Japanese have beaten even the Swiss with watches ranging from Citizen to Seiko. Unhappily, the British never did regain confidence in the British watch, even though the Armed Forces adopted British instead of Swiss watches in the '60s. Could an industrialising country produce its own watches? India did, learning the craft rapidly from Japanese tutors, but then the Indians have a craft culture that goes back for centuries.

Other Objectives

A few examples have been discussed above, but there can be many more, and the reader may find it instructive to list those which apply to his own organisation, or to any other to which he may apply this exercise. Some may concern other matters such as the recruitment of staff, the launching of a share issue in a public company, the explanation of the services of a government department, the role and needs of a charity, or simply the success story of a go-ahead organisation.

Defining the Publics

It is all very well knowing what the situation is, and setting down objectives to achieve in order to deal with the situation, but to whom do we need to communicate the message?

We do not address 'the general public'. Nor do we address the broad market, as with advertising. Nor, as with so much advertising in industrialising countries, are we limited to media which perhaps reaches only a minority of the population. By that, the contrast is made with industrialised countries where there are thousands of newspapers read by people of different class or with special interests. As we shall see, public relations uses a diversity of media to reach all kinds of people, even in less sophisticated societies.

We have to define publics, or separate groups of people to whom messages should be directed, according to the nature of our product or service, and the demographic make-up of the country — what sort of people live in it. As a result the list of publics will differ. There is, however, a basic list of publics which can be looked at as a starting point. This can be adapted for any particular public relations programme in any particular country.

Basic List of Publics

The following are the eight standard publics.

1 The community   The community consists of our neighbours, the people living nearby who are affected by what the organisation does, or who may not know or understand what it does. Their attitudes could be very important, and these attitudes could be hostile or friendly. The community could be a source of staff or customers. The behaviour of the organisation could arouse hostility or respect. The behaviour of the people towards the organisation could affect the successful operation of the organisation.

Let us take some examples. Suppose the organisation was an airport. People living nearby might object to the noise of aircraft, traffic on the roads to the airport, or plans to extend the runways. The community surrounding an airport is as important a public as airlines, travel agents and passengers who may be impossible to service if there are not good relations with the local public. It may be necessary, for example, to ban or restrict night flights.

Another example might be a manufacturing company which has unpleasant effluent or waste, and in the interests of the community it may have to listen to complaints, and adopt measures to avoid pollution or damage to the environment. It will need to explain these measures to the community.

2 Prospective employees   Where do they come from, and how can they be reached? Do they live locally, are they employed by rival firms, are they students in schools, colleges or universities, and are they far away and perhaps overseas? The organisation has to make itself known and understood as a desirable employer by all these people, whoever they are and wherever they are. Recruitment advertising is not enough, and it could fail to attract the right response if the organisation is not known and properly understood.

3 The staff   This public can be sub-divided into as many publics as there are grades of staff. Some messages may apply to all, but different messages may have to be aimed at, say, executives and transport drivers or salesmen.

4 Suppliers of goods and services   All organisations buy numerous goods and services, from public services to raw materials and professional services. They are better able to supply if they understand the buyer and the buyer's needs. This can apply to the waste disposal service as much as to the supplier of ingredients, chemicals, parts and accessories or outside services such as lawyers, accountants and advertising agents. They all need to be kept informed.

5 The money market   As the commercial structure develops, and banking, insurance, shareholders and stock exchanges become increasingly important facets of business, those in the 'money market' combine as a public. Ultimately, this can lead to financial relations of seeking shareholders, annual reports and accounts, dividend distribution, mergers, amalgamations and even take-over bids. Very often, money may have to be borrowed by one means or another, and the good reputation of the organisation will be vital. But how well is the organisation known and understood?

6 Distributors   Trade may depend on simple bargaining and on buying cheap and selling dear, and that may be all right at the level of street markets and bazaars, but if one is setting up a factory or any other business a different situation exists. Profit depends on regular sales and the take-up of capacity. That capacity may consist of the seats on the aircraft of an airline, the rooms of a hotel and the seating of the restaurant, the number of rolls of cloth produced by a mill, the crates or barrels of beer produced by a brewery, or the number of cars that come off the production line. The ability of the supply to be taken up by demand depends on the efficiency of the chain of distributors. That chain may consist of wholesalers, agents, retailers and possibly exporters and foreign importers. Three things are usually fundamental to the efficient operation of the chain of distribution: a well-trained, enthusiastic and well paid sales force to sell to the distributors; good trade terms (supported in some cases by good after-sales service); and effective advertising to persuade consumers to buy the goods from the shops. Public relations is necessary to perfect the chain. The distributor needs to understand, trust and respect both the supplier or manufacturer and his products and services. In so doing he will be better able to sell to the customer. Thus, as part of the marketing strategy, successful salesmen and satisfied customers depend on good dealer relations, and part of the public relations programme can be aimed at this public with the aim of achieving good dealer relations.

Suppose the organisation is a national tourist organisation. One of its publics will be those who distribute transport and holiday services, the airlines and travel agencies. If the man behind the counter selling air tickets and packaged holidays is knowledgeable about the destination he will be better able to convince the customer and sell his agency services. But how well does he know the attractions of Mauritius, Barbados or Thailand, beyond what he can read (like the customer) in the holiday brochure? Many tourist boards arrange visits to their country by parties of travel agents and travel journalists.

7 Customers and users   Now we come to those who buy the product or service, but this is not just the broad general public who read the press advertisements, watch or listen to broadcast commercials, or see the posters. This buying public can be broken down into many categories such as children, housewives, husbands, specialist buyers and those of various incomes.

8 Opinion leaders   Finally we come to all those people, with authority and knowledge or otherwise, who express opinions which can damage or benefit the organisation and its products or services according to the advice they give to other people. This advice can be laced with hostility and prejudice or sympathy and understanding. The correctness of the advice will depend on the extent to which they have been informed and educated. That is a public relations task. Opinion leaders can be anyone who is in a position to give advice or express opinions. They can include parents, teachers, clergymen, politicians and so on as well as journalists and broadcasters. It is therefore essential to define who are the people most likely to influence others with opinions about a given product or service. They may be people who are already expressing opinions or those who might or should.

Such people are not always deliberately antagonistic. Very often, and this is a public relations failure, they have never been properly informed by the source of information. For example, in Britain the press got to know that St. Ivel Ltd., the food manufacturers, was launching a new product. They described it as 'a new margarine' but it was an entirely different product to spread on bread which was neither margarine nor butter but contained butter milk and other ingredients. This misinformation had to be rectified. In this case the opinion leaders were journalists who wrote about food. An important fact, apart from the excellence of the product as a health food, was that it was priced between that of margarine and butter. Consequently, it became necessary to put the record straight before the press created misconceptions which would have damaged the national launch. This was done with a press reception which included a film, a question and answer session and sampling of the product. Today it is a well-established product called Gold.

The Media and Methods

The fourth element in the planning model is how we reach our publics to achieve our objectives. This covers the media and the techniques with which the media may be used. For instance, a film or video is a medium (singular of media), and it may be shown at a press reception when news is being presented to another medium, the press. A news release is a method of distributing news to the media of press, radio and television.

Public relations contrasts with advertising yet again in both its choice and range of media. An advertising campaign will use the fewest number of media to reach the largest number of potential buyers. A typical advertising media mix might consist of press, television, posters and point-of-sale display material. But in public relations, the range of possible media includes commercial media as used for advertising purposes plus private, created media like the documentary film and the video already mentioned. Moreover, in industrialising countries the mass media so plentiful in Europe and America may scarcely exist or exist only for an elitist educated urban minority. Other media, such as the mobile film unit, may be the answer.

There are thus two groups of media available for public relations purposes, and they may be classified as follows:

EXISTING COMMERCIAL (UNLESS STATE OWNED) MEDIA

The press – newspapers and magazines; news stories, articles, pictures.

Television – news, interviews, magazine programmes, etc.

Radio – news, live and taped interviews, etc.

Public and trade exhibitions which usually have press officers and press offices with which the exhibitor can co-operate to his advantage.

In all the above media we are concerned with the public relations opportunities within the editorial, programme or press office side, not with the buying of space, the buying of airtime or sponsoring of programmes, or with taking exhibition space. There may be some organisations which will exhibit for public relations reasons, but generally public and trade exhibitions are advertising media. These distinctions should be clearly understood.

PRIVATE CREATED MEDIA

House journals – internal for employees, external for special readerships such as distributors, customers or other outside publics. They may be newspapers or magazines, and may be published daily, weekly, fortnightly, monthly, two-monthly, or quarterly.

Documentary films Sometimes called sponsored or industrial films, these are non-fiction films as distinct from the entertainment films seen at the cinema or on television. They are much shorter than commercial entertainment films, usually not more than 20 minutes in length, but preferably shorter still if the audience is unsophisticated like villagers. It is a mistake to make films too long: their content should be simple and they should be well-edited. They can be used to demonstrate the use of products, describe tourist attractions, show how products are made, explain the purpose and policy of an organisation, and they exploit the realism of movement, sound and colour.

Videotapes Film can be transferred to video and vice versa, whether the subject is shot on film or videotape. Films will continue to survive because projectors are usually universally available, and films can be shown on larger screens to larger audiences. Video requires a video cassette recorder (VCR) and a television set, while the small screen is suitable for only a small audience. And whereas films and projectors are usually the standard 16mm kind, there are incompatible video and television systems. Good quality 'industrial' video, Sony Umatic, may meet the problem of finding a suitable VCR; the domestic VHS, Betamax and Philips systems are more common, with VHS being the more popular. Video productions include house magazines as well as the equivalent of documentary films.

Private and mobile exhibitions These are exhibitions mounted by one sponsor, and they can be housed permanently on company premises, shown at various places such as hotels, or toured on special vehicles such as caravans or trailers, or larger specially designed vehicles or converted buses.

Educational literature Not to be confused with sales literature, this kind of print may consist of explanatory leaflets, folders, brochures, books or posters. They can explain how a product or service works, or perhaps tell the story of an organisation or industry.

Sponsored publications   Some organisations sponsor books, guides, maps and so on (published either by themselves or by a commercial publisher), and they may be given away or sold in bookshops or other appropriate places. Food companies sponsor cookery books and oil and tyre companies publish tourist books and maps.

Seminars   Under this general heading come various invited assemblies for the purpose of making presentations with speakers, slides, films, videos, displays and demonstrations. A larger assembly would be a *conference*. Such functions may be accompanied by suitable hospitality according to the time of day, and there might be a bar and buffet. These events are especially useful when communicating with special interest groups or publics. They should be strictly functional, that is, informative and educational and free of blatant advertising and salesmanship.

The Innovator Theory   The innovator or dispersion theory is one which has been applied very successfully in developing countries, although its origins lie in Europe and America. The method is to seek an influential person who is prepared to support a new idea, and is willing to demonstrate this to others.

An early example was the way McCormick introduced farm machinery to farmers in the American mid-West. These farmers had acquired vast areas of land but their only labour consisted of themselves and their families. Power farming, leading eventually to the tractor and the combine harvester, was introduced by one farmer buying the equipment and permitting other farmers to attend a demonstration on his land. First came the early adopters of the machinery, then the late adopters, and finally the laggards. The stages and proportions of this procedure are shown in the following model.

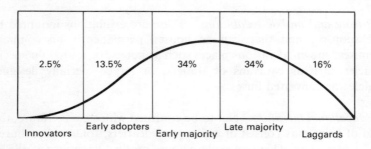

Fig. 2.1 Innovator or dispersion theory

In the industrialising South, this device has been used to promote all kinds of public relations campaigns from family planning to efficient farming, family hygiene and adult literacy. In rural communities, the innovator theory has been applied with the co-operation of local rulers and leaders such as emirs, obas, kings and village headmen or other elders. Taken up by someone with authority and influence, the new idea becomes adopted, whereas had the message been broadcast to the whole community few, if any, would have found it credible. People, especially country folk, are often set in their ways and unwilling to make changes. In an industrialising society, new ideas (like electricity, liquid gas, piped clean water supplies, insecticides and fertilisers) can bring about dramatic changes in life styles as well as improved health and prosperity.

Folk media   There are some other interesting ways of communicating public relations messages to rural people, some of which are useful when there are local tribes or mixed ethnic groups with different languages and dialects. These people may live in remote places and perhaps be beyond the reach of the mass media. They may pay little attention to radio beyond listening to music. They may also be disinterested in the affairs of the cities and here the negative state of *apathy* applies, so that news bulletins produce little interest.

The *puppet show* is a medium used in many parts of Africa and Asia, and the message is communicated by a playlet acted out and mimed by puppets. Since there is no spoken word, the message can be conveyed to people of any language. However, language can be used in the *village theatre* where, again, the public relations message can be presented in the form of a short play. These methods are entertaining and make an impact.

An interesting form of folk media is *gossip*. In many non-Western societies gossip is important where people congregate. It may be the gossip that takes place in markets and bazaars where people meet regularly, or which occurs in restaurants, or when friends gather at home. In large cities, with family networks, news travels fast. In the above instances we have ranged over African, Arab, Indian and Chinese situations where gossip flourishes. Public relations messages can be communicated by feeding these systems of gossip.

Mobile units   To distant places the public relations message, whether commercial or non-commercial, can be carried by land-rover, specially built vehicle or river boat. A screen can be erected on top of the land-rover, and a film show can be given to assembled villagers.

To this may be added other features such as music and dancing, product demonstrations, poster displays, sampling or fashion shows and distribution of leaflets. The puppet theatre or village theatre methods can also be mobile, and can be associated with any of the features mentioned above.

In Malawi, David Whitehead, the textile company, has a specially designed large van with a side which drops down to form a platform. Two girls model dresses made from Whitehead fabrics. This popular show travels from village to village throughout the country. In Kenya, film units travel the country in a similar way with monthly programmes of commercial and documentary features. There is a government information service on similar lines in Zambia, augmented by motor-boats which visit communities on lake islands. The Malaysian government information service has a very extensive mobile system which is described more fully at the end of Chapter 4. Nigeria is another country where mobile units, either commercial or government, tour villages with films and demonstrations, often supported by song and dance teams. In Zimbabwe, sky shouting from helicopters has been adapted from military use to advertising and public relations purposes.

Budgeting

The fifth consideration is the budget, and the plan must be costed per item and as an overall budget of all the items. The three areas of budgeting are man-hours, materials and expenses. The following factors emphasise the need for budgeting.

1 It establishes what resources there are and how they may be employed, and also what additional resources may be required. These resources include both manpower and equipment, and the possible need to augment existing resources with outside services and equipment. For the purpose of the exercise, in-house public relations is now being discussed but later on we shall consider the budgeting of consultancy services. Unlike advertising, most public relations is conducted in-house whereas most advertising is conducted through advertising agencies. This becomes obvious when we realise that a great deal of public relations is concerned with non-commercial organisations which do not or rarely use advertising.

2 The budget may be given or proposed. This must be determined. Are we working to a laid-down fixed budget, or are we calculating what it will cost to achieve set objectives?

3 When it is known that certain expenditure will be incurred a time-

table can be produced to show the expenditure and corresponding action. For instance, if money is allocated for a monthly house journal a series of actions must be planned to coincide with the costs, otherwise the costed issues will not appear on time. Thus, one of the advantages of careful budgeting is that it encourages the planning of a timetable of things that have to be done as well as being an estimate of costs.

4 The budget is an estimate of the cost of the plan, and nothing must be omitted or forgotten. There should also be a contingency fund of, say, 10 per cent of the total to cover unexpected costs or price increases. The contingency fund does not have to be spent, and is merely a safeguard.

5 When presenting the plan to management it shows that the public relations officer is businesslike and this will be appreciated. If the public relations officer presents management with a proposal the first question he is likely to be asked is 'What will it cost?' The public relations officer should know. He should have done his homework. His budget should not consist of guesses, but figures based on quotations which he has obtained from suppliers. Nothing should be left to chance.

THE THREE ELEMENTS OF THE BUDGET

Three costs have to be estimated.

1 Man-hours   Time is often the biggest single cost, unless perhaps a lot of money is to be spent on house journals, films or video. Public relations is mostly hard work and is therefore labour intensive. Labour must be available to carry out the plan or, conversely, no more can be carried out than is possible with the available manpower. This cost is represented by salaries, and the time consists of the total number of working hours of the public relations officer and his staff. It follows the simple principle that when one is doing one thing one cannot do another.

However, what can be done, and how well it can be done, depends on the knowledge, experience and skill of the public relations officer. The well-paid proficient public relations officer is consequently more economic than the ill-paid inexperienced one. It pays to employ a qualified person, and the only way a public relations officer deserves to be well-paid, and to enjoy high status, is if he is well-trained, qualified, experienced and very good at his job.

relations officer who is appointed simply because he has some sort of degree, but nothing else, cannot expect more than a lowly salary and status. While the CAM Diploma may be rather difficult for overseas students to attain, the LCCI Diploma is a worthwhile attainment.

As an example, let us say that after deducting weekends and holidays and assuming a seven hour working day five days a week, a public relations officer's working hours might be about 236 days or 1452 hours a year. That is his 'time bank'. What can he do in this time? Here is an example of what he can do with this time, and if the plan requires that more shall be done he will need an assistant. If there is a public relations staff everyone's time can be allocated in a similar way.

Allocation of 'Time bank'

Researching, writing, distributing 25 news releases	100
Researching, writing, arranging publication, 4 Feature articles	252
Daily information service — answering calls	500
Writing film treatment, script, working with film unit	21
Handling public relations for 2 exhibitions	126
Editing monthly house journal	252
Attending photo sessions	30
Organising three press receptions	63
Organising works visit	21
Preparing annual report	21
Briefing meetings with management	66
	1452 hours

(N.B. 1452 hours represents one year's working hours, the cost being annual salary).

This is a fictitious time budget, but it is remarkably like the work-load of a typical public relations officer. In fact, it both implies that it may require a good deal of unpaid overtime since other demands on time can crop up unexpectedly! It also justified the need to forecast one's work-load, and to emphasise that the work will not be carried out successfully if additional demands are made by management. Moreover, when management is presented with an estimate like this it will be revelation of what the public relations job entails. It follows that time control requires the use of daily time sheets, and these will show whether time is being rationed properly so that the total programme can be achieved.

that time control requires the use of daily time sheets, and these will show whether time is being rationed properly so that the total programme can be achieved.

In the above example, the cost is the public relations officer's salary, to which must be added all the fixed costs of his office, secretarial salary, and the costs of all materials and expenses incurred. All these have to budgeted too. The time factor applies to the consultant also, except that to his costs must be added profit. The consultant operates on an hourly rate covering salaries, overheads and profit, after which he charges for materials and expenses.

In the example of the time bank given above, the public relations officer is working full-time for his organisation. It is only on large accounts that a consultant provides a full-time service. If, for the sake of demonstration, the consultant undertook the same workload of 1452 hours this would be multiplied by the consultant's hourly rate to arrive at the fee. Remember that the in-house public relations officer's salary cannot be matched against the consultant's fee for the public relations officer still has to add on his office overheads. The only real difference between the two (assuming that the public relations officer and the public relations consultant earn equal salaries) is the consultant's profit. A false idea sometimes persists that consultants are expensive by comparison with the cost of employing an in-house public relations officer, but it is necessary to compare like with like. For instance, a poorly paid, inexperienced public relations officer is obviously 'cheaper' than an experienced consultant.

2 Materials   The material costs to be budgeted will be everything that has to be bought and used for the campaign such as news release headings, photographs, photo captions, printing of house journals, making of films or videos and so on.

3 Expenses   Here we include catering and hospitality, travel and overnight costs, and other expenses which may be incurred.

4 In-house public relations department or outside consultancy?
The two are different and one is not necessarily better than the other. Large companies often employ both, and this emphasises that each can offer special services.

5 Advantages of in-house public relations department   But its very nature, public relations calls for close contact with everything that goes on in an organisation, and being part of the organisation is one of the public relations officer's strengths. He may also be familiar with the industry. For example, a bank public relations officer has usually begun as a bank employee and has probably taken banking examinations before specialising in public relations. He can therefore act as a very authoritative spokesman for his organisation. The consultant will lack these advantages.

Advantages of the outside consultant   The consultant also has his strengths. His wide experience based on working for other clients will help him to give professional advice, and to be familiar with a great variety of techniques and media. He is not limited to the experience of the in-house public relations officer who is familiar only with his special organisation and industry. There are therefore differences between the two which are important in their own ways.

The larger public relations consultancies employ specialist staff who are competent in special areas such as corporate and financial public relations, Parliamentary liaison (e.g. advising clients on government procedures and legislation), and creative work such as producing house journals, videos and films. But overall, the public relations consultant can be a useful independent outside adviser who can advise on many business matters.

MEDIA RELATIONS

The range of media which can be used for public relations has already been analysed. It may seem to be a formidable list but of course selections have to be made according to the objectives, publics to be reached, and the budget. Here we shall concern ourselves with the existing commercial mass media, the press, television and radio. We are not dealing with the advertising side of these media, but the editorial and production sides and with the news, feature and programme aspects; how to publish or broadcast public relations messages.

The first consideration is that material must be provided which will be of 'interest and value' to the readers, viewers or listeners. This essential criterion was first laid down by the American public relations consultant, Ivy Ledbetter Lee, as long ago as 1906, and it remains the first rule of successful public relations. It is a very sensible rule. If the editor or producer does not please his readers or audiences his newspaper, magazine or programme will fail. They are his first consideration.

A great deal of submitted public relations material fails to get published or broadcast simply because it interests no-one except the sender. Employers and clients sometimes demand that unusable material is sent to the media, and it is rejected. If the public relations practitioner issues only usable material he will please everybody including his employer or client.

For instance, there is a special way to write a news release. It can be learned simply by reading newspapers. The rules are as follows:

1 The subject must be stated in the first few words. Usually, it is not the name of the organisation but what the organisation has done or will do. For instance, if the story is about a new aircraft going into service it should read: 'The Airbus will replace older aircraft on the daily service operated between Lagos and Kano by Nigeria Airways'. Not the other way round!

2 The opening paragraph should 'give away' the whole story in the form of a brief summary. This is the most important part of a news release. It may be all that gets printed if space is scarce.

3 There should be no puffery, that is use of advertising language. A news release is not an advertisement. It is a piece of factual information, no more. There should be no boasting, no comments, few, if any, adjectives. The story should be written as a journalist would write it, given the same facts.

4 Nothing should be emphasised, such as by writing names entirely in capital letters, or putting names in inverted commas, or by underlining. Capital letters should be reserved for proper nouns and place names, and not for business titles like managing director.

5 There should be no full points or full stops between abbreviations — UNESCO, not U.N.E.S.C.O.

6 Dates should be written month first, e.g. April 30, 1986, not 30th April, 1986.

7 Numbers should be spelt out one to nine, then 10, 54 or 106.

8 All but the first paragraph should be indented, like this book.

9 Embargoes should not be used, unless the editor is being privileged with advance information (such as a speech yet to be delivered), or unless there is a genuine reason such as time differentials between different parts of the world. Editors are not obliged to honour embargoes, and frivolous ones will be ignored.

The following is a useful model for news release writing.

Seven Point News Release Formula (SOLAADS)

1 Subject
2 Organisation
3 Location of organisation
4 Advantages — what is new, special or different
5 Applications — how or by whom the product or service may be used

6 Details — prices, colours, sizes, specifications
7 Source — full name and address of organisation

The opening paragraph should consist of the subject, name of the organisation, location (which could be different from the head-quarters address), and the highlight of the story. This paragraph will thus summarise the essentials of the story.

This formula provides a checklist of information required to write the release, a synopsis or framework for the logical presentation of the information, and finally a checklist to make sure that all the information has been given. The story should be written as briefly as possible, using short words, short sentences and short paragraphs. Most releases can be written on one sheet of paper. At the end should appear the writer's name, his telephone number and the date.

It should look and read just like a typical newspaper report, and require little if any sub-editing or re-writing. However, it should be typed with double spacing, with good margins on either side, and be typed on one side of the paper only. The press release heading should be as simple as possible, allowing the story to start high up on the sheet, and for this reason it is a good idea to print the sender's name, address and telephone number at the bottom. The release heading should not look like an advertisement.

One of the easiest ways to establish good media relations is there-fore to supply the media with what it wants, how it wants it and when it wants it. Timing is also important, and this means knowing how far in advance a newspaper or magazine needs to receive press material for the next issue. The copy date will vary from one publication to another, and from one country to another. In Nigeria, for instance, because of the hundreds of miles separating Lagos in the South and Kano in the North, the *Daily Times* requires copy 48 hours in advance, because it prints the Northern edition at noon on the previous day.

PRESS EVENTS

The three main kinds of press activity are the press conference, the press reception and the facility visit.

Press Conference

This is an informal press gathering, perhaps held at short notice as when an important announcement has to be made. Governments and their ministries may hold regular press conferences. A spokesman will make a statement, issue a news release, and answer questions from assembled journalists. Hospitality will be minimal.

Press Reception

Now we have a more formal and organised press party, ideally with a programme of activities which may include a speech, demonstration, film or video presentation, and hospitality such as a bar and buffet, or perhaps lunch. The extent of socialising may be greater in African than in European countries, partly because there are fewer journalists and the two sides know each other well and partly because parties are a way of life. In Britain, where there are thousands of journals, journalists are busy people who do not have time to waste, and host and guests may not always know each other, press receptions are very businesslike. Moreover, a London journalist may have to choose between several conflicting invitations, whereas in industrialising countries journalists receive far fewer invitations and a more free and easy atmosphere may be acceptable.

Press Facility Visit

The object of a facility visit is to take journalists to see and report a topic of news value. This could be to visit a factory, or other premises, or to see a product being used by a customer (such as a piece of equipment), or to experience a journey on a new bus, aircraft or ship.

The programme has to be carefully arranged to allow time for travelling and the actual visit, and will involve hospitality such as meals and possibly overnight accommodation. Guests and speakers will have to be organised, and perhaps demonstrations, slide/film/video presentations. A lot of organising is required, with careful timing. Rehearsals may be advisable. The organiser should go to the place to be visited and make sure that everything is well prepared for the day. This is where the organising ability of the public relations officer will be tested, and it calls for meticulous attention to detail so that the guests are unable to criticise the visit. They should return with a good story, and well satisfied that the visit was worthwhile. The success of the trip will help to enhance the image of the host organisation.

PHOTOGRAPHY FOR PUBLIC RELATIONS PURPOSES

Pictures can often convey a message more effectively than words. They can be used for many public relations purposes, supporting news

releases, accompanying articles, and illustrating house journals, annual reports, educational literature and other publications. Some pictures can be used many times over. They differ from advertising pictures, and from mere record pictures taken for industrial purposes. Public relations pictures should contain no blatant advertising, like the bold display of names. They should be interesting and well composed, perhaps with some human interest such as people actually using the product or playing a useful role.

The mistake should not be made of hiring a photographer and expecting him to produce the required picture. He may be an expert with a camera and a darkroom, but it is no good leaving him to take what he thinks suitable. It is the responsibility of the public relations officer to give the photographer precise instructions. The public relations officer should decide what story he wants to tell in pictures. He has to use the camera as a medium of communication. The photographer cannot guess what this story might be. Suppose the picture is to be of an airliner. The story might be that it has four engines instead of three, or that it is a wide-bodied jet with a large roomy cabin, or that it has a new system for stowing luggage. These will be the special aspects of the airliner which should be photographed.

The public relations officer should always try to accompany the photographer, and to act as a stage-manager, making sure that there are no untidy obstructions to spoil the picture, checking to see that people are correctly or tidily dressed and doing the right jobs, and generally helping the photographer by setting the scene. He will need to tell the photographer whether pictures are to be in black and white or colour. For press work, black and white pictures are usually required unless the editor has specially asked for colour pictures.

Captions

When pictures are sent to editors they should have captions fixed to the backs of the prints. The wording of the caption should explain what the picture cannot say for itself. What kind of aircraft is it? Who owns it? How many passengers does it carry? On what route does it fly? The information on the caption will depend on the story the picture aims to tell. The caption must also give the name, address and telephone number of the sender. Remember, a photograph may be put in a photo library and looked at in the future when it is separated from the news release, and the caption must be able to explain what the picture is all about.

There are two kinds of caption, the one on the back of the original photograph, and the one which is printed when the picture is published. The editor will base his caption on the wording given on the back of the picture.

From this description of the role of public relations it will be realised that this is a very complex subject requiring training, knowledge and skill. It is not just about 'mass communications' but how to use all kinds of communication techniques to create understanding.

The attributes of a good public relations practitioner are:
1 Ability to communicate;
2 Ability to organise;
3 Ability to understand and get on with people;
4 Personal integrity;
5 Imagination.

3
The Role of
Advertising

Advertising and public relations are quite different, and public relations is not a form of advertising. They are both forms of communication, but they each serve very different purposes. Public relations deals with news and strictly factual information aimed at educating in order to create understanding. Advertising consists of selling messages aimed at persuading people to buy. The writing styles are different as can be seen by comparing the editorial and the advertisement columns of a newspaper, or by comparing the content of radio and television news bulletins with that of the commercials.

They have to be different if they are to work. It does not mean that one is true and the other is false. But no editor wants to print, and no reader wishes to read, an advertisement in the news columns of the press. The advertisement has to use more exciting words because it has to compete for attention with both the editorial and other advertisements. People seldom buy newspapers to read the advertisements so advertisements have to be written and designed to capture attention. The advertisement can make emotional claims, and declare that a product is the best or better than others. But press relations material must state facts only and make no claims. Thus the writing of news releases and advertisements require different skills and they are usually written by different people. Journalists and copywriters write in their own special ways.

Advertising becomes necessary when the sales message has to be transmitted to a large number of people who may be scattered over a large area. The salesman in the market place can only talk to a limited number of people, however loud he shouts. Advertising reaches hundreds, thousands, perhaps millions of people. The cost of advertising may seem high but it can be a cheap way of reaching a very large number of prospective customers. The shoe-maker can make a pair of shoes and sell them to passers-by, but a shoe factory has to sell to thousands of people all over the country. Advertising can reach them.

As a country becomes industrialised and goods are made in factories in large quantities advertising becomes increasingly necessary, otherwise they would have to close down. No-one would know the goods existed, and no-one would go on buying them unless they were constantly reminded of their existence. One of the world's most successful companies is Coca-Cola, and it is also one of the biggest advertisers.

Some of the world's most famous names such as Ford, Cadbury-Schweppes, Guinness, Nestlé, Dunlop, Singer and Lipton are all household names which would be unknown but for advertising. Once-famous names which are no longer advertised like Hillman, Gold Flake, Oxydol, Selo, Bile Beans and Matchless are forgotten. During the Second World War, although it was not available, Stork margarine was advertised continuously so that the name would not be forgotten.

Advertising is not only to do with increasing sales but with maintaining them. It has to remind people to buy again, perhaps by building brand loyalty. It is part of the economics of industry. A factory will make a profit only if its production capacity is taken up regularly, and production is maintained. Economics of scale operate because a price may be as low as it is as a result of mass production. A Rolls-Royce motor-car is expensive because only a small number are made, but a Nissan is relatively cheaper because a large number are made and sold, and techniques such as robots can be used in their manufacture.

However, a major part of price is packaging and distribution, and the latter includes everything such as warehousing, transportation, salesmen's commission, discounts to wholesalers and retailers and advertising. If these costs were not met the goods would stay in the factory. The cost of advertising is included in the price. The customer has to pay for advertising, as he does for everything that is involved in getting the product to the point-of-sale and into his possession. That advertising increases the price, or that the price could be reduced if there was no advertising, are both false arguments.

It is significant that the prosperity of a country can be measured by the extent of advertising. As industrialising countries prosper so advertising increases because more goods and services are available and more people have more money with which to buy them. Advertising is the lubricating oil of trade.

Reverting to public relations, advertising is more likely to be successful if readers of advertisements understand what is being advertised, and the manufacturer and the supplier enjoy good reputations and corporate images. Heavy advertising will not sell misunderstood products made and supplied by firms with bad reputations. It was very difficult at one time to sell Japanese motor-cars in Eastern countries which had been occupied by the Japanese during the Second World War. Even as late as 1969, the first Datsun motor-cars to arrive in Britain were met with suspicion for no-one in Britain had ever heard of Datsun. In 1983, Canon sponsored the Football League because Canon cameras were not as well-known as Olympus.

ACCEPTANCE OF ADVERTISING IN INDUSTRIALISING COUNTRIES

Two problems occur in some industrialising countries, especially in Africa. These are the attitudes of businessmen on the one hand, and the attitudes of the public on the other, towards advertising. There may also be some resentment because it is a feature of the industrialising world, introduced into industrialising countries mainly by multi-nationals. There may therefore seem to be something 'foreign' about advertising. It is, of course, foreign to traditional methods of selling, but so are all forms of industrialising. But let us discuss the two major problems or handicaps which beset advertising, and operate against its effective use. Advertising is effective if it oils the wheels of exchange, bringing manufacturers (and their distributors) and customers together.

The Business Attitude

Businessmen are inclined to be cautious about investing money in advertising. Is it really necessary, they ask. They tend to see the cost of advertising coming out of their pockets, out of their profits, instead of budgeting it as part of the price so that it puts money in their pockets. Where would the big merchants of Africa be, the Levantis, Ibru, UAC, UTC, East African Industries, Food Specialities, whether indigenous or multi-national, but for advertising?

In a world where a quick sale and a quick profit is normal, where the market place and the bazaar are the traditional places of sale, or in Arab countries where window shopping is rare, and a Western-style housewife market hardly exists, advertising may seem a strange aid to selling. Advertising requires forward planning, the forecasting of sales, and an investment in a future sales target. In Moslem countries this may conflict with the Islamic code that money should not make money, a problem that Arab banks have over interest which has **not** been earned by work.

However, if the economy is to be industrialised, mass production and mass selling will be its very nature. A factory owner has to estimate demand and also to produce supply. He will not use expensive machinery and labour to produce one quantity of goods, sell them, and close down the factory. He has to manufacture and sell continuously, and both production and sales must extend into the future. He has to plan at least a year ahead. If he does not he will go out of business. He will expect to obtain orders regularly, the shopkeepers will expect to receive stocks regularly, and customers will expect the goods to be available whenever they want to buy them. Advertising fits into this production and trading pattern as the means of creating and maintaining the demand.

To some extent, the manufacturer and the shopkeeper have been spoiled by having a seller's market when goods were in short supply and customers had to accept what they could get. But an industrialising society means an expanding market because the more people there are in employment the more money there is to buy goods, and a buyer's market occurs because goods are more abundant and there is greater choice. Now, advertising is not only concerned with creating and maintaining sales, it has to vie with rivals in a competitive market. Advertising becomes a way of providing choice. We have seen this happen in Nigeria with the growth of state breweries and many competing brands of beer.

The businessman, if he is going to run a successful company, has to plan the whole sequence of the marketing mix. This takes in developing the product, naming it, designing packaging, pricing, organising a sales force, finding distributors, warehousing and transport, and advertising the product to the trade and to the public. At various stages he can perfect the process, and reduce risk, by using the various forms of research discussed in Chapter 7. throughout this process public relations will apply because many aspects of the marketing mix (e.g. the product name) are forms of communication. Moreover, the advertising could fail through lack of understanding of either the company or the product or service, unless there has been advance market education which is yet another form of public relations.

It will be seen that advertising is part of marketing, but a weakness in many industrialising countries is that there is no marketing. Salesmen are wrongly called marketing managers when they market nothing. They rely on advertising and salesmanship to sell goods without first finding out whether anyone wants them, or what preferences people have. Often, they merely sell imports which are irrelevant to the local markets.

How many foreign motor-cars, even if assembled locally, are suitable for, say, African conditions? The suspension may be too soft, the back of the vehicle may be too low, the upholstery may be unsuitable, the metal unprotected against rust, and they may come with heaters and heated rear-windows instead of air-conditioning. There is no marketing involved in selling motor-cars that were intended for London, Paris, New York or Tokyo. They can be foisted on a seller's market, but not on a buyer's market.

To have confidence in advertising, to regard it as a necessity, to spend wisely on it, and to buy advertising efficiently, the businessman needs to study the subject. He may need to use experts, just as he engages accountants, lawyers or architects, and an advertising agency may be required to plan campaigns, create advertisements and buy media. But he must know what he wants the advertising to achieve. An advertising agency can certainly advise him, and it can spend his money, but the advertising is more likely to be successful if the businessman is sure of his market and can guide the agency. To do this he should employ a qualified and experienced in-house advertising manager who can work with the agency. We shall deal with the advertising department and the advertising agency later in this chapter.

The Public Attitude

Advertising tends to arouse suspicion and scepticism among readers, viewers and listeners in industrialising countries. Again, the problem may be that advertising is regarded as a foreign and unconventional way of selling. But why is there such widespread mistrust of advertising? It is partly the fault of advertisers and partly because people are not conditioned to advertising as they are in industrial countries.

While it is true that good advertisment copy should say what it has to say in the fewest necessary words, the copy that one generally sees in the press in these countries is either brief to the point of banality, or claims are made in too blatant a tone and with too much emphasis. They may not be exaggerated claims but they are often too bombastic, and emotional. An advertisement should make a promise, but not seem to offer the impossible. The writers of these advertisements underestimate the intelligence of readers, and so destroy credibility. In fact, a good many of these advertisements would be banned under the British Code of Advertising Practice. This is a pity because it ruins the good name of advertising, and encourages people to disbelieve what they read in advertisements. It is bad advertising, not that advertising itself — if properly created — is bad.

At the same time, there is also the attitude of many readers, viewers and listeners that advertising is an unnecessary evil, that it is practised by big, wealthy companies which have money to waste. This is a social attitude, held by people who are not wealthy themselves and who are antagonistic to businesses that are prosperous. There is a misunderstanding here about the nature of big business which is big only because it has succeeded in satisfying the needs of its customers. If people like the taste and the quality of the beer they will buy it and the company will grow. Only a small fraction of the money it makes goes to shareholders as dividends: most of it goes in wages, raw materials, production and distribution costs (which include advertising).

Consequently, advertising has to work in a difficult atmosphere. The advertising has to be somewhat more enthusiastic than in older more-advertising-conscious countries yet it must be believable, and it has to use language which is readily understood by the majority. Often, it is promoting new products and new life styles to people with limited incomes, and the sales message has to be convincing.

Another criticism in poorer countries is that advertising arouses the expectations of people who cannot afford to satisfy them, and that this causes resentment and jealousy. This, of course, is true the world over in the sense that we would all like to have more of all sorts of things, but advertising is aimed at those who are prospective buyers, and it may even encourage others to earn or save more money in order to satisfy their desires. As already said, the extent of advertising is an indication of the prosperity of a country. The streets of Hong Kong are a mass of advertising signs, all lit up at night, and there are thousands of shops crammed with goods. It is a shopper's paradise, not just for visitors but for the local population. The Chinese work hard, and earn the money to buy what they can afford. Many of them were once poor peasants in China.

Advertising, therefore, can be an incentive to enjoy a higher standard of living. Let us remember that in both Europe and America a hundred years ago, when mass production really began, most people were poor country folk. The factories would never have sold their goods if people had not worked harder in better paid jobs (such as in the factories), and if advertising had not made known the goods that were in the shops in the growing cities and towns. Perhaps this is a lesson for people in industrialising countries. They are experiencing today what the British, the Germans and the Americans experienced a century ago. The first popular British national daily newspaper was the *Daily Mail*, launched in 1896 and packed with advertisements.

THE THREE SIDES OF ADVERTISING

Advertising comes about by the blending of three different interests. First, there is the advertiser. He may produce his own advertising but he is likely to reach a stage when he needs more skilful planning, creative and media buying skills. He can find these skills in our second side of advertising, the advertising agency. Third, there are the media owners who sell advertisement space in the press or on poster sites, airtime on radio and television, screentime on static or mobile cinema, or stands at exhibitions.

All three are quite different and require special skills, but they combine (together with the supporting services of printers, photographers, film makers, exhibition stand designers and so on) to make up the complex world of advertising. Let us examine each one in turn.

The Advertising Department

The advertising department, under the control of the advertising manager, may be responsible for planning, creating and placing the company's entire advertising campaign. The advertising manager may therefore handle both above-the-line media (press, radio, television, outdoor and cinema) and below-the-line (direct mail, exhibitions, point-of-sale displays, sales promotion schemes, sales literature, give-aways and so on, but not public relations, which is a separate activity). This is not to say that in the absence of a public relations officer the advertising manager will not also handle public relations, but this requires separate planning and budgeting and should not be confused with advertising. The advertising manager is also responsible for interpreting management's policy, and he may come under the direction of the marketing manager. Obviously there can be many variations on the organisation and responsibilities of the in-house advertising department.

In large companies which use an advertising agency (and perhaps a public relations consultancy too) it is possible that the agency will be responsible for above-the-line or 'media' advertising, and the in-house advertising manager will deal with below-the-line advertising. Much depends on the kind of company, what it makes, and how it affects distribution, while some advertising agencies may also offer public relations services.

Above-the-line and below-the-line media are simply different media, and one is not superior to the other. Agencies usually concentrate on above-the-line media because these are the ones which pay commission, and commission may be the agency's main source of income. But some companies (e.g. mail order or direct response businesses) are likely to devote most of their advertising to direct mail, catalogues and sales literature, and not use any of the five above-the-line media.

The media used as the spearhead of a campaign are called *primary* media, and those used to support them are called *secondary* media. Television might be the primary medium for a beer, but direct mail for an insurance company. In industrialising countries the choice of primary and secondary media will depend on what is available. Radio and posters could be more important than either television or direct mail.

When an agency is used the advertising manager will be responsible for interpreting company policy to the agency and working with the account executive or agency representative. He will also have to supervise the work produced by the agency, approving media schedules, checking artwork, copy and proofs, and controlling the budget. He will need to understand how an agency operates and work closely with it. An harmonious relationship is essential, and the agency should be seen as an extension of the advertising department and the opportunity to enjoy a share of the resources and expertise of the agency. The advertising manager and the account executive must be able to work together. This point is emphasised because bad advertising can result from poor agency/client relations, misunderstandings leading to unnecessary changes of agency.

From the above description it will be seen that the role of the advertising manager is a very important one. His knowledge, experience and skill is vital to the success of the advertising campaign, and this calls for getting the best out of the agency. Advertising managers are often former agency account executives who have moved over to the client side, bringing with them the necessary training, qualifications and experience.

The Advertising Agency

Originally, advertising agencies began as space brokers who earned a commission from publishers on the space they sold to advertisers.

Gradually they became involved in offering advisory, planning and creative services to advertisers. Strictly speaking, they remain agents of the media rather than of the advertisers although they will buy the media of greatest advantage to their clients. They are still 'middle men', linking advertisers with the media. They may derive all their income from commissions on whatever they buy for clients, but when commission income is inadequate they will charge their clients service fees. Legally, the 'agent acts as principal' and is responsible for paying for whatever is bought for the client, even if the client goes bankrupt. It is therefore necessary for the agency to have sufficient cash flow to pay for purchases, often before being paid by the client.

Recognition or accreditation means that the agency has been approved for the purpose of receiving commission on space or airtime purchases, not that it is recognised as a good agency. Recognition is granted by media owners, not advertising trade associations. In Britain the law has been changed so that agencies are not guaranteed a particular rate of commission, but have proven credit worthiness and are able to pay their debts to the media owners. They must also accept the British Code of Advertising Practice. Different recognition or accreditation systems will operate in other countries, but the main objective of such approval is to make sure that the media owners get their bills paid promptly.

The role of an advertising agency is to advise clients on how to plan their advertising campaigns (and this may involve research), to create advertising, to plan media schedules and buy media, and to supply the media with copy, layouts, camera-ready copy, or radio and TV commercials, or printed posters or signs, according to the needs of the campaign. It will employ specialist staff who will undertake all these tasks, the account executive being the liaison man between client and agency. Large agencies will have specialists such as media planners, media buyers and copywriters who write the wording or the scripts, visualisers who draw roughs of proposed advertisements, layout men who prepare the final designs for printing, typographers who select type faces, a television producer who creates commercials for filming, and production men who supply typesetting, blocks or finished camera-ready copy to the publishers. Smaller agencies will have fewer specialists and some members of the staff will be responsible for more than one specialist function.

Generally, the agency is a team of experts. It would be uneconomical for the advertiser to employ all these people full-time, but by using an agency he can enjoy a share of their services according to the demands of the campaign. It is therefore a mistake to imagine that it is expensive to use an agency since it is obviously cheaper to share the agency's expertise. Moreover, the agency probably employs people of higher calibre than could be employed in an advertising department, and this quality has to be paid for.

Media Owners

These are the publishers of newspapers and magazines, television and radio stations, and cinema and poster advertising contractors. This is a selling operation; they do not just take orders from advertisers and agencies. The selling of media is consequently a highly organised selling operation, and space, airtime or sites will be sold on the basis of arguments about their advertising value. These sales propositions are usually supported by data about the size and nature of circulations, readerships and audiences, and where circulation figures are audited, and readership and audiences are researched, each media owner will exploit the figures available. The advertiser or the agency will buy the media which are most cost-effective on the basis of the evidence provided by the media owners, or by independent research where this exists.

A problem in many industrialising countries is that there may be no independent readership or audience surveys, and reliance will have to be placed on statements by media owners that could be rather optimistic assessments which need to be accepted with care. For instance, the number of copies printed is not the same as the number of copies sold.

However, when the *South China Morning Post* in Hong Kong claims it has an ABC (Audit Bureau of Circulations) figure of 68,940, or the *Trinidad Guardian* claims an ABC net sales figure of 51,340, this is an authenticated average daily net sale figure.

Characteristics of the Media

Each medium has its own special advantages and disadvantages which must be understood when planning an advertising campaign, and they will differ from country to country and must be judged according to the conditions which prevail. The following is a brief summary of these assessments.

Press advertising's value rests with its ability to reach a large number of readers, and relies upon the extent of literacy and the ability of people to buy publications. It can be one of the cheapest ways of reaching a big readership. But journals may be short lived and an advertisement may survive no longer than a day in the case of newspapers. However, a press advertisement is capable of conveying detailed information. The response is measurable if it produces direct enquiries or orders.

Radio has the advantage of sound and spoken sales messages, and it can reach distant audiences including illiterates who do not read newspapers. But it is ephemeral, and it is difficult to retain advertising messages except that they can be repeated so that listeners remember them.

Television depends on people owning receivers, or being able to view at community centres, and perhaps on the availability of electricity, batteries or generators. The big advantage of television is its realism through the use of colour, sound and movement and its impact can be great.

Posters, signs, transportation and other forms of outdoor advertising carry limited advertising messages, but size and site can present advertisements to large numbers of people. They are usually exhibited for weeks or months, or permanently, and simple messages using pictures can be absorbed by people irrespective of literacy or language.

Cinema advertising has the characteristics of television, but the audience is captive and will absorb advertisements together with the main programme. Moreover, cinema advertisements are seen by a receptive audience in an entertainment atmosphere.

Direct mail can be directed at selected prospective customers, and if lists of addresses are available and there is a reliable postal service, it can be a very powerful medium.

Exhibitions usually enjoy a pleasant atmosphere because people enjoy attending shows where they can actually see products being displayed or demonstrated.

Sales promotion schemes include prize contests, free gifts, special price offers, and premium offers of items at special prices if applications are accompanied by evidence of purchase. However, in some countries there are legal restraints on some forms of sales promotion.

Point-of-sale material consists of advertising material supplied to shops to promote goods and may include posters, showcards, display models, dummy packs and so on which attract the attention of people when they are shopping. This display material can reinforce other forms of advertising at the point of purchase.

Advertising media must therefore be evaluated carefully, and the media mix will be based on the choice of media which will achieve the greatest result at the lowest cost. Familiarity with all the available media should be one of the greatest strengths of the advertising agency.

If we close with the definition used by the Institute of Practitioners in Advertising it will be seen how successful advertising can result from a combination of research, creativity and media buying skills. The Institute of Practitioners in Advertising is the British trade association of advertising agencies, and this definition defines advertising from the point of view of the agency.

Advertising presents the most persuasive possible selling message to the right prospects for the product or service at the lowest possible cost.

MAJOR DIFFERENCES

What are the major differences between advertising in the old and the new nations, bearing in mind that advertising grew up alongside the development of the industrialised world over a period of some two hundred years? Ready-made advertising media and techniques were there to be adapted or adopted. The only things special to the industrialising countries were that commercial radio had arrived long before it came to Britain, and mobile cinemas were a feature of these largely rural countries.

We have already discussed the quality and the circulations of the press, and it is sometimes a surprise to people in, say, Nigeria to learn that the biggest selling daily, the *Daily Times* has a circulation similar to the small circulation of the British *Times*, which is wrongly believed to be Britain's leading newspaper.

While poster advertising is a useful medium, there are remarkably few poster sites in industrialising countries. Unlike British cities, one does not see a variety of poster sizes on every available space including the side walls of houses. Poster sites tend to be mainly beside main highways, and they are usually of supersite size.

Few countries have double-decker buses which provide such prominent advertising sites in Britain, although in some countries there are buses and trams where the whole vehicle is monopolised by one advertiser.

The biggest single difference is television. In Britain there is commercial television, meaning that programmes are the total responsibility of the station, and a limited amount of time is permitted for commercial breaks in which short advertisements appear. The situation is different in industrialising countries where, in addition to commercials, there is sponsored television. An advertiser can sponsor a whole programme, also inserting some commercials. Often, the programmes sponsored are major sports events. For example, Dunhill have sponsored the FA Cup live by satellite on Malaysian television.

The expression 'sponsored' creates some confusion. During the broadcast of the 1985 FA Cup it was noticeable that Manchester United were wearing red shirts bearing the word Sharp. Their strip was sponsored by the Japanese electronics firm which has a factory in Manchester.

This is a different kind of sponsorship and the two need to be clearly understood. Many events, especially sporting ones like golf, tennis, cricket, football, horse and motor racing are sponsored by commercial firms. They may sponsor players, as Dunlop sponsored McEnroe, or racing cars as Marlborough do, or prizes such as the Schweppes Gold Cup, and all 92 clubs of the Football League as in the case of Canon.

Thus, events, prizes and participants may be sponsored irrespective of whether the event is televised. If, in Britain, it is televised the television company is responsible for doing so and the programme time is not paid for by the sponsor of the event. For example, in Britain the FA Cup was presented by both the BBC and ITV over both networks. It was also sold to television stations in 50 countries, and as already mentioned, one was Malaysia where Dunhill sponsored the whole programme, and took full colour whole page advertisements in the daily papers to say so.

USE OF SYMBOLS

In Chapter 1 reference was made to the use of animals, birds and other creatures as communication symbols, for instance, Black dog beer as the means of communicating Guinness stout to the Chinese in Malaysia. It is necessary to avoid double meanings, and Nigeria Airways, probably from want of the most elementary copy-testing, had two disasters with 'Flies All Over Africa' and the 'Flying Elephant'. Compare these idiocies with 'The Golden Service' of Malaysian Airline System, when gold infers quality and is particularly meaningful to Asiatics.

4
The Role of
Media Relations

The media of communication follows the demand for it, and this is provoked by the needs of government to communicate, the extent of literacy, the economic situation and the ability of the media to reach people, which may include physical communications such as transport. The way in which the media grow depends on these considerations in each individual country. That is why the student has to be careful when he reads British or American books on advertising, marketing and public relations because the media situations are not the same, and chapters on media could be irrelevant to the situation in the reader's own country. This is also a problem when students go abroad and study in, say, Australia, Britain, Canada and the USA.

Probably only a few things are common. The basic principles that the mass media should inform, educate and entertain persist except that their order of importance and their nature will vary from one part of the world to another. In some countries political information will come first, whereas it would be a poor runner-up in Britain. An example of this is news-reading on television. The British news reader wears colourful clothes and even tells jokes at the end of the bulletin, and there is a distinct element of entertainment in programmes like ITN's *News at Ten*. Not so in most industrialising countries where news readers dress discreetly and read the news very seriously.

To define the role of media relations it is necessary to understand the characteristics of the media, and not only mass media, in the industrialising countries. Mass communications studies are often the subject of university degrees and polytechnic diplomas in these countries, but they may not be wholly relevant to the practice of advertising or public relations since they deal more with the sociology and mechanics of media rather than how they may be used for advertising and public relations purposes. The syllabus of the British CAM Diploma is totally different from that for a mass communications qualification.

The practice of journalism will be common, almost as if all

Fig. 4.1 The inverted triangle for news report writing

journalists were trained in the same school. Newspaper reports the world over follow the inverted triangle principle (which is not unlike the public relations Seven-Point Formula for news releases given in Chapter 2).

The essence of the story leads so that the first paragraph is a summary or complete story in itself. The next paragraph may set the scene, describing the person or where the event occurred. Then follow supporting facts, and finally less important background information. Again, this follows the principle that the story can be cut from the bottom up so that, if necessary, the opening paragraph remains and is a digest of the whole story.

However, although the press officer, who is professionally trained, will endeavour to write his news releases in this fashion there is a universal antipathy by journalists towards public relations officers which has become known as the 'adversarial situation'. It is even expressed quite bluntly in textbooks for the training of journalists.

The following example is quoted from an excellent manual *Here's the News* published by the Asia-Pacific Institute for Broadcasting Development[1]. The manual is the product of tests carried out in Malaysia, Thailand, Nepal, the Philippines, Sri Lanka, Papua New Guinea, Fiji and Western Samoa, and was largely sponsored by UNESCO. These are the opening words of the chapter on handouts, news releases, statements:

'One of the worst developments in all countries is the growing power of public relations as a source of news and information. It is a serious restraint on the media's healthy development.

'Journalism is not the same as public relations. Journalists can make careful use of both government and non-government public relations handouts as a source of news, but the reporter has to avoid the pitfalls of the handouts'.

The writer goes on to add: 'Sometimes they are deliberately written in a way to obscure the news. At other times, the statement is so ineptly written and offered to news media for one purpose only: to promote something of interest to the dispensing agency. Whenever possible, seek additional information that is almost always hidden or simply absent in the handout'.

Note the use of the derogatory word *handout*, which no professional public relations officer who issues news of interest and value to the media would use.

Paul De Maeseneer, the writer of the manual and a UNESCO associate-expert, continues by describing how to edit 'handouts', and gives a check list of five questions:

'i) What does it mean?
ii) What is the effect of it?
iii) What is not clear and asks for explanations?
iv) Find out all you can about what is *not* in the handout.
v) Why do they want the information in this release disseminated?'

Well, they are questions which any self-respecting public relations officer should have asked himself before issuing the news release. Unhappily, this is not always so and the bad public relations officer (perhaps directed by masters who misunderstand public relations) earns the criticism and suspicion of sceptical journalists who are daily bombarded with unpublishable releases. The public relations officer has to understand and supply what the media want and are most likely to use. Otherwise, public relations deserves the bad reputation it so often earns from the media.

A master who is frequently the chief culprit is the marketing manager, and it is unfortunate if the public relations officer has to serve the marketing manager rather than report to the chief executive. The placing of public relations within the narrow confines of the marketing department has been the cause of much of the conflict between public relations and the media. This is not surprising when marketing managers rely on the concept of public relations expressed in Philip Kotler's widely published and nonsensical definition[2]:

'Non-personal stimulating of demand for a product, service or business unit by planting commercially significant news about it in a published medium or obtaining favourable presentation of it upon radio, television, or stage that is not paid for by the sponsor'.

Public relations practitioners do *not* 'plant' news, which implies unethical behaviour!

Kotler's total misunderstanding of public relations, his relegation of it as publicity where it is wrongly placed under the promotion 'P' of the Four P's, is worsened by this cynical definition which defies the professional ethics of public relations. It is not the place of public relations to use underhanded methods as suggested by the word 'planting', nor is it not paid for. Public relations costs money just like anything else, but it is mostly the cost of time and expertise.

THE PRESS

The quality and nature of the press depends on the pressures it receives economically or politically. In Europe and America the press is big business, even if some newspapers have lost money through loss of popularity and advertising revenues coupled with, in Britain, restrictive trade unionism. It is paradoxical that Malaysian dailies can boast Atex computerised newsrooms and offset-litho machines when London's Fleet Street retains archaic methods and produces badly printed newspapers. Nevertheless the newspapers of Europe and America are usually free from political interference, have big circulations and offer ready media for hundreds of public relations stories. An analysis of the situation elsewhere makes some striking comparisons, and suggests the opportunities or handicaps which exist.

1 In the Caribbean, small populations occupy islands and the volume of local news may be fairly small, especially if the news is not dominated by political statements. West Indians are also very world conscious. They may have travelled to Britain or North America, or they may have relatives and friends who have emigrated. They are surprisingly world conscious and their newspapers are well served by CANA, the West Indies news agency. As a result, newspapers like the Trinidadian *Guardian* and *Express* carry international news. They also name local public relations officers who have given them news stories. Caribbean newspapers seem to welcome good public relations stories.

2 The newspapers of African countries tend to be government owned or subject to control or censorship. They carry a lot of political news, and space for public relations material is very limited. Of course, readers may be interested in the political development of the country and enjoy reading statements by politicians or reports on what the government or ministries are doing on behalf of the nation.

More often newspapers are platforms for governments or parties and are little more than propaganda sheets. An aside to this is that the *Rand Daily Mail*, which did not always support the South African government, lost circulation and money and folded in early 1985. It is also significant that the *New Straits Times*, in which the government party holds shares, prints a pro-government front page lead story every day which would kill the sales of most of the popular British newspapers. So, very different situations prevail although when the author was visiting Zambia, and a major speech by Kenneth Kaunda filled the Lusaka daily for three days running, a Zambian told him how much he envied the British newspaper reader. Imagine all the pages of a London daily paper having to carry the full speech made by any British prime minister!

3 The number of pages may be small and this will reduce the possibility of publishing news releases. The reasons for small editions could be lack of advertising (reflecting the state of the economy), poor sales due to illiteracy and poverty, or small circulations because different newspapers have to serve a number of ethnic, religious or language groups. These situations can be seen in Nigeria where the biggest circulation newspaper sells 60,000 copies in a country with a population of up to 100 million, whereas the leading paper in Peninsular Malaysia sells well over 100,000 copies with a population of only 14 million.

4 Another reason for poor circulations, few pages and also a scarcity of publications is lack of foreign exchange, and the rationing of imports of newsprint.

5 Long distances, bad weather conditions, and poor roads can make distribution very difficult. In Nigeria the *Daily Times* does not reach Kano, some 700 miles to the north, until the following day. The AI road to the north has bad surfaces, and burnt out wrecks of oil tankers, lorries, buses and cars by the roadside. Nigeria's plans to extend its expressways have been hampered by both corrupt practices and economic conditions. Other African countries as different as Kenya, Malawi and Zimbabwe have good roads. The length of the Malaysian peninsular is served by excellent roads, and to improve them even further a toll system was introduced in 1985 to provide a road building fund.

The author's experience of driving from Lagos to Kano raises the hope that Nigeria will build better roads. Communications, whether mass media or physical, are vital to a country's development, and the potential in a great country with vast natural resources and intelligent people, is enormous once its strength ceases to be sapped by corruption. The day when an avaricious minority ceases its admiration of Swiss bank accounts will be the greatest day of progress Nigeria has ever enjoyed.

6 Printing quality varies enormously in spite of new offset-litho presses having been installed in many industrialising countries. The reasons vary from poor workmanship to poor quality newsprint, while the reproduction of pictures is often abysmal. Trinidad and Kuala Lumpur newspapers are well produced, but some Nigerian newspapers have to be seen to be believed.

7 Low standards of journalism can also be a problem, although this is where the good public relations officer can score by supplying well-written stories which merit publication. Journalistic standards vary tremendously from country to country. When there are only a few small circulation journals it is difficult for young journalists to gain training and experience. The author has been interviewed many times by journalists who knew no shorthand, unheard of with a properly trained and skilled journalist.

Public authorities, since they serve the nation, are subject to constant criticism. Some of it may be justified, some of it not. Electricity failures may be the result of negligence or over-consumption by users who either fail to replace their own faulty equipment or to conserve electricity.

In Nigeria, the public relations unit of the National Electric Power Authority (NEPA) makes sure that its top officials are aware of what is said in the media by producing regular digests of press reports in the form of a Weekly Press Review. The report carries subject titles in the left-hand margin, while in the right-hand margin are set out the initials of the general manager, assistant general managers and directors who should take special note of the reports. This is an excellent feedback system which enables top officials to be aware of press reports in newspapers which they may not necessarily see. The reports show both praise and criticism of NEPA and provide a concise picture of how the authority is regarded by both journalists and members of the public.

HOUSE JOURNALS

This form of created, private public relations media is introduced at this point because, in a number of countries, house journals may supplement the commercial press and be sold at bookstalls. The house journal is popular in all industrialising countries. Some may suffer from poor writing, design and printing, but there are many very good ones.

RADIO

In most industrialising countries radio is a long-established and popular medium, and personal receivers may be augmented by the 'box radio' or rediffusion services, frequently in public places like cafes. Unlike the press and television, radio is comparatively simple and inexpensive to broadcast.

Whether or not it achieves the penetration that is claimed for it is another matter. Weak signals, lack of transmitters, broken sets or the high cost of batteries, disinterest in programmes from a remote city, preference for music programmes, and use of radio as a companionable background noise, all tend to reduce its effectiveness.

Nevertheless, radio is a medium which people can often afford, it can be listened to on portable sets not requiring electricity, broadcasts can be made in many languages, and it can be listened to by the illiterate. It is also a medium with which many people have been familiar for a long time. Moreover radio can be listened to in places, such as in a car, when television cannot be watched.

News bulletins, interviews, magazine programmes and so on can be interested in public relations material. Some services give information on local events, road traffic conditions, flight arrivals, police notices, stock market prices and other topics and this information may have to be supplied by the public relations or press officer of the organisation concerned. Interviews can be live, taped in the studio or supplied from a public relations source on tape.

PAYING FOR THE PRIVILEGE!

A practice which would surprise public relations officers in the industrialised world, and probably in a good many developing countries, has become normal in Nigeria. Due to the economic situation, and the need to raise revenue, a charge is made by Nigerian television companies for any public relations news story which they broadcast.

This preposterous denial of the criterion of newsworthiness is hard to believe. The media *buy* news by employing journalists or subscribing to news agencies. They receive public relations news free of charge. It is a bonus. Even the curse of the 'brown envelope' is scorned by professional editors. Now the Nigerian television companies charge one of its sources of news instead of welcoming stories it might otherwise not have known about. Business news is no less news than political or social news. It may be even more interesting.

Perhaps this has been encouraged by the poor quality of public relations news releases. Editors do not like puffs. But the answer to the puff is to reject it. Nigerian public relations officers (and their employers) who have insisted on submitting unpublishable stories have only themselves to blame, and with Nigerian television companies making charges for even usable stories they have created their own penalty.

When the author visited a Nigerian television station in September 1985 the general manager admitted that the practice of charging for the broadcasting of business news was unethical.

TELEVISION

Although there are still a few countries, such as Malawi and Botswana, which do not yet have their own television stations, television is widespread and is rapidly becoming less of an elitist medium than it used to be. The reasons for this are quite different from those in, say, Britain where television is the mass market medium, extremely popular with the working and middle classes, and watched by people of all ages. Up to 20 million people may watch a major programme.

Television has reached larger audiences in some industrialising countries, in spite of electricity being unavailable, by means of 16 volt battery powered sets and by the use of generators and community centres. For some years Indonesia has carried television to its people spread over an area as wide as that of the United States and with three time zones, using a satellite and 90 earth stations. For the past few years, commercials have been banned in Indonesia because they raised the expectations of the people during a period of economic recession. When commercials were permitted, they were assembled in special segments, mostly at 6 pm and interspersed with pop records to attract viewers. But people with batteries which have to be recharged periodically are selective about their viewing!

This is seldom the case in Nigeria where the television set seldom seems to be switched off, and in large families it is left on to amuse the children, even though this may contribute to the frequent power cuts.

But why blame advertising for worsening the economic situation? Indonesia has acute problems which affect its economy. First, the country is largely an amalgam of lands and islands acquired from neighbours, colonial powers and occupiers including the Dutch, British, Japanese and Malaysians. Consequently, as *The Economist*[3] has said, 'Although nine-tenths of Indonesia's 165 million people profess to be Moslems — making it the world's biggest Islamic nation — most of them are "statistical Moslems".' The ruling party, United Development, has stamped on fundamentalist Islamic activists rather like it kept the Chinese under control by banning the use of Chinese names and the display of Chinese signs. In a country which 'contains almost as many ethnic groups as islands' President Suharto has introduced the Pancasila doctrine which is a semi-religious philosophy aimed at creating national unity and keeping the Iran-type Islam influences at bay. This is perhaps not too difficult in a country where the Moslem religion has been imposed upon the original Buddhism of Java and is a long way from the Islamic version.

Advertising, therefore, has to contend with the effects of religious strife on the economy, but worse than that is the deep-rooted corruption and the vagaries of the taxation system.

President Suharto, faced with the urgent need to improve his country's overseas trade situation, is having to combat corruption. It is significant that, while international trade exhibitions are being held in Jakarta, the biggest worry of the foreign exhibitors is not how to sell to the Indonesians but how to deal with Indonesian corruption. In 1985, President Suharto was bold enough to dismiss 13,000 customs officials (if only on 'indefinite paid leave') who were believed to be taking £200 million a year in bribes. The Société Général de Surveilance of Switzerland was brought in to handle customs inspections.

Public relations in Indonesia suffers from the peculiarities of the tax system to the extent that it could attract the attention of the inland revenue if a company success story was published in the press. As a result, press relations can be inhibited.

If anyone has benefited from public relations in Indonesia it has been the Japanese. Whereas Indonesia had thrown off the yokes of the Dutch colonists and Japanese occupiers, and welcomed the English-speaking Americans, Australians, British and Canadians, there was hostility towards the Japanese when they first tried to sell motor-cars in Indonesia. Over the years goodwill has been won, through good use of public relations techniques such as charitable sponsorships, until today the streets of Jakarta are as dominated by Japanese motor-cars as those of Hong Kong, Singapore, Kuala Lumpur and Bangkok.

Attitudes to television vary remarkably. Africans tend to believe that television is for young people. In Malaysia, partly for similar reasons but mainly because prime time is taken up with locally made programmes in Bahasa Malay, strong imported drama series or American soap operas like *Dynasty* and *Dallas* are shown at 11p.m. Malaysian programmes are of good quality, and an annual Academy Awards ceremony is held, covering both radio and television productions.

Most television in industrialising countries is state owned and controlled, either as a national television company or as part of the Ministry of Information. It does not have the autonomy of the BBC which, while being a public authority, can present programmes critical of the government if it wishes. This can have a very limiting effect on the acceptance of public relations material, although there are still the news bulletins which may accept business news. It is also possible that public relations documentaries of wide audience appeal will be accepted, especially where the television station has limited resources for producing films. The British Central Office of Information has a film acquisition department which distributes non-advertising public relations films to television companies world-wide.

But to return to the question of ages of viewers. In these countries audiences are mostly aged between 20 and 40 years of age, whereas European and North American television is watched by a very large number of people older than 40. Extended families do not exist in Europe and North America and many viewers may be living alone, and be elderly. The population triangles given in Chapter 6 help to explain this. In societies where 50 per cent of the population is under 15 years of age, and the elderly do not form a large proportion of the population, the ages of adults who watch television seriously will be between 20 and 40 years of age.

Sport is an extremely popular television subject. This includes football, either local or foreign, particularly British. Special sports programmes are compiled by the BBC and syndicated to overseas television companies. The FA Cup Final is seen in 50 countries, often live by satellite, and that includes a number of industrialising countries where the whole programme is usually sponsored by an advertiser. World Cup football is likewise seen in this way, and also major sporting events like the Olympic Games, when a series of programmes will be sponsored night after night by a company such as Coca-Cola.

Returning to attitudes, television has very much suited the life style of Arab families, and this has also been extended to video cassette recorders and cassettes. Kuwait has become one of the world's largest markets for video. There are two reasons for this. Women may seldom go out, and families and friends gather in the home in the evening. Arabs are not great readers, and this is partly due to lack of time spent alone.

Advertising has a big influence on television in industrialising countries. In Zimbabwe such is the demand for prime time that to satisfy advertisers there are large clusters of commercials during the mid-evening. This is foolish because although it pampers to the demands of advertisers, and so sells airtime and provides much needed revenue, it is boring and frustrating to viewers who may retaliate by not watching, switching off, or playing videos.

MOBILE UNITS/CINEMA

Perhaps one of the most interesting forms of public relations in industrialising countries is the way in which information, both government and business, is conveyed to people in the countryside and often in very remote areas. This has been practised for many years. There are mobile film shows (and nowadays it is becoming more convenient to transport videos). Commercial shows may include singers and dancers, product demonstrations and the handing out of sales literature and samples. These are common in Nigeria and Kenya, and we have already mentioned the fashion shows which are toured in Malawi by the Whitehead textile company. In Kenya there are private commercial operators of mobile cinemas, such as Katex, and also those toured by large companies such as the Unilever organisation and East Africa Industries. Government information services may use local village talent to augment talks, films or video. Land Rovers and similar pick-up vehicles are used, while motor launches are used on waterways and lakes.

In Malaysia, government information services were intensified following the May 13 1969 incident when fighting broke out in Kuala Lumpur between Malays and Chinese who protested that they were treated as second class citizens, with the government favouring the Malays. Public relations services were developed by the Ministry of Information and the individual ministries to keep people better informed and to create racial harmony.

The following is an account of the work of mobile units in Malaysia, where today the more portable video cassette recorder and video cassette are replacing the screen and film.

An Example of Mobile Units

Long established in Malaysia by the British, and continued since independence, is the government information service of mobile film units which visit villages even in the remotest parts of the country. Until a few years ago, Malaysian information officers came to Britain for training with the Central Office of Information, but more recently training has been centralised in Malaysia, and in October 1984 the state government of Sarawak announced an increase in its internal information services under the direction of the Chief Political Secretary, Tuan Haji Khaider Zaidell. There are today some 350 mobile units operating in Malaysia.

In Sarawak, once a British colony on the island of Borneo but now part of Malaysia, there are 62 mobile units.

These units operate Land Rovers, the Riverine service with wooden and fibre-glass long boats powered by outboard motors plus fibre-glass speedboats, and occasionally they hire light aircraft and helicopters. The units are manned by teams of three or four people.

The purpose of this field service is to explain government policies and actions to the people who may be of many races including the indigenous Ibans who live in longhouses which accommodate from 50 to 100 families.

Public assemblies are called to discuss government policy which has been already announced on the radio. An excellent example of the innovator or dispersion theory is practised, local opinion leaders (briefed by the information officers) explaining the government policy. A version of the 'village theatre' conducted in Nigeria is followed with the performance of sketches which present the message dramatically. These playlets usually consist of three short scenes of ten minutes or less duration. The scenes are interspersed with music and songs performed by both the visiting artists (mostly information personnel) and locals. The information service tours the players in a separate vehicle. Film shows are also given, either on the day before the stage show or the day after.

In the middle '60s and '70s, when the border was threatened by Communists, one programme aimed to demonstrate the consequences of supporting the infiltrators. More recently, there has been a programme to explain the resettlement scheme associated with a hydro-electric project.

An interesting example is the Heart and Mind project to encourage local people to take up organised community work, such as making footpaths or river cleaning to improve the amenities. These groups may be led by the local member of parliament and the sketches are a practical medium for showing the sort of community work that can be undertaken in the public interest. Thus the 'self-help' principle is encouraged.

A Nigerian Example

In the mid-'80s the Ministry of Health in Nigeria conducted an interesting public relations campaign which demonstrates how this country has made excellent use of public relations through the government information services. In Nigeria, public relations has been used in the public sector to conduct numerous services in the public interest, such as changing over from driving on the left-hand side of the road to driving on the right; adult literacy campaigns; the introduction of Universal Primary Education for all children of five years of age or more; personal health and hygiene campaigns; and many others. In each state there are local information officers who coordinate national information campaigns.

The example given here is of a campaign to make available to every village in the country vaccines supplied by the Federal Military Government for the immunisation of babies and pregnant women. The infant mortality rate had been very high for the past 20 years, while many women died during pregnancy or lost their babies six months after delivery.

The expanded programme of immunisation (EPI) sought to educate Nigerians about government efforts to stop or minimise the calamities which had struck mothers and babies in the past. Primarily, the programme offered vaccines for the prevention of measles, poliomyelitis, dyphtheria in children, whooping cough, and also the immunisation of pregnant woman against any of these diseases while their babies were still in the womb.

Committees were formed at federal, state and local government levels for effective public enlightenment. One reason for this was that in a large country with some 62 languages and dialects, a national campaign in one common language, even English, was not possible. It had, therefore, to be a grass roots programme if it was to be communicated effectively. In the main, the programme was conducted in the four principal languages, English, Hausa, Yoruba and Igbo, plus local languages where necessary.

Radio and television (both state and national television), and the press (which has vernacular newspapers) played important roles, together with the public enlightenment unit of the Ministry of

Information. The innovation theory technique was very well applied by engaging the traditional local rulers in the education of their subjects at village level. Market women associations, the 'market gossip' medium, also played a useful part. Church leaders and teachers in primary and post-primary schools also contributed. Other public relations efforts included leaflets and brochures, and feature articles in the press supplied by the Ministry of Health at federal and state level.

Roads, bridges and culverts were specially built on some state roads to provide easier access to rural areas by the medical team.

The complete programme was well organised to explain the need for immunisation of every child and pregnant mother, and to win the co-operation of every Nigerian citizen in carrying out the scheme in the belief that prevention is better than cure.

The War Against Indiscipline Programme

During 1984 the Buhari military government in Nigeria, which had replaced the corrupt civilian government, introduced the war against indiscipline public relations programme. The objective was to encourage new values that would help the country in its efforts to deal with an economic situation which the world saw primarily as Nigeria's prodigious $15 billion foreign debt.

The war against indiscipline campaign sought to bring about a more responsible work force and a more productive economy. It urged punctuality, queuing in orderly fashion (how Nigerians love horizontal queues!), and patriotism.

To this end public meetings, shows, debates, poster displays, and even war against indiscipline buttons, were used. The results showed in the new attitudes it encouraged. People did adopt proper queuing, did arrive at work on time, and became optimistic in spite of the government's tough edicts. It was reminiscent of Roosevelt's exhortations to the American people in the depression years of the '30s. But such a campaign is not easy to conduct in a large multi-cultural country like Nigeria, and probably only evidence of a recovering economy will sustain enthusiasm for it, in spite of the dictates of a military regime. Nevertheless, the better educated new generation has probably lost patience with the inefficiencies and corruption of the past, and a turn round in Nigeria's prosperity will be stimulating to the whole of black Africa.

Nigeria celebrated 25 years of independence in October 1985. From a colonial administration which had brooked no opposition Nigeria entered upon 25 years of unsatisfactory government. Both British and American democratic systems were tried and both failed, the latter inviting the corruption which the Americans had perfected for more than a century. Military governments also came and went with assassinations, coups and palace revolutions. In a country which dissipated ₦ 43 billion of oil revenue between 1979 and 1983 when Nigeria's 'total oil' revenue from 1958 to 1979[4] was ₦ 41 billion, and with a population of 100 million, expected to expand to 220 million over the next 25 years[5], press relations between government and media are apt to be erratic and inadequate.

At least the new military government of Major General Ibrahim Badomosi Babangida, when he deposed his predecessor Major General Muhamadu Buhari on August 27, 1985, showed a new attitude to the media. The infamous Decree No 4 (Protection of public officers against false publication) was proscribed and six imprisoned journalists were released. The next step, about a month later, was to appoint a very experienced and respected journalist as press secretary to the Head of State. This was Chief Duro Onabule, editor of the *National Concord*, a comparatively new newspaper which had grown in status in a very few years.

Taking up his new job (at less pay) at Dodan Barracks, Onabule set out to emulate Ogbuefe Alex Nwokedi, the famous press secretary to General Olusegun Obasanjo from 1976 to 1979, who achieved excellent rapport between the government and the media. In an interview published in the Nigerian *Sunday Times*[6], Babangida's chief spokesman stated:

'In this position I'm supposed to serve as a link between the government and the people.

'It is well-known that even if you have the most performing government and there is no communication between it and the people through the media that is, the government efforts won't be appreciated. So I'll try to establish that link'.

He went on to promise:

'I will do my best to avoid the misunderstandings of the recent past between the government and the media, an example of which was that some sections of the press were seen to belong to an enemy camp while others, who were more or less court jesters, were treated like spoilt children'.

The British *UK Press Gazette*[7] also reported the repeal of Decree No 4, quoting a statement by Bola Adedoja, president of the Nigerian National Union of Journalists. Adedoja said: 'The abrogation of Decree 4 is a vindication of the stand of NUJ over measures calculated to muzzle the press and deprive the people of their natural rights to free speech and the right to information'.

CASE STUDY

Here is an interesting case study in 'crisis public relations' which has been contributed by Femi Ogunleye, public relations officer, Nigeria Airways.

Sustaining Public Confidence in Nigeria Airways F28 after November 28, 1983 Crash

On November 28, 1983, Nigeria Airways recorded an air disaster which claimed 53 lives.

A Fokker F28 aircraft operating a Nigeria Airways domestic service between Lagos and Enugu, crashed at Emene, two kilometres from the Enugu airport terminal building, leaving only 19 survivors from the 72 passengers on board.

The captain of the flight, the first officer and head of cabin crew were among the survivors.

The November 28 accident was the second major crash in which a F28 aircraft was written off in an accident. The earlier one was an air collision with a military jet in Kano in March 1978 in which 25 people were killed. Before then there had been minor incidents such as over-running/overshooting, tyre bursts and so on. All the accidents and incidents had at one time or the other attracted press coverage.

Before the November 1983 accident, there had been some suppressed insinuations questioning why smaller aircraft, such as F28, should ply one route when bigger aircraft, such as the Boeing 737 and the Boeing 707, ply others. Even when explained that the distance, traffic volume and available facilities at airports determine aircraft schedules, the critics saw no reason for sending 'smaller' aircraft on their routes.

The November 1983 accident, however, appeared to be the climax of public conjectures and misgivings on Nigeria Airways rationale for scheduling F28 aircraft on certain routes within the domestic network.

Perhaps because the accident occurred within the area almost turning to a buffer-stock for the then ruling party, the then Minister for Transport and Aviation, Umaru Dikko, cashed in on the emotion and sentiment of the people, and ordered the immediate withdrawal from service of the remaining seven F28s in the fleet of Nigeria Airways.

That decision, which was made without reference to any known law or advice, became the climax of the crisis of confidence in Nigeria Airways and F28 aircraft in particular.

Public Relations Objectives and Strategies

How to restore public confidence in the national airline, and F28 aircraft particularly, so as to re-introduce it into service, became the task of public relations.

Nigeria Airways public relations strategies included a massive publicity campaign to disabuse the minds of the public that the F28 aircraft in the fleet of Nigeria Airways were old and unserviceable.

In doing this, records of the aircraft since the date of purchase, maintenance schedule, hours flown and so on, giving supportive correlations with other F28s in service with other airlines in various parts of the world, were placed before the public.

Besides regular informative press releases directly written by the internal public relations team, special media writers were encouraged to give independent accounts of the aircraft through records which were made available to them. Key groups, such as pilots and the engineers association, flight engineers and other interested bodies, were encouraged to organise talks and symposia on relevant subjects such as 'air safety in Nigeria'. During these talks the characteristics of different aircraft and other equipment in aviation management were discussed, and F28 aircraft were particularly given prominence.

The Transport and Aviation committee members of the parliament were approached individually and collectively with a view to educating them on the intricacies and complexities of airline management, during which the F28 issue was exhaustively discussed.

The manufacturers of F28 were not left behind in the exercise. Fokker sent in documents and films/video and other data on the aircraft to support Nigeria Airways' public relations effort in educating the public about the safety and reliability of F28 aircraft and, in particular, those in the Nigeria Airways fleet. Eventually, the Federal Government instituted a judicial enquiry into the causes of the accident. This provided the opportunity and the avenue for the airline and Fokker to officially and publicly denounce public insinuations about the unreliability of the aircraft and any other political undertones.

By the efforts of Nigeria Airways public relations, the public was convinced that the decision to ground all the remaining F28s without any proof of technical faults in them was political, and not realistic nor economical. A hypothetical example was made of a car accident

— 'if a man crashes his Volkswagon car, can it be realistic to say all the Volkswagon cars bought by all individuals or groups in the country should be scrapped'? The public response was 'No'.

The public was also made to understand that even before the accident, the airlines had had a fleet plan to phase out F28s and two other models, Boeing 707s and Boeing 727s, so as to minimise the types of aircraft in the fleet for economical maintenance and management.

Public opinion monitored after three months of campaign showed that passenger confidence in the aircraft had been regained, and on May 26, 1984, exactly 180 days after being grounded, the F28 roared into the airspace of Nigeria. Before this day, test flights had been made and adequate press coverage had been made of those flights for passengers' awareness.

Although the F28 planes are returned to service with Nigeria Airways, they generated new media coverage as the national airline sought buyers in conforming to its policy to phase out the type.

References

1 De Maeseneer, Paul, *Here's the News*, Asia-Pacific Institute for Broadcasting Development, Kuala Lumpur, 1982.
2 Kotler, Philip, *Marketing Management*, 3rd ed, Prentice-Hall, London, 1976.
3 *Economist, The*, 'Emasculating Islam? London, May 25, 1985.
4 *Sunday Times*, interview with Professor Alaba Ogunsanwo, Lagos, September 29, 1985.
5 *Sunday Times*, report of speech by Professor Adebayo Adedeji, Executive Secretary of the Economic Commission for Africa, Lagos, September 29, 1985.
6 Odunfa, Shola, article, 'Babangida's Chief Spokesman', *Sunday Times*, Lagos, September 29, 1985.
7 *UK Press Gazette*, report, 'Infamous Decree No 4 is Repealed', London, September 30, 1985.

5
The Role of Propaganda

DEFINITION AND BRIEF HISTORY OF PROPAGANDA

Three methods are basic in any attempt at convincing people of one's attitude of mind or line of argument. These are coercion (force), corruption (bribery), and persuasion (psychological motivation). The central objective behind propaganda, which is persuasion, is to make a person, a group of persons or an entire population do what the communicator intends them to do. This strategy has been referred to as mind management by Ugboajah[1]. However, the subject of propaganda is difficult to discuss in meaningful terms because of its spurious and abstract nature. One definition of propaganda is: 'a systematic attempt to influence opinion or attitude in the interest of some cause.'

Martin[2] traces the history of propaganda to the era of Pope Gregory XV. He founded the Sacre Congregatio De Propaganda Fide in 1622 to do missionary work abroad to propagate the Gospels and win souls. By the early 19th century the term 'propaganda' had acquired a derogatory connotation. W.T. Brande[3], describes propaganda in the following way: 'Derived from this celebrated society, the name propaganda is applied in political language as a term of reproach to secret associations for the spread of opinions and principles which are viewed by most governments with horror and aversion.'

There is today, in London, the United Society for the Propagation of the Gospel. It employs a press and publicity officer with a worldwide mission, and his job is to 'write press releases, feature articles, interview visitors and answer enquiries from the press'[4]. What is his job, public relations or propaganda? This is an interesting question. Such a person could perform both tasks, that is, disseminating factual information about Christianity (public relations), and disseminating information aimed at converting people to Christianity (propaganda).

Organisations representing various denominations and creeds are concerned with both. It is public relations to create understanding of a church as a religion, that is informative and educational, whereas it is propaganda to seek to attract members and believers. The difference may seem marginal but it is, nevertheless, crucial. For instance, it is sensible that Christians should understand the Islamic faith, and vice versa, but they do not have to change religions. However, the effort to change people's beliefs would be propaganda.

Another definition of propaganda is that it is *the means of gaining support for an opinion, creed or belief*. This support may be by way of membership, subscriptions or donations, voluntary work or votes. There is no exchange, and the support is all out-going and often sacrificial with no reward other than perhaps mental satisfaction. Unlike public relations, it is a one-way, biased form of communication , although the cause which is served may be a good or a bad one. Much charity propaganda aims at saving lives, whereas political propaganda may seek to promote undesirable regimes where life is at risk.

Systematic propaganda started during the first World War. It was then discovered that total war could be waged not only by attacking the physical body of men but also by attacking their minds. By the early '50s, the Hoveland's Communication and Attitude Change Programme at Yale University, USA[5], was instituted to study and perfect propaganda. Also Columbia University, New York, started a Bureau of Applied Social Research under the leadership of an eminent social scientist, Paul Lazarsfeld. The Bureau made major contributions in the area of challenging the assumption of the instant effect or 'hypodermic needle effect' of persuasive communication. Significant early British contributions in this respect are traced to the work of Trenamen and McQuail[6] in their studies of media impact on knowledge levels of individuals about election issues.

IS IT GOOD OR BAD?

Unlike public relations, but like advertising, propaganda is naturally biased in favour of its sponsor. Some of the well-known uses of propaganda have been disliked, but mainly because the organisation issuing it was disliked. Adolf Hitler was a master of propaganda, with the infamous Dr Goebbels heading his Department of Propaganda and Social Enlightenment. Every German was obliged to own a radio set so that he or she could receive Nazi propaganda. During the Second World War, Lord Haw-Haw made propaganda broadcasts for the Germans, and Tokyo Rose did the same for the Japanese.

But equally, the British had their Ministry of Information which issued propaganda both at home and abroad. During the Second World War, the Ministry of Information displayed posters bearing messages such as *Dig For Victory* (to encourage people to grow vegetables), *Be like Dad, Keep Mum* (to discourage people from gossiping and perhaps inadvertently giving away vital information to an eavesdropping spy), and *Is Your Journey Really Necessary?* (to discourage people from wasting public transport resources such as trains). This propaganda was done humorously with cartoon illustrations. However, during the First World War there was the often criticised and rather sinister Kitchener Army recruitment poster with the general pointing his finger and the message *Your Country Needs You!*.

In times of war, both sides in the conflict issue propaganda to maintain morale, stir up patriotism or demoralise the enemy. This propaganda often indulges in downright untruths such as fictitious atrocity stories. Both sides depict the other as evilly as possible. Then the politicans sit down and sign a peace treaty and everyone is friends again! As George Viereck said in 1931, 'Without hate there can be no propaganda'.

That may be true in wartime, but in peacetime governments indulge in propaganda to inspire love, admiration, trade agreements, emigration, tourism and so on. Exaggerated claims may be made to this end. The best side of things is presented in advertisements, films, political speeches, exhibitions and other forms of propagandist information. Every country in the world indulges in propaganda which may be fanciful but not evil.

Propaganda is also employed by numerous societies and voluntary bodies, such as charities or ones representing special interests. For instance, there is the Tobacco Advisory Council representing the tobacco industry. The Freedom Organisation for the Right to Enjoy Smoking Tobacco (FOREST) which presents the interests of smokers, and Action on Smoking and Health (ASH) which opposes smoking. Thus there are organisations which propagate all kinds of interests, some supporting, some attacking certain topics.

In many respects such organisations represent democratic society and the right of people to promote their beliefs, many of which may be good, if one-sided. For example, people who enjoy field sports will not like organisations like the League Against Cruel Sports. Many people in Britain who love animals object to the hunting of wild animals such as foxes, otters and deer, but in developing countries where wild animals may be a danger or nuisance such a point of view may be difficult to understand.

All charities, which perform valuable social services, adopt propaganda techniques to obtain funds, members, helpers and sympathisers, and to get government support for their aims. In this sense, propaganda can be a very good thing, even though it is obviously biased in favour of particular interests.

It is mainly in the political sphere that propaganda provokes distrust. Naturally, politicians seek to present the best case for their policies, and are apt to make big promises in order to win votes or continued support if in power. This is acceptable in a democracy where there is freedom of expression, and the electorate can believe or disbelieve as it wishes, and vote accordingly. But where there is a one-party or military government, and virtually a dictatorship, the propaganda can be abused and either swallowed whole because there is no alternative information, or distrusted because opposition is disallowed.

This is where government control of the media is dangerous, and where independent media are superior. When the press, radio and television are state-owned, the public can only know what they are told. But even in industrialised societies the independent media can be biased because they may be owned by, or represent the interests of, political parties, trade unions, churches or other organisations with vested interests. Even in Britain the media are sometimes accused of being biased. However, the BBC has always striven to maintain its independence, for while it is a public service it is not controlled by the government. In spite of a government having a difficult time or being unpopular, the BBC (and also ITV) will present the facts in news bulletins and invite opposing people to take part in studio interviews. This is very different from radio and television (as, say, in Russia) which broadcasts only the official view.

Propaganda is thus more like advertising than public relations in that to succeed it is bound to be biased. While it seeks to achieve belief, it does not require the credibility which is the hallmark of public relations, nor must it avoid the exaggeration which would make advertising ineffective. Often, it is cajoling, deceptive or aggressive in its desire to influence, assert its point of view or gain adherents. In so doing it may well use the communication techniques of public relations and advertising, but for its own special purposes.

To adopt a broader view of propaganda Jefkins defines it as 'the means of gaining support for an opinion, cause or belief'. This extends propaganda beyond the more commonly accepted religious and political users to all those non-commercial bodies which seek supporters, members and financial contributors. This includes voluntary bodies, special interest societies, and charities whose objectives may be sectional and biased or desirable and laudable. Great propaganda efforts have been used to raise funds for the social disasters which have ravaged the world, such as famine, flood, earthquake and volcanic eruption. Live Aid was Bob Geldof's major propaganda effort which inspired the world's greatest charity response.

Propaganda is one of the oldest forms of communication. It is quite different from either advertising or public relations with which it is often confused. The expression 'trade propaganda' is wrongly used to describe the trade advertising which manufacturers address to wholesalers, retailers and agents through the trade press or by direct mail. Journalists, when they are being cynical about press relations, sometimes refer to news releases or press receptions as propaganda. The word is so loosely used that it produces frequent misunderstandings about its real nature and purpose.

One of the problems is that public relations practitioners, such as government information officers, may be engaged in a mixture of public relations and propaganda. It is necessary for them to distinguish between which form of communication they are using, and for the public to recognise which form of message they are receiving. Both produce publicity. The dilemma is not helped when a government information service is called the Department or Ministry of Public Enlightenment!

A WEAPON OF POWER

According to the late J. B. Whitton[7], propaganda is a valuable weapon of power, as evidenced by the powerful effect of the BBC and Voice of America. Even with small states, ideological warfare may be their only weapon in the absence of other military, economic and diplomatic capabilities.

Without the invention and universal use of wireless communications, propaganda would have been less effective or less widespread or even impossible. The Germans learnt the first lesson when, by a not unusual historical coincidence, they found themselves cut off from the rest of the world at the beginning of the war. The Allies were in control of the cables. The Germans were therefore forced to turn to wireless communications and, by 1915, amateurs and agents abroad were receiving daily news bulletins from Germany. The propaganda activities of Bela Kun, the Hungarian Communist leader, after the First World War, worried Austria and Switzerland to such an extent that they protested vigorously. Kun was addressing his propaganda broadcast to proletariats all over the world.

The credit for the development of international propaganda as an instrument of foreign policy in peace time is generally attributed to Hitler and Lenin. But it was Lenin and Trotsky who originated the idea of broadcasting to foreign peoples over the heads of their governments. Propaganda messages of this type are usually directed against real or imaginary enemies or at neutral target audiences who might be won over. International broadcasting effort is usually directed to the latter audience and is also aimed at reinforcing positive and friendly images held about the propagandist nation.

The developing world is completely encircled by foreign media activities, particularly broadcasts. For example, 52 countries direct English broadcasts to Anglophone Africa where English is spoken primarily, due to historical or colonial circumstance. Boyd and Mackay[8] emphasised that broadcasts segment a class which is most desirable as a target audience of international communication. Certainly, international English broadcasts create linguistic and cultural assimilation of the elite in industrialising countries. Some of the international radio stations that beam English language broadcasts to Africa are Radio Peace and Progress of USSR, Radio Moscow, Voice of America, Radio Netherlands, Radio Canada International, the Israeli Broadcasting Authority and the Broadcasting Service of Saudi Arabia.

The British Broadcasting Corporation is either relayed or monitored and rebroadcast by many Anglophone countries of Africa. Such relays of the BBC are going on Radio Gambia, which tunes in BBC for World News and News of the African World. Radio ELWA (Eternal Love Winning Africa) of the Sudan Interior Mission in Liberia, also relays the BBC. So does Sierra Leone Broadcasting Service (SLBS) which also relays Voice of America and Radio Moscow. Liberia Broadcasting Corporation relays Voice of America from 2300 – 2358 daily. These international stations are designed to be used by the stations of the African continent.

Mention should be made here of the incessant hostile propaganda mounted by South Africa through its mouthpiece, Radio South Africa, against neighbouring African states. Radio South Africa strives daily to confer prestige onto the South African system, drive fear and insecurity into the populations of neighbouring states, as well as divide the people's collective resistance to the apartheid system of

South Africa. Radio South Africa uses hostile communication, what can be regarded as defamatory propaganda, against the leaders and institutions of the neighbouring states. The African leaders are called illiterates. The UN is described as an illegal and hypocritical organisation lacking in prestige. Such inflamatory propaganda tends to degrade, revile or insult foreign independent states, their institutions, leaders and people. Whitton[9] makes this clear: '... Despite frequent violations, it is clear from review of customary international law, the writings of publicists, the relevant treaties in this matter and the decision at Nuremberg, supported by pertinent analogies to domestic laws everywhere, that the act of engaging in subversive propaganda (as in the case of Radio South Africa) except when within the limits prescribed by precedent and principle, is contrary to the law of nations.' South Africa, being the outcast of the world community, might care little about respecting international law, ethics, and agreements.

PROPAGANDA MODELS AS BASIC MODELS IN THIRD WORLD BROADCASTING DEVELOPMENT

Colonially speaking, British and French governments saw radio broadcasting primarily as an extension of their political and cultural influence. The Second World War provided the impetus for the development of radio broadcasting in the colonies in that it was used as a propaganda organ to inform the colonies about the war. Thus after the war the format of propaganda broadcasting was grafted onto the colonies. Radio broadcasting became well established, with about 12,000 radio sets and 3,000 wired boxes in Nigeria in 1948. Programmes were broadcast for 18 hours daily, of which 17 hours were relayed from the BBC Empire Service. Broadcasting structures in the British colonies were modelled on the BBC format. There was a deliberate extension of the BBC model to British expatriates in the colonies, and the development of local services by the colonial administration accompanied the transfer of broadcasting.

In the French colonies, the French model of broadcasting was patterned to relay metropolitan services aimed primarily at expatriates and local urban elite. In Algeria, programmes were relayed directly from France, while in West Africa the territories were served by Radio Afrique Occidentale Français based in Senegal. The staff were trained in France at the ORTF. Television services were introduced years after independence. The French Département des Affairs Extérieures et

Coopération (DAEC) offered consultation and advice to the newly independent countries and equipment was supplied by Thomson-CSP of France. Elihu Katz and George Wedell[10] have written exhaustively on the promise and performance of broadcasting in industrialising societies. Much of the thought in this section of the chapter is drawn from their reliable observations.

The propaganda structure of broadcasting in industrialising countries has aided the spread of cultural imperialism and the creation of a sophisticated urban elite who are the main actors in national and international politics and diplomacy. It has also created an unfair urban-rural imbalance where a larger portion of the population, mainly less literate and poor people living in very underdeveloped areas, is cut off from mass communication.

At independence the new rulers embraced the propaganda role of the mass media and forgot that they could be restructured for development purposes and for integrating the rural areas into the nation. As Katz and Wedell[11] point out, although most developing countries have introduced radio and television broadcasting, little effort has been made towards formulating explicit policies to relate the media to development goals. The aims set for broadcasting in these countries have been narrowly fashioned after the West, namely, to inform, to educate and to entertain. Even then these aims are hardly pursued. Kwame Boafo[12] has this to say:

'For the most part, communication projects have been isolated attempts at change. Communication projects in sub-Saharan Africa have tended to operate over and above basic structural elements which constrain development. Also development-oriented communication projects undertaken in the region have been short-lived, ad hocish, limited in time and scope and have not been sustained or built into permanent national and comprehensive planning for development.'

Boafo notes that the ruling elite, who dominate the synchronic, hierarchical and centralised information systems in African societies, have the prerogative of determining what is politically and socially desirable information to transmit to the bulk of the population. Often the information transmitted is political in nature, propaganda-laden and has minimal significance or relevance for development.

Much of the modern communication media in Africa have been consciously used by political leaders as instruments for building personality cults, an enterprise which does not promote development. A broadcast director friend once told the author that he does not request huge budgets in between election years. He asks for and receives promptly more than his normal budget from the government during an election year. This period is when he is provided with new vehicles, outside broadcast equipment and new staff.

Communication is important to leaders in industrialising countries at a selfish level. Soldiers find it expedient to barricade broadcasting stations during and after a coup, for fear that opposing groups might vie for the control of this potent agent of public information. If governments would capitalise on the power of the mass media during critical periods of coups and elections, why should they not apply the same attitude to the problems of socio-economic development borne out of the promises made on their platforms and in their manifestos?

Katz and Wedell[13] note additional policies which guided the introduction of broadcasting to the industrialising world as the following:

1 enlistment of loyalty;
2 promotion of tranquility and unity in a grossly pluralistic nation;
3 preservation of autonomy or independence;
4 the achievement of modernisation;
5 the encouragement of indigenous creativity.

Still additional to these aims is the promotion of the profit motive (capitalism) as is the case in Peru, Brazil and Thailand.

Late to arrive in the industrialising world was television broadcasting. And where it appeared it seems to have been propelled:

1 as an opiate and diversion for the people;
2 as a symbol of nationhood;
3 as a projector of the image of leadership;
4 as part of the national celebration to transmit festivals, such as sports;
5 as a result of an attractive proposition by a foreign broadcast equipment merchant or manufacturer;
6 as a result of an educational prodding by UNESCO or other donor agencies;
7 as an answer to the cosmopolitan expectations of the urban elite whose tastes are teleguided from abroad and whose wishes are to be entertained in a cosmopolitan manner.

Of course, big-city or urban location of television stations automatically denies communication access to a great majority of the rural population who would have benefitted from television broadcasting, geared to rural reformation. In such a situation, what is left of the mass media is propaganda and information gaps.

In the industrialising world, particularly in Africa and Asia, the broadcasting systems are controlled by governments. Broadcasting mainly reflects metropolitan structures. In other words, it is a big-city phenomenon. The only difference between the African and the Asian broadcasting systems is that, with some exceptions such as the Philippines, South Korea and Lebanon, to a certain degree broadcasting stations are allowed to operate on the American model, a multi-operator commercial format. In South America there are many broadcasting stations — mainly small-scale types operated by private individuals. In Brazil alone there are about 1,200 radio stations. Only a token few are government-owned but all broadcasting operates under the supervision and regulation of a government agency, the Telecommunications Department.

Broadcasting technology depends on three types of activity: production, distribution and reception. It has been conclusively proved – later chapters will dwell more on this point — that the production technology of broadcasting is from the West; America and Europe; we add Japan. This technology is expensive to acquire, which has placed restrictions on the number of stations the industrialising world can have. Except for the OPEC countries, broadcasting stations average not more than one per country. Local programmes are very costly to produce, thus making it cheaper and easier to slot in imported foreign programmes. Only India, among industrialising countries, can produce its own programmes. The rest depend on foreign imports for most of their broadcast programmes, especially those on television. This heightens propaganda and entrenches cultural imperialism.

Radio broadcasting in the industrialising nations is mostly done on medium wave or short wave transmitters because of the large areas to be covered. Transmission and frequency problems result because of the use of wireless transmission, which suffers both tropopheric and ionospheric interferences. Additionally, there is the presence of ground conductivity which makes coverage of large geographical areas problematic.

An example of this problem is Radio Botswana which, owing to technological incapability, has deferred its role to Radio South Africa's propaganda machine, which is more clearly received in Botswana than the national broadcasting system. All transmitting outlets are concentrated in Gaborone, the capital, and most of the country receives a very poor signal from Radio Botswana, particularly during the day. Radio Botswana's coverage is poor because it broadcasts on medium-wave with a 50 kw transmitter and on short-wave with two 10 kw transmitters. It also has a VHF/FM 50 watt transmitter in Gaborone. This is not the type of equipment with which to counter Radio South Africa, or for use in national mobilisation.

Unreasonable fiscal policy, such as high taxes on books, films, radio and television receivers and video cassette recorders, impedes ownership of receivers by the vast majority of the population, particularly those living in the rural areas. Citizens are denied access to meaningful participation in the affairs of the nation, not only by such indefensible official policy but also by the absence of infrastructures such as electricity and good all-season roads in the rural areas.

The western format of broadcasting in the industrialising countries is fostered also through the training and professional styles of the personnel. Engineering and production staff are trained in the countries where the equipment originates. The methods and systems of work are imported, thus establishing dependence and cultural domination. The broadcaster depends on the West for such things as spare parts, retraining and acquisition of new generations of compatible equipment. Production and content are also imported, even the norms, unwritten rules, style of production and transmission, professional values and codes, expectations, beliefs and attitudes to service, indeed the entire format of propagandist broadcasting.

Once the transfer of the metropolitan model is complete, the rural sectors of the industrialising world, the real inhabitants, are written off the national agenda. One can cite the case of South and Central America, where the proliferation of small commercial radio stations was gradually forged into formidable family empires thus establishing the US model.

The pluralistic system of Dutch broadcasting still persists in places like Indonesia, where some 700 small radio stations are issued with licences to operate. Developing countries that were not formally colonised adapted broadcasting directly to local conditions and voided it of the propaganda element. Iranian and Thai radio structure co-opted American commercialism. There are about 200 to 300 broadcasting stations in Thailand with the spectrum heavily loaded with signals. Iran co-opted the American model despite the presence of government control. About 70 per cent of its programmes were American products before the revolution of the mulahs, headed by Ayatollah Khomeini. Libya, Iraq, Jordan and Syria operate government-owned broadcasting systems that are unitary in structure but also metropolitan in outlook. Jordan, Egypt and Syria still maintain American and British advisers in their broadcasting development. The structural problems are perhaps the major obstacle in the way of broadcasting for effective communication in industrialising countries.

THE DAWN OF DEVELOPMENT COMMUNICATION

High hopes were placed by early experts on the impact of the mass media in national development. To this end we credit foremost the work of Wilbur Schramm[14-21], who wrote massively on this subject in the early '60s. Schramm's ideas were sold to UNESCO which vigorously promoted the concept throughout the industrialising countries, with projects and other forms of assistance. By the late '70s it began to appear that the hopes on the big mass media as a potent agent of development were misplaced, as most industrialising countries were not responding to the mass media doses administered to them.

Indeed the African world was fast deteriorating instead of developing. It was discovered that too much emphasis was placed on the mass media instead of on general communication, meaning all forms of communication that can be found in the context of development. This has meant that all along, the hypodermic or propaganda principle of the mass media as a message injection process had been in use.

Chapters 8 and 9 of this book will hold that the 1970s was a decade of reawakening and rethinking about the concepts of development. This led to the movement for a new world information and communication order (NWICO), an emphasis on cultural consciousness and self identity of all nations and total restructuring of the information media to make them pertinent to development. Scholars are now directing their attention to underscore the myth of the mighty media and reassess their power.

The concept of oramedia has been advocated for African development by Ugboajah[22]. There are suggestions for the democratisation of communication by White[23], and total delinking of development from that of the West by Hamelink[24]. Some industrial countries have found the NWICO concept offensive because it poses formidable opposition to imperialism and neo-colonialism. Both the United States and Britain have pulled out of UNESCO, accusing it of incompetence and fronting for communism and backwardness.

France is not leaving UNESCO but neither is she going away from Africa. The dominance of the colonial cultural heritage remains clearest in those countries that were colonised by France, and we might add Portugal, Belgium and Spain. Few of these countries have developed national languages and cultural programmes in the mass media as have countries of the Anglophone group. Notwithstanding the nationalism of Guinea, which unilaterally pulled away from the rule of France in 1958, two years prior to the blanket granting of independence to all West African Francophone countries, its official language is still French and local languages are yet to be integrated into broadcasting development. Even at this point, when the consciousness of non-alignment and Panafricanism is having firm grip on the industrialising world, including Africa, France appears reluctant to see the writing on the wall.

A crusade has been launched by French officals to defend French language and culture in Africa, singling out what they see as the 'dangerous influence of American television programmes'[25] according to a report in the *Daily Nation*. Within this crusade, France will work with African governments to train language teachers, develop local French language television programmes and promote creative writing in French under a scheme sponsored by the Ministry of Co-operation. French is spoken by some 110 million in a total population of about 520 million Africans. French constitutes the official language of 12 African countries.

The mass media in the industrialising countries have failed in the process of socio-economic development because they have neglected the indigenous cultural contexts and functioned, so far, along a propagandist format. Andrew Moemeka[26] reminds us that 'the oftenforgotten fact is that modern media technologies, modes and models of communication are products of (distant) Western culture and, therefore, have resulted from measures under very specific economic, social and cultural circumstances, quite different from those existing in countries into which the new media were introduced to aid development.' He asserts that this constitutes the major cog in the wheel of progress towards effective use of the mass media because it has meant that insufficient attention was paid to the socio-cultural and psychological environments and contexts.

The tendency to adapt broadcasting for educational purposes has not been very successful or conclusively achieved in most African, Central and South American countries, according to an observation by Katz and Weddel[27]. This is as a result of inadequate planning evident in poor reception, as was the case in Nigeria, lack of support materials, poor programme production, low audience participation, as was the case in Senegal and problems of co-ordination, production and transmission, as in Botswana, Thailand, and South and Central American countries.

Nora Quebral[28] of the University of the Philippines, has supported a concept of development communication which is aimed at reducing propaganda on issues of development. According to her:

'The purpose of development communication is to advance

development. Development requires that a mass of people
with a low rate of literacy and income and the socio-economic
attributes that go with it, first of all be informed about and
motivated to accept and use a sizeable body of hitherto unfamiliar ideas and skills in very much less time than that
process would normally take. This then is the job of development communication: to inform and motivate at the national,
sectoral and project levels. Stated in these terms, the job of
development communication is the process of development
itself.'

Development communication, interpreted differently, would involve all the marketing strategies which would map out territories and
have quality ideas or products to sell. It would also map out targets
and use salesmen and advertising strategies to make the ideas and
products acceptable to the clients and use public relations as the principal motivator for the acceptance of change needed for progress.
Such a strategy would involve all the media, particularly traditional
media structures known to the people, to generate interaction among
them. Development communication would involve research or fact
finding. Research attempts, such as cultural indicators, are important to understand and keep in view the specific cultural worlds in
which socio-economic development takes place. It is the absence of
such consistent research and profile studies that has converted socio-
economic development in the industrialising world, particularly
Africa, into revolutions of rising frustrations.

Nearly all development campaigns in Africa that emphasise rural
focus, for example, Nigeria's 'Operation Feed the Nation' and 'Green
Revolution', and Ghana's 'Operation Feed Yourself', have foundered
because of a lack of useable basic data or systematic information to
properly back these attempts at introducing progressive behavioural
change.

And in Nigeria's 'War Against Indiscipline' (WAI), the operators
of this campaign have confused cognitive shifts with behavioural
change and are celebrating a success that has not yet been achieved.
Transactions are lacking because of the limitations of the infrastructure. You cannot ask citizens to be disciplined and wait in line to
purchase 'essential commodities', such as rice, if you have only ten
bags of rice for 200 people and you expect each person to wait his turn
to collect one bag of rice. You cannot ask them to respect being in a
queue to enter a bus when you have just one bus for every 1,000

passengers. Condoms should not be scarce items in family planning campaigns.

Political will, not selfish ends, are important in applying communication strategies to socio-economic development. In the West, the market principle that backs free enterprise does the work for the profit motive. Buyer behaviour must be researched and appropriate communication strategies, in the forms of salesmanship, advertising, publicity and public relations, applied for competitive corporate survival. The government is spared the headache of this responsibility while it focuses its attention purely on administrative matters.

A few countries in the industrialising world have applied political will by using broadcasting to accomplish specific tasks. After the triumph of the Front de la Libération Nationale (FLN), Algeria decided to use radio and television intensively to raise the indigenous cultural level of its population, as well as to provide massive adult education services. In Cyprus, the broadcast media played an important role in the adoption of a new post-colonial dual Cypriot identity — Greek or Turkish. Nigeria has used decentralised television and radio broadcasting in the establishment of various regional or state identities since the early '60s.

Other countries of the industrialising world, where broadcasting is being adapted as an instrument of cultural, political and economic development as well as unity and national integration, are Iran, Thailand, Indonesia, Peru and Brazil. The new breed of leaders, on taking over power, realise the threat to indigenous cultures and economic development in the transmission of foreign programmes through indigenous broadcasting systems. They go for new broadcasting, as well as cogent information policies, that will enhance the realisation of their objectives, which are cultural, political and economic development as well as national integration.

Tanzania has succeeded in raising the educational and awareness levels of her citizens by activating and applying all the communication structures in the country along a multi-media approach. Botswana has applied the potency of the popular arts, in which it is so rich, to back communication for development. India adopts traditional media of the opera, music and dance as an official policy in communication development. Nigeria will now officially integrate traditional media (oramedia) in her public enlightenment efforts. In the industrialising nations, development communication, which involves development as strategic planning in the cultural context, constitutes an answer to propaganda. Ugboajah[29] recommends a strategic model of communication for development in Africa.

STRATEGIC MODEL OF COMMUNICATION FOR
DEVELOPMENT

Successful diffusion or transfer of innovation (agriculture, health,
taxation, management, education, science and technology, sport,
politics, social welfare, community development, etc.) depends upon
the priority given to strategic communication planning. Childers[30]
advocates a national systems approach to co-ordinate and develop
communication delivery services aimed at direct contact with those
groups of people who are willing to participate in the implementation of
the development plan. This would be preferable to, and more effective
than, relying entirely upon 'hypodermic' mass media publicity to gain
support for socio-economic development priorities. In fact, such
groups of people should be located along what Ugboajah describes as
'concentric cultural diameters' (see Fig. 5.1) to facilitate a horizontal
and holistic socio-economic development.

In this figure, A–F represents the cultural diameter (CD) of an
African nation. B–C represents the cultural diameter of the states or
provinces of the country. D–E represents the cultural diameter of the
villages which is the soul of the states and the nation. D–E cultural
diameter is made up of over 70 per cent of the human, physical and
psychological geography, the targets for whom communication for
development is directed and the targets which are needed for social
mobilisation through the process of communication. The rural-urban
ratio of settlements in Africa is always heavily skewed to the rural.

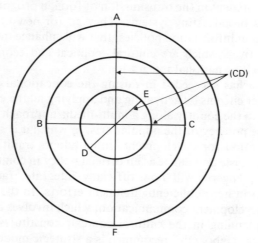

Fig. 5.1 Concentric cultural diameters

The cultural diameters would demarcate different communication modalities, objectives and strategies for socio-economic development. Projects of national character, for example, should be supported by communication requiring inputs from the cultural diameter that cuts across the entire nation (A–F). Provincial developments should emphasise the B–C cultural diameter. A–F projects would require a type of communication needed to bring about, for example, national unity in a multi-ethnic and pluralistic situation. Here the communicator would contextually use the electronic mass media, magazines and newspapers, as well as opinion leaders, as primary and not supplementary channels. But for decentralised matters of community and rural development, the D–E sectors would be reached through a communication strategy which de-emphasises the electronic and paper media.

Efforts should be made, primarily, to locate and use the most accessible and closest channels which are oramedial in nature. Oramedia are interpersonal. They are great legitimisers because they are highly distinctive and credible, unlike the electronic media which can be elitist, mighty, vicarious and urban.

The electronic media have been over-emphasised in Africa's public enlightenment and development campaigns. They are often very expensive, miss their target and fall on deaf ears because they cannot be fully integrated into psycho-cultural contexts. The result is that our well-intentioned development campaigns have become a woeful waste of scarce resources.

Decentralisation of the gatekeeper responsibilities, and of the media facilities geographically in the form of local radio or rural press, brings the media systems much closer to local interests and involvement, issues and problems. Such horizontal communication leads to quick and effective socio-economic planning and development. It creates an effective integrated multi-media approach and leads to easy mobilisation of the people. Of all electronic media, the radio would certainly be the most effective in the D–E sector in the African situation. Radio is oral and has linguistic adaptability. Its decentralisation would enhance its impact and usefulness for national mobilisation and grass-roots appeal.

An example of an integrated multi-media model, for an effective cultural diameter campaign for mobilisation, is illustrated by Fig. 5.2. This involves a well-researched, well-prepared, well-packaged and planned information campaign, decentralised from the central campaign headquarters of A–F or B–C to link up with the mass media and the oramedia and D–E group channels. Then, through the complex nexus of the various communication channels contained within the

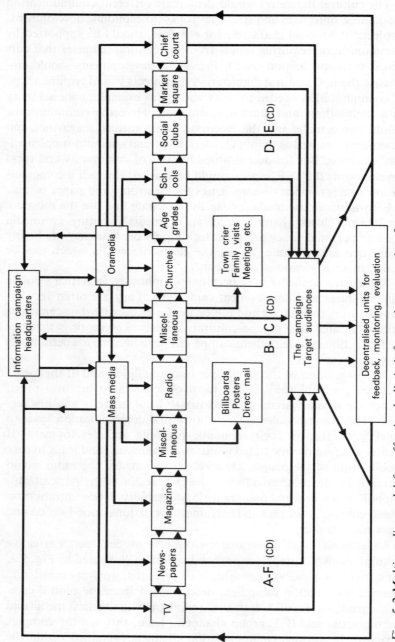

Fig. 5.2 Multi-media model for effective holistic information campaign for socio-economic development

two broad channels of mass media and oramedia, effective reward-oriented information gets to the target audiences along the various cultural diameters.

Continual reference to the campaign objectives and strategies is assumed through constant monitoring of campaign tactics, coupled with evaluation and feedback. Ordinarily, in the cultural diameters of A–F and B–C, more emphasis and strategic planning would be on the mass media, whereas if the campaigns were to have been limited or focussed on the cultural diameter of D–E, the emphasis on planning would have been weighted in favour of oramedia. One ought to supplement but not supplant the other.

Planners of development campaigns should think of integrated communication rather than about the use of specific media. As long as communication is extended, the action energised, the psychological mood set, the socio-cultural context identified, and the audience mobilised, it is unnecessary to worry about any given media. But planning and management are vital in locating the correct cultural diameter or diameters and the pertinent psychological field of the campaign, to aid media selection and strategy. In such a process, innovative communication and research are needed. The concentric cultural diameter model is a proposition that requires experimentation to save Africa and the industrialising world from the frustrations of development.

References

1 Ugboajah, Frank Okwu, 'Mind Management: An Analysis of South African Broadcasts Into Neighbouring African States', *Current Research on Peace and Violence*, Vol. IV, No. 4, pps. 287–309, Tampere, Finland, 1981.

2 Martin, Leslie John, 'International Propaganda in Retrospect and Prospect,' in Fischer, Heinz-Dietrich, and Merrill, John C., (eds), *International Communication*, Hastings House, New York, 1970.

3 Brande, W.T., *Dictionary of Science, Literature and Art*, 1942.

4 Advertisement, United Society for the Propagation of the Gospel, *UK Press Gazette*, London, October 21, 1985.

5 Hoveland, C.I., (ed), *Order of Presentation in Persuasion*, Yale University Press, New Haven, 1957.

6 Trenaman, J., and McQuail, D., *Television and the Political Image*, Methuen, London, 1961.

7 Whitton, John B., 'Hostile International Propaganda and International Law', in Nordenstreng, Kaarle and Schiller, Herbert I.,

(eds). *National Sovereignty and International Communication*, Norwood: Ablex Publishing Corporation, New Jersey, 1979.

8 Boyd, Douglas, and Mackay, Donald, 'English Radio Broadcasts to Africa', *Communication and Development Review*, Vol. 2, No. 2, pps. 29–32. Teheran, Summer, 1978.

9 Op. cit., Whitton, John B. Note 9.

10 Katz, Elihu, and Wedell, George, *Broadcasting in the Third World: Promise and Performance*, The Macmillan Press, London, 1978.

11 Ibid.

12 Boafo, Kwame, 'Utilising Development Communication Strategies in African Societies', 35:83–92, *Gazette*, Amsterdam, 1985.

13 Op. cit., note 12.

14 Schramm, Wilbur, 'Newspapers of a State as a News Network', *Journalism Quarterly*, 35:pps. 177–82, Minneapolis, 1958.

15 Schramm, Wilbur, and Carter, R.F., 'Scales for Describing National Communication Systems' (mimeo), Institute for Communication Research, Stanford, California, 1959.

16 Schramm, Wilbur, *One Day in the World's Press*, Stanford University Press, Stanford, California, 1960.

17 Schramm, Wilbur, *Mass Communications*, (Second Edition), Univeristy of Illinois Press, Urbana, 1960.

18 Schramm, Wilbur, 'Mass Communication', *Annual Review of Psychology*, 13:pps. 251–284, New York, 1962.

19 Schramm, Wilbur, 'The Newer Educational Media in the United States', working paper for Paris Conference of Experts on Educational Media, published in *New Methods and Techniques in Education*, pps. 5–17, UNESCO, Paris, 1962.

20 Schramm, Wilbur, and Winfield, G.F., 'New Uses of Mass Communication for the Promotion of Economic and Social Development', paper presented at the United Nations Conference on the Application of Science and Technology for the Benefit of the Less Developed Areas, Geneva, 1963. US Papers for the Conference, Vol. 10, Washington, D.C, 1963.

21 Schramm, Wilbur, *Mass Media and National Development: The Role of Information in the Developing Countries*, UNESCO, Paris, 1964.

22 Ugboajah, Frank Okwu, '"Oramedia" or Traditional Media as Effective Communication Options for Rural Development in Africa', *Communication Socialis Year Book*, Vol. 11, Rome, 1982–3.

23 White, Robert, 'Contradictions in Contemporary Policies for

Democratic Communication', paper presented to the International Association for Mass Communication Research Congress, Paris, September 5–10, 1982.

24 Hamelink, Cees J., *Cultural Autonomy in Global Communication: Planning National Information Policy,* Longman, New York, 1982.

25 *Daily Nation,* Nairobi, August 23, 1985.

26 Moemeka, Andrew A., 'Socio-Cultural Environment of Communications in Traditional Nigeria: An Ethnographic Exploration', *Communication Socialis* (16/1983/4), Aachen, January 1983.

27 Op. cit., note 12.

28 Quebral, Nora C., 'What Do We Mean By Developing Communication?' *International Development Review,* Vol. XV, No. 2, Paris, 1973.

29 Ugboajah, Frank Okwu, 'Mobilising African Resource for National Communication Strategies', *Media Development,* Vol. XXXII, No. 4, pps. 31–33, London, 1985.

30 Childers, Erskine, and Vajrathon, Maldica, 'Social Communication Components in Development Programmes', in Jamais, Juan F., (ed), *Readings in Development Communication,* University of the Philippines at Los Banos, Laguna, Philippines, 1975.

6
The Role of
Marketing

INTRODUCTION

The extent to which marketing exists in industrialising countries has been questioned already in the chapter on advertising. The term 'marketing' is often used glibly because it sounds more impressive than selling, and there are people with marketing titles which are at best optimistic descriptions of their responsibilities. The title may just sound better, and give greater status than that of 'sales manager'. To what extent, if any, are companies in industrialising countries concerned with researching the market, discovering what the market wants, and contributing to the development of products or services which will both satisfy customers and prove profitable to the company?

The success of a company, and the progress of industrialisation leading to the prosperous economic development of a country, depends on the adoption of marketing techniques. This does not rest with appointing a marketing manager and setting up a marketing department, but with management applying a marketing philosophy right at the top. This requires a business management approach beyond finance, production, sales and distribution. A businessman may decide to go into furniture making, but what kind of furniture is he to make for whom, if he is to be as financially successful as possible? This goes a long way beyond craftsmanship and selling. He may be capable of producing excellent furniture, but does anyone want it, or will anyone pay the price that his quality demands?

Imagination helps, and an interesting example at the time of writing is the idea to supply sparkling cats-eye garters to make camels visible to motorists on unlit roads in Saudi Arabia. The need is there because when a motor-car hits a camel both animal and occupants can be killed. It was holiday tour operator, John Ashby, who had the idea, and the clip-on prototypes were tested on camels at Dudley Zoo.

The camel is also a means of overcoming the milk problem in arid countries where cattle suffer badly during droughts. A camel has a milk yield similar to that of the popular Friesian cow, but it calves infrequently and so is an expensive animal to buy compared with a cow. Camels as milk producers are not uncommon in some parts of the world (such as Mongolia, where there is also mare-herding), while the King of Saudi Arabia has a camel milking parlour which supplies the needs of his many children. Two things have coincided which could enable good marketing to offset famine in the drought areas of Africa. Scientists have bred a camel which calves as frequently as a cow, while the Reading firm of Gascoigne has been developing markets for its camel milking machines.

TOURISM

It is a truism that people often know little about their own country, but some of them have travelled abroad for education, business or holiday reasons. Even in Britain, thousands of people are more familiar with Spain, France and Italy than with their own country as a holiday attraction. In industrialising countries there have been problems in the past of transport and accommodation, but countries with natural and historic attractions have been opened up to overseas tourists, providing excellent hotels and internal travel services. The Caribbean, East, Central and Southern Africa, and most parts of Asia have done well. With the possible exception of Kenya, the inhabitants of countries famed for wild life have rarely ever seen it, except perhaps in zoos in places like Ibadan, Kano and Lusaka.

Home holiday tourism requires good marketing, and in May 1985 there was an enterprising exercise by the Tourist Development Corporation of Malaysia. It was based on three marketing considerations:

1 that in 1983 2.4 million Malaysians, out of a population of only 14.9 million (including Sabah and Sarawak), took holidays abroad resulting in a big outflow of money;

2 that many Malaysians like to travel but have limited budgets; and

3 that the majority of Malaysians were unfamiliar with their own very attractive country.

In the past, the Tourist Development Corporation had concentrated on promoting Malaysia to overseas tourists, giving support to the country's fine hotels and national airline. As an editorial in the

Malaysian *New Sunday Times*[1] said, 'It was assumed that Malaysians with money would spend their holiday abroad and those without would stay at home'.

The 1985 *Great Value Holidays in Malaysia* campaign applied good marketing thinking and the promotion included press advertisements such as a full-page, full-colour advertisement in the *New Straits Times*[2], which consisted largely of a pictorial map, and the offer of a free booklet describing 32 holidays at reduced prices at 13 destinations. The advertisement carried a coupon and listed 13 telephone numbers. The headline read *The fun is right here*! Below the map was a bold sub-heading *From as little as Rgt 96.00*, and the main copy theme was *Take a break and see your own country*.

The editorial in the *New Sunday Times* complemented this by saying:

'. . . The TDC has painstakingly put together 32 packages to 13 local destinations at prices that would either discourage Malaysians from vacationing too often abroad or encourage those who have never travelled to begin doing so now.

'For Malaysians who have been travelling, the TDC packages will remove the guesswork each time a family or group sets out to reach a particular destination. Equally important, such tours, no doubt brief and selective, would be a history and geography lesson for children. How many have seen the home of Princess Cik Siti Wan Kembang in Kelantan or the Portuguese fort built in the 16th century in Malacca?'

The above is quoted not just from a report in the columns of a newspaper, but from the main editorial feature, demonstrating prime editorial support.

Indicative of the well-planned marketing strategy was the campaign's combination of the resources of the Malayan Railway, the Malaysian Association of Hotels and the Malaysian Association of Tour and Travel Agencies. Here, then, is an example of studying the situation and applying a combination of marketing methods.

Holidays at home can be a valuable contribution to the economy because domestic airlines are often loss-makers, railways may be under-used, and when the tourist season is slack reduced prices can be offered at hotels and unused capacity can be taken up. There is good marketing sense here, but it is necessary to study the market, and market education may be necessary to break down the inherent immobility of people within their own country. This sales resistance exists whether it be a small Caribbean island or a large African state.

MARKETING PROBLEMS

While marketing ideas may be borrowed and loosely applied, there are significant problems which handicap the application of marketing in countries where it could be beneficial.

Absence of Marketing

In another book[3], the author has quoted Gordon Draper, marketing lecturer at the University of the West Indies, Trinidad, who has said that in industrialising countries marketing does not exist, only advertising and selling. He referred to the importation or assembly of foreign products no different from those sold in the original home market, which were advertised and sold, with no research into their suitability, in the importing market. This is supported by a Nigerian who wrote to the *Sunday Concord*[4] saying:

'... this country is a dumping ground for several unsuitable and inferior vehicles. And the vehicles that are alright, quality-wise, often come loaded with unwanted accessories. Conversely, they do not have those items of equipment which are necessary in the Tropics.

'Cars have been imported into Nigeria for many decades and they have always come with heaters and heated rear windows. The practice continues. A heater and a heated rear window are, naturally, of no use here. The resources used to produce and fit such items of dubious value should have been employed to install more useful equipment'.

Obviously, there are some products, such as cameras, calculators, computers or Coca-Cola which are standard world-wide. But Guinness brewed outside Dublin and London (or exported) is usually stronger, combine harvesters are designed for different crops, detergents are formulated for washing in cold water, and some products are packed in containers such as pails so that they have a secondary use. While it would be foolish to say there is absolutely *no* marketing in industrialising countries, Gordon Draper is more often right than wrong. Caribbean countries are subject to an influx of foreign goods because, with the possible exception of Trinidad, these island communities have very little local manufacturing.

A sub-continent like India, with great manufacturing capability, can withstand imports and out of economic necessity may have to. It can borrow the expertise of Seiko and build its own watch-making industry. It took cotton making away from Lancashire long ago. But what about a country like Nigeria, a vast state with a population probably exceeding 100 million, and not short of raw materials? Bata

Shoe Company has long boasted of making shoes with wholly Nigerian raw materials. Is it untrue to say Nigeria has no real marketing when it has its own Institute of Marketing? To a large extent it is true since, until the mid-'80s, Nigeria did import hugely and was content to advertise and sell a great variety of purely foreign products, and to make under license, or through locally established expatriate companies, products originally intended for northern hemisphere markets.

There are contradictions, of course, but the need is for all companies, whether expatriate or indigenous, to spend more time finding out what will really satisfy customers. A criticism of locally produced goods is that they are not as good as imported ones, and this is chiefly a criticism of workmanship, and lack of confidence in the home-produced article. But home-produced goods could have superior claims if they were seen to respect local needs and demand.

Business Attitude

Without repeating too much of what was said on this theme in the advertising chapter, it does need to be emphasised that the idea of investing in future forecasts is unconventional for businessmen in industrialising countries. They have the market place mentality of transacting swift trade, resulting in immediate profits. That is not marketing.

The caravan that travelled thousands of miles to bring its wares to distant buyers had no difficulty in achieving sales because of the scarcity value of its goods in countries where they were not available. Another example is the age-old trade in leather goods made in Northern Nigeria which were carried across the Sahara to North African states and sold in Europe as 'Moroccan leather'. Nobody went to the final market to find out what kind of products the people wanted: there was simply a universal belief that people would buy spices, silks or leather goods because there was no alternative, no competition.

Similarly, motor-car manufacturers, British, French, German, Swedish and Japanese, have sold their vehicles in Nigeria simply because (unlike the Malaysians and the Koreans) they have not yet designed and built their own. But one should remember that having industry, as we know it today with all its international trade, is a post-MacArthur phenomenon of modern Japan. Before the '60s no-one in Europe had heard of a Datsun car, and the pre-1939 image of Japanese industry was one of paper and celluloid toys. 'Made in

Japan' was once derisory. The Japanese were very clever in marketing to Europe cars which resembled makes such as Ford, but which were cheaper and more reliable. Today 'Made in Japan' is no joke. Months before the Proton Saga motor-car was on sale in Malaysia there was an agency for it in Britain!

A significant reason for the success of the big Japanese companies has been their reliance on bank finance rather than shareholder finance. This enabled them to concentrate on designing saleable products and the marketing of them, for they were not constrained by the short-term profit demands of shareholders.

Already, we have touched on marketing in two areas, internal and external, but for the moment let us concentrate on the problem of persuading the indigenous businessman to expand his mind beyond straightforward selling and immediate profits. No doubt this calls for a mental somersault for the merchant mind. For the African this is sometimes very difficult because he usually has little sense of history, finds it hard to contemplate the future, and tends to live for the present. He is not, by nature, a planner. He has not, for instance, the foresight of the Englishman scores of years ago who would plant a plantation of trees which would mature in 20 years and, when felled, provide a dowry for his daughter when she married. The counterpart of that today might be to invest in an endowment life insurance policy. It is that forward-looking mentality that is required for marketing.

For example, a famous international margarine company decided to diversify since it had achieved a major share of the market, and it would be uneconomic to compete for the remainder. What should it now make, bearing in mind it already had selling and distribution resources directed at food retailers? Much time was spent in researching the possibilities. Eventually, it decided on a soft drink. In spite of there being 400 brands on sale in the UK, this product was chosen because research showed that housewife mothers would pay the higher price of a well-identified quality product that could benefit from national advertising. Many of the existing brands were poor-quality, low-priced, locally-made, small volume production drinks which could not afford to benefit from advertising. The reader will see how the marketing, and not just the selling, aspects of the product were shaping up.

But the market had to be satisfied even further if the project was to succeed. Research was conducted stage by stage to decide the flavours, the product name, the shape of the bottle, and the style of the label. This research produced three flavours for the launch (but others were added later), a name which suggested quality, a tall bottle with a measuring cap which was long enough to obscure the 'ring' which looks like sediment at the top of the contents, and a label which distinguished the product. Finally, they had to find a new factory and equip it.

Before the national launch, the drink was test-marketed in a typical sales area to see whether the desired share of the market could be won, and the result exceeded expectations. Only then did they put the product on sale. All this took about two years. All very different from setting up a bottling plant and distributing a product in the hope that it might sell.

If the businessman can apply this sort of patience and meticulous care over detail he is a marketing man. Moreover, he will need to be prepared to cut his losses and abandon his venture. This again is asking him to take an unfamiliar risk. When one criticises large multinational corporations as capitalist monsters it is worth remembering that they are as big as they are in spite of having lost money on abandoned projects. Some, like Ford, have even believed a product to be marketable and failed, as they did with the Edsel sports car. It is said that the majority of new products launched suffer failure, and Nielsen have said that even 50 per cent of those test-marketed failed. So it is still a high-risk operation, but that is the nature of business.

Many industries and services like energy, transport and telecommunications are state-owned in the industrialising world. It is the stultifying unwillingness to take risks of state and parastatal enterprises which inhibits their progress and saps their strength. Politics and business seldom mix, except for corruption. In Britain, public enterprise has benefited by being able to pay high salaries to successful businessmen to run it. Such businessmen seldom exist in industrialising countries or, if they do, they see little profit in accepting the yoke of government service. Moreover, in Britain, public authorities have considerable autonomy which encourages marketing strategies, as has been seen with British Gas, British Airways and British Telecom, even though the Thatcher government decreed they should be privatised to control government borrowing. In a number of industrialising countries privatisation is the 'in' word, where it is believed that private ownership can bring greater efficiency than civil service administration. The case is different from the British and it could be true.

The marketing-oriented businessman cannot afford to play hunches. The most successful product (or service) is one which fills a gap in the market, or is superior to anything currently available.

This 'plus' is what the marketing mind seeks to discover. Put a clumsy, breakable, spillable liquid medicine into tablet form and pack it in a handy blister pack; put powdered coffee in a sachet to make a single drink; put a large quantity of soft drink in an extra-large light-weight plastic bottle; make an electronic camera that does not need film; produce a flat-screen, portable, miniature television set; substitute a plastic card for money; design a telephone that can be used in a car or carried anywhere; or simply grow a crop which has a higher yield or which will resist disease.

None of these products would have come about if producers had been content to sell what they had and not study the market to find out what would sell even better and make a bigger profit.

The industrialising world does not have time on its side. New opportunities exist, and if they are to be exploited the lessons of marketing have to be learned to minimise risks and to create and supply the right products as soon as possible.

Size of the Market

The size of the cash economy sets yet another problem. In higher urbanised, literate, industrial countries, everyone except small children, are in the cash economy. Their income may range over wages, salaries, social benefits, dividends, pensions and even pocket-money. A totally different situation occurs in industrialising countries where only a minority may possess monetary income. Others may live by subsistence farming and have no surplus produce to sell. In Zambia there are small farmers who will not grow surplus crops for sale because they see no use for money.

However, the most significant factor is the population triangle which shows that in many industrialising countries, particularly in Africa, 50 per cent of the people are below the age of 15 and have no income. With 50 per cent of the people outside the cash economy, and with only a minority of the remaining 50 per cent in the middle to upper-class bracket, the buying market can be very small. Population triangles are not strictly triangles of the familiar three-cornered shape. Rather, they have mounting sections or layers which represent the number of people in different age groups. A European population triangle shows a preponderance of old people at the top of the triangle, whereas an African population triangle shows a large volume of young people, 15 years old or younger, at the base.

The two triangles can be drawn as shown in Fig. 6.1.

Thus the size of the cash economy, that is the number of people with money to spend, is not only huge in an industrialised economy but also includes many young people, whereas in most industrialising

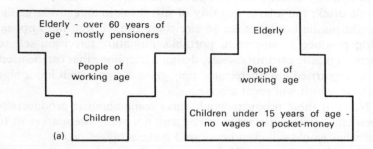

Fig. 6.1 Population triangles:
(a) industrialised country of the North;
(b) developing country of the South

countries it is half the size, of which less than half of that consists of
the middle-class or wealthy. The rest of the 50 per cent are very poor,
and have little buying power. It is possible that in most African
countries less than 20 per cent can be reached by the mass media and
are financially able to respond to press and television advertising.
Small unit consumer goods such as beer, cigarettes, washing powder
and simple remedies, can be advertised on posters and at point-of-sale
and so extend the reach to those who do not read newspapers or watch
television. Self explanatory packaging can be very important.

The situation imposes two marketing contradictions. The market is
comparatively small, although the population may be huge. Even then
this 'small' market may be counted in millions. The literate population of India is equal to the whole of Nigeria's which is twice that of
Britain, and even 20 per cent of the Nigerian population is around 20
million, which is almost equal to the total population of Malaysia.
The almost wholly Chinese population of Hong Kong is under 6
million but most of them are within the cash economy, however little
they earn.

The proportionately small markets are definable but they will vary
within the same country. Energy resources such as liquid gas may
have reached the Nigerian hinterland, but in Jos you will see women
carrying washbowls full of coal on their heads, and men pushing
bicycles loaded with firewood. It is in the cities that homes are equip-
ped with colour television, Hi-fi, air conditioning, electric fans,
refrigerators and electric cookers, to the despair of the Nigerian Electric
Power Authority and causing constant power cuts.

MARKETING DEFINED

After this discussion of some of the peculiarities of the marketing scene in countries where its application may or may not be happening, let us consider the Institute of Marketing definition. Is this what is meant by marketing in the countries which are developing production and distribution, as well as importing or assembling standard foreign products? The definition reads: 'Marketing is the management process responsible for identifying, anticipating and satisfying customer requirements profitably'. It contains four vital words: *identifying, anticipating, satisfying and profitably*.

The words 'satisfying customer requirements' invites us to look at the products which lack marketing expertise and are merely advertised and sold. Why do they lack marketing expertise? There are at least two reasons: for the original home market, marketing techniques were applied, but the mistake was made in not realising that the exercise was necessary again for overseas markets. On the one hand there was contempt for the special needs of foreigners, and on the other it was rarely appreciated that few products have universal appeal and that there are national (or regional) rather than global markets.

Some companies make goods to satisfy the home market, and then seek to sell surplus production overseas. Others can satisfy a small home market only provided they have sufficient overseas sales to justify volume production. This is true of the industries of both Scandinavia and Japan, where high standards of living are possible in the home country, provided goods are exported. In Japan there is also need to sell abroad in order to buy both raw materials and energy fuels. While company fortunes may well depend on exports, and markets abroad may be cultivated and exploited to this end, the short-sightedness of home-based management has resulted in a failure to really profit from supplying what is most likely to satisfy customers. The Institute of Marketing concept scarcely crosses the English Channel and the North Sea, let alone the Atlantic, Pacific or Indian Oceans, or the Mediterranean or South China Seas. What do those businessmen really know of the markets thousands of miles from Geneva, Paris, London or New York? Often, nothing. If they have travelled, they have often returned with cynical and contemptuous attitudes towards the non-European races. They are content to forget marketing principles, and to indulge in deals which are little more than dumping. They even have the audacity to send home market commercials and artwork for re-use in these territories, as can be seen on television and cinema screens and in the press where local advertising agencies are permitted little creativity. It does not seem to occur to these alleged marketing experts that their very short sighted view of the international scene dilutes the sales effort and minimises sales.

So much for the foreign firms which have forsaken their privileges. What about the indigenous businessmen who may have been bewildered by the clumsiness of foreigners thought to be experts in marketing? If the great multi-nationals can afford to be so foolhardy, what evidence is there that marketing can be rewarding? Presumably all those mighty tomes of Philip Kotler and others are not to be trusted if exponents of marketing theory can make such a bad job of the practice in international terms!

What does marketing involve? As the definition implies, it is necessary to *forecast* what can be sold – is there a gap in the market which can be satisfied, is an entirely new product required to meet an unsatisfied demand? When this has been identified, research must be undertaken to see whether such a product or service can be produced or supplied at a profit. Then the process of distribution must be planned if the project is feasible. The whole requires an investment in initial research, product planning and development, production and distribution, with a calculation of the time it will take to recover these costs and make a product profitable.

Some sophisticated products like pharmaceuticals, computers or aeroplanes will take many years of development, and, according to the pricing policy envolved, may take years to recoup investment and make a profit. Again, much may depend on the cost envolved in setting up the manufacturing plant, for which finance will have to be raised. But more simple products will require less investment in time and money. Alternatively, initial research could show a demand for a product which already exists abroad, or which could be modified to suit the market, or which could be produced with existing plant, and it could be either imported or produced locally under license. For instance, in Nigeria there are breweries throughout the country which brew beers based on foreign formulas, and there are proprietary medicines based on foreign formulations. In both cases the basic research has been done already by the original foreign firms. An appropriate local name can be given to such a product. This is different from, say, Guinness or Pfizer setting up a plant to produce and sell an existing line, since the procedure has been to anticipate and identify the customer requirement before looking for a means of satisfying it at a profit.

MARKETING MIX OR STRATEGY

American marketing textbooks tend to rely on the Four Ps (product, place, price and promotion) approach to the marketing mix, but this is an oversimplification with two major weaknesses.

First, it suggests that the four areas of marketing strategy can be isolated or grouped when in reality it is more practical to have a stage-by-stage time-scale of activities. This natural build-up starts with the creation or development of the new product and ends with after-market services and efforts to maintain customer interest.

Second, writers such as Philip Kotler[5] make the gross mistake of confusing public relations with publicity and relegating it to mere product publicity or virtually 'free' advertising. However, public relations can be part of most stages of the marketing mix, to mention only branding and packaging which have considerable public relations implications. How well does a name communicate? Does the package create ill-will or goodwill?

Elsewhere[6], the author has developed an extensive marketing mix of 20 elements, arranging them in a chronological order which is a complete dismissal of the Four Ps concept. Here, we shall consider a shorter version which is more suitable for the enterpreneur in an industrialising country where conditions call for a less complicated approach, and certain aspects such as financial public relations, test marketing and advertising research may be less appropriate.

The selected elements are therefore:

1 New product development;
2 Marketing research;
3 Naming and branding;
4 Market segment;
5 Pricing;
6 Packaging;
7 Distribution;
8 Sales force;
9 Market education;
10 Advertising;
11 The after-market;
12 Maintaining customer interest and loyalty.

(Public relations is not listed separately but is implicit throughout, except that if a company already exists there should be internal and external public relations in practice already, and certainly corporate public relations on behalf of the company as a whole. If it is a new company, set up to market a new product, then it would be wise to set up a separate public relations department, answerable to the chief executive, and servicing all functional divisions such as the primary ones of production, marketing and finance.)

Of the 12 elements of the mix, marketing research and advertising have their own separate chapters. Marketing research is listed only because research may be required in connection with items which appear later in the list.

1 New Product Development

It may be an invention, but such absolutely new products are rare nowadays and most 'new' products, or services, are usually modifications of old ones or innovations which are product developments. A better product or service, or one which satisfies a previously unsatisfied segment of the market, is more usual. The Japanese have invented nothing, but have produced and marketed better watches, cameras, motor-cycles or motor-cars. Better workmanship has been achieved by introducing automation, computers and robotics which have replaced the uncertainties of human labour. In an industrialising country the businessman faces a dilemma regarding workmanship. It may pay him to exploit available labour and to use intermediate technology, but this could invite poor workmanship and inefficient or uneconomic production. In Nigeria, the *Daily Times* installed modern printing presses capable of producing better quality print and even full colour, yet the *Daily Times* does not compare with newspapers printed elsewhere with the same presses.

Choice of product must be reconciled with ability to produce it. What shall he produce — a different paint, drink, foodstuff or textile? He would be foolish to take on a product where the expertise was monopolised elsewhere, unless he could make a deal with the owner of the technology, as the Malaysians have done with Mitsubishi for their Proton Saga motor-car. It may be sensible to produce an *economical product*, that is one which makes use of existing resources such as production plant, labour and know-how.

Situations are changing which make for new marketing opportunities. A new economic nationalism is asserting itself in countries as different as Nigeria and Malaysia. Thanks to importers (and multinationals with local interests) Nigerians had paid through the nose for many household products which the import restrictions of the military government have now denied them. Such goods have not been difficult to produce by Nigerians. Similarly, Malaysia, with its wealth of natural resources, has also been able to ban imports of goods it can produce for itself. Zimbabwe has proved itself to be remarkably self-sufficient even in the days of the Rhodesian UDI regime. These changing economic situations make it possible for indigenous enterprises to flower and flourish.

But we are confronted again by fatalistic attitudes. As Nonyelo G. Nwokoye has written 'The Nigerian businessman operates on relatively short time horizons and wants quick profits to accrue from his business dealings, as in importation, supply contracting and transportation. In short, he has to learn the patient cultivation of profits'. And that starts with the planned development of products that will satisfy marketing requirements.

Perhaps the tighter, more demanding economic climate which followed the overthrow of an Amercian style political system, which (as in the USA) invited corruption, will force his hand. He must import less and produce more, but now he has to answer the marketing-oriented questions of what, why and how?

Not only that but he can adopt a form of marketing that goes beyond that defined by the Institute of Marketing. This is to produce and market what a company does best, and to exploit this strength. Traditionally, if only on a small village scale, many industrialising countries have been good at farming. Product development could follow the lines of developing better crops or livestock on large farms, adopting the ranch or plantation instead of the smallholding. This could satisfy the 'Feed the Nation' and 'Green Revolution' campaigns which have foundered in the past.

Already quoted is the Whitehead programme in Malawi which not only enthused farmers to profit from achieving higher yields of cotton, but helped the national economy by reducing the need to import cotton. In this case the product development was more and better cotton. A country like Nigeria, a net exporter which became a net importer, could reverse the situation as the Ivory Coast did with the export of bananas to Europe, or emerge into international trade as Burma is doing with the development of a higher quality of rice to satisfy the Malaysian market. Another interesting trade between neighbouring countries is the giving of copyright protection to books produced by Asean countries (where there has been pirating of books), and the co-publishing of Indonesian and Malaysian books. The marketing strategy here is that larger sales of books permit more economical production and lower prices. Active in promoting these books is the National Book Development Council of Malaysia.

But, as with the Malawi example, it has been shown in Nigeria that beer can be made from a locally grown substitute for costly imported barley, while in Malaysia soft drinks are made from local fruits such as coconut, watermelon, star fruit or mango. There can be alternatives to Coca-Cola, Fanta, Sprite and Solo, or even to beer so far as young people are concerned.

As is described at the end of this chapter, product development is following two interesting paths in industrialising countries. There is the transfer of technology which allows imported products to be made locally (perhaps with national modifications), and there are the 'Made in . . . . .' campaigns to encourage both better locally made products and the purchase of them.

There are, therefore, on-going examples of product development which utilise national resources and skills for both internal and external trade. Inevitably, their development involves marketing considerations, and this is encouraging challenge to the reluctance of businessmen to accept the necessity for long-term planning. It does require a mental somersault, and a new kind of business confidence. Belief in the old saying 'you have to speculate to accumulate', the willingness to take a calculated risk, and to do so by exploiting both opportunities and marketing techniques, are the makings of the entrepreneur.

2 Marketing Research

The methods of conducting market research, and a discussion of the problems related to marketing research in industrialising countries, is the subject of the next chapter, but here we shall just mention how marketing research can be applied to the marketing mix.

New products cannot be developed unless research is carried out to identify and anticipate market requirements. If a new brewery is planned, do people prefer a light or dark coloured, a sweet or bitter, beer? Should the beer be bottled, canned or draught in a cask? Thus the research can be extended to examine the branding, market segment (e.g. socio-economic or ethnic group) pricing policy, packaging, forms of distribution (and to what extent they exist or have to be created), recruitment and training of the sales force, market education required, the most cost-effective media, and the need for after-sales services. All of these topics are capable of some kind of study, no matter what the difficulties compared with the ease of conducting research in Europe or America. It is no use making assumptions. Marketing research is a form of insurance to minimise risk. It shows responsible management.

3 Naming and Branding

In the first chapter examples were given of the communication problems arising from the use of names, words and colours. Once chosen, it is difficult and often unwise to change a name, unless there is a very good reason, as when a country adopts a new name. This occurred with the change from Rhodesia to Zimbabwe and the desirability of changing company prefixes from Rho to Zim. Again, political niceties made it advisable to change Barclays Bank in Nigeria to Union Bank, and in Trinidad to replace the same bank name with Republic Bank. An unwise change of name may damage confidence, whereas a sensible one can enhance national pride.

The choice of either company or brand name is a vital piece of communication, but goodwill is also implicit in it. When British Leyland decided to close down the MG sports car factory there were indignant protests from MG enthusiasts, and no doubt this influenced the company to head the range of the Maestros with an MG version, just as there had been a Riley version of the Mini. Motor-car marques have a habit of dying hard.

In the industrialising countries which have won independence it is common for company names to include the name of the country, for example Nigerpak, Nigerlink, Nigersteel, Nigerian Textile Mills or Nigerian Ropes.

Whatever the name, it should be easy to pronounce, spell and remember. It should not be ambiguous or confusing, and if possible it should be identified with the product or service, or quickly associated with what it represents. There can be subtle uses of a name, as in the case of the United Africa Company which became UAC because its operations, were extended beyond Africa to countries like Malaysia. P & O (adopted many years ago) originally stood for Peninsular and Oriental, but the shipping line has long since ceased to be associated only with ships sailing to the Malayan peninsular and beyond. It operates, for instance, P & O Air Tours.

Some of the best names are those which contain two or three vowels and two or three syllables, giving them a helpful rhythm. In spite of their foreignness, several Japanese names have benefited from this device, for example Honda, Fuji, Toshiba, Hitachi, Kawasaki, Minolta and Yamaha. They are all easy to pronounce, spell and remember and yet they are characteristically Japanese.

But there are some famous names like Audi, Guinness, Peugeot, and Singer which are subject to a variety of pronunciations and spellings. Some generic names achieve phonetic spellings like 'larger' for lager. This happens in reverse when a foreigner will pronounce soft-vowel Nigerian names like Ife and Ibadan as in knife or garden. There are even deliberate changes of pronunciation as when Kenya (Keenya) became Kenya as in yen. As in all forms of communication, simplicity is the key. Oddly enough, one would be correct to use the English pronunciation and not the French for Hine brandy because the original Hine was an Englishman.

Names can be of four kinds: family, personal or place names like Ford, Rowntree, Kano, Egyptian or Hindustan; invented names like Coca-Cola, Ovaltine, American Express or Seven Up; initials such as BMW, IBM, ITT and KLM; or acronyms which are derived from a number of words such as Sabena, Toshiba, Rentokil, Fiat, Esso and Caltex. Few people may know what the initials stand for, or from what names or words acronyms are derived, but they will know what products or services are associated with these names. Esso is a very clever one, based on Standard Oil.

However, sardonic jokesters can play havoc with acronyms and initials, to quote only *Perhaps I Arrive* for PIA (Pakistan International Airways), and *Fiat Is Always Trouble* for FIAT!

Imagination and inventiveness can be introduced into naming and branding, provided it is not too clever and does not result in a misleading name, or even one which has unexpected meanings in other parts of the world. Even a familiar name like Swan, which is given to a number of British products from matches to saucepans, can be meaningless in countries where the bird is unknown, Africa for instance. For that matter, how many people outside South East Asia know why the bird name Garuda was chosen for the Indonesian airline? Even Malaysian Airline System's attractive 'flying kite' symbol could be misunderstood to represent the bird of that name, and not the kind of kite which people fly.

When choosing a name it pays to write out a long list of possible names. It may be found that some names are already registered by other companies, and so legally protected. It is also useful to research names and find out which one is most favoured. A name may result from a public competition, as with Proton Saga for the Malaysian motor-car. Some famous names have come about by accident like Oxo, which a book-keeper was found to be using instead of 'ditto', while Elf was produced by a computer and it is only by chance that in Britain an elf is a tiny fairy.

Care has to be taken that a name does not provoke legal proceedings as once occurred between Coca-Cola and Pepsi-Cola, and between

Granada Television and Ford over the naming of their Granada motor-car. Even the wine growers of various countries such as France and Spain have taken action against other producers using names like champagne and sherry. There are also registered names which belong to certain manufacturers who insist on them being capitalised like Pop rivets, Coke, Vaseline and Sellotape. Generic names having no protection are ones like aspirin, instant coffee and perhaps, surprisingly, hoover which is derived from the Hoover vacuum cleaner company.

4 Market Segment

It is important to define the precise market. Unless it is the sort of product found in a supermarket or general stores, there are usually special markets for particular products or classes of product. For example, the market for a Mercedes Benz is different from that for the bottom of the range Nissans or Mitsubishis, whereas the market for a drink, cigarette or detergent could be very wide.

The market segment may not only be socio-economic; it could be cultural. Different ethnic or religious sections of the community will have their preferences or taboos. There may be an Islamic ban on alcohol, and the visitor to Kuwait may be surprised to find no bar at his hotel, yet find the North Brewery in Moslem Kano in Nigeria. There used to be posters advertising Scotch whisky on the road to Cairo airport, but they have been banned for religious reasons.

As societies grow more prosperous because more employment and higher wages expand the cash economy, there will develop a greater variety of income groups with their separate demands for goods at corresponding price ranges. The market segments will grow with their special demands for different products of varying qualities and prices. The shrewd businessman must observe these differentials carefully and supply accordingly. In fact, such developments may well direct him in his product development so that he can enter the market with new products or services hitherto unavailable. Selecting the right market segment is therefore an important element when planning the marketing strategy, and it is an excellent example of the value of the marketing concept. Without this consideration the businessman could be misled into producing and trying to sell the wrong product to the wrong people. In fact, if his study showed that there was no market segment he could satisfy he would do well to drop the product he had in mind and start again.

5 Pricing

The basic theory of profitable selling is to buy cheap and sell dear, but there is more to it than that. Price could be the deciding factor in whether a product is sold at all or in what volume, whether costs were recovered and a profit was made, whether the price affected the product image and also what effect the price had on goodwill and reputation. Picking the right price can therefore be a delicate matter. Again, it may be necessary to design and cost a product so that it satisfies a certain price bracket.

An example of bad pricing can be taken from the British watch industry. It was decided to design a very reliable watch which would compete with more expensive Swiss and Japanese watches whose prices were inflated by import duty. The British watches cost half the price of the foreign watches. The watch failed to sell because buyers judged the quality of the watch by its price. There is a saying 'You get what you pay for', and buyers thought the cheaper British watch must be of inferior quality than the more expensive foreign one. Had the British watch cost the same as the others it would have competed better and would probably have succeeded. As it is, the British watch is no longer made and the company now imports and sells a foreign make. This was tragic pricing.

Four kinds of pricing may be considered, namely economic, market, psychological and skimming (or creaming).

Economic pricing means that the price will recover all costs and show a desired percentage of profit.

Market pricing means charging the price that people expect to pay.

Psychological pricing means that the price will have the right mental appeal. This could be bargain appeal or a quality appeal that bestows status on the buyer or recipient. It is also possible to make a very small reduction which suggests that the price is less expensive than it really is. For example, 9 sounds a lot less than 10, and 99 sounds much cheaper than 100!

Skimming or creaming means selling dear at first in order to recover costs of, say, research and developing or, in the case of a book, the typesetting costs. These costs may be recovered by first selling a hardback edition before introducing a cheaper paperback edition.

Price may also be subject to controls, regulations and taxes which will vary from country to country. Prices may be guaranteed by the government on the basis of subsidies. There may be a system which permits only 'recommended prices', with the retailer able to offer discounts on list prices so that the manufacturer has no control of the price paid by the final customer. There could be some kind of sales or value added tax which hikes the price beyond what the manufacturer already charges. The government may impose 'price control, and regulate the maximum prices that may be charged. A foreign product could be subject to an import duty. The ultimate price could therefore be beyond the control of the manufacturer, and it might even deter sales or make it necessary to cut costs in the attempt to keep the price down. Any purchaser has limited money to spend, and in the case of expensive goods we move from staple products to those which compete for the spending of discretionary income, that is what remains after necessities have been paid for. The buyer may have to decide between buying a car or taking a holiday, but cannot afford both.

6 Packaging

By packaging we mean the way in which the product is presented in its container (including any labelling), but this can be taken more broadly to include the outward appearance of a product. However, we normally mean a container of some sort which can be designed to help sell the product. Years ago many products arrived at the shop in a large quantity, and the shopkeeper packed or wrapped the quantity required by the customer. Today, and this is especially necessary for stores which display goods and for supermarkets, goods are packed individually. Some goods like sweets are even packed separately inside a main container.

There are some primary conditions which will be discussed in detail, but first let us consider three special values of packaging.

i) *Convenience*   The goods have to be put in something if they are not to be sold loose like fruit and vegetables on a market stall. Can they be packed in such a way that is especially *convenient* to the buyer? A liquid medicine may not only be converted into tablet form but supplied in a press-out blister pack; a product which has to be used in measured quantities can be put in sachets containing the right amount for each use; stretch plastic film can be used to cover and protect items such as foods which are supplied on plastic trays; all kinds of products such as adhesives, sauces, or toothpaste can be packed in squeeze-out tubes; loose ironmongery items like screws can be put in small plastic bags; and the aerosol is useful for paints, insecticides, shaving cream and deodorants.

Cafinol is an example of a product which is carefully packed in cards of four tablets for two doses so that the African, irrespective of language, knows how to use the pain reliever safely and correctly.

A form of *new product development* might therefore be the packing of a product in a more convenient package.

ii) *After-use* In many parts of the world, purchase may be encouraged if the container has a secondary use. Can it be used afterwards, say, as a bucket or for storage purposes? Cans with lids or handles, and jars with screw-tops, may be put to many after-uses. In countries like Bangladesh, where little is wasted or discarded, useful containers are prized.

iii) *Advertising* Does the package distinguish the product and lend itself to display at the point-of-sale, and to advertising which creates pack recognition? A distinctive shape, colour or design can help to sell the product. The original pinched-sided Coca-Cola bottle is a good example.

These three factors can be essential to the success of a product. There are, of course, some packs, like those for expensive perfumes, which cost more than the product itself. Such extravagance may seem absurdly wasteful, but it may add to the enjoyment of the product if it represents the giver's generosity and affection and his regard for the recipient. Marketing is about achieving satisfaction. If the product satisfies someone's love, pride, vanity or pleasure it will be satisfaction enough.

A good package may also have to do other things such as *protect* the item in transit, storage or while being used, and this can include keeping it in good condition. The method of packaging may also make it easy or cheap to *transport* because of its shape, strength or lightness. It may also bear a family *likeness* to other products in the range. Colour coding can be used to link a range of products as with batteries.

There can also be alternative materials from which a package can be made. Shall it be paper, card, wood, aluminium, plastic, metal foil, or glass? Cost is a major factor, but fitness for purpose and ability to satisfy could be more important even if it raises the price. Many people like aerosols, but they are costly containers which increase the price, yet people are prepared to pay for the extra convenience. The pack can add value to a product and help to sell it, even if the price is higher than if some ordinary container were used. As with prices, there is a psychology of packaging.

Another point is the ease with which the contents are extracted or the container is opened. Customers can grow impatient with something which is difficult to use. Rip-pull opening devices are handy for cans and ejectors for razor blades. Conversely, vandal proof lids are useful for products which could be wilfully contaminated, and pills and tablets can be packed in tubs which can be kept safe from children because they can be opened only by turning the lid to a marked point.

This is a subject which has benefited from great ingenuity by the packaging industry, and part of the marketing strategy will be to explore the great variety of ways in which the product may be packed most effectively.

It is interesting that in countries where 'made in . . .' campaigns are being run to stimulate substitution of home-produced goods for imports, attention is being paid to good presentation and packaging as well as to quality of national products. This much has been learned from the importers.

7 Distribution

By this we mean the process of transferring the product from the factory to the final customer. The chain of distribution, and the number of people through whose hands the product will pass, will depend on two things.

First, what system of distribution already exists? Ultimately, the last distributor will be a shopkeeper, broker, direct response trader (mail order) or perhaps the manufacturer's own salesmen or shops. Goods may be sold through all possible outlets, or only appointed dealers.

Second, it all depends on the nature of the product. Small unit goods are usually sold to wholesalers who break bulk to supply the smaller orders of retailers, but bulk supplies, at virtually wholesale prices, will be sold to the central warehouses of chains of multiples and supermarkets who then supply their own branches.

The use of wholesalers may be economic and convenient, but it does mean loss of contact with the retailers, and reliance on the wholesalers to promote sales to them. But against that is the cost of maintaining a large field sales force. The cost of discounts and other trade terms have to be included in the final selling price.

Where there are good postal services, a reliable telephone system and, in those countries where television is well established, a teletext service, it is possible to sell direct. Direct response marketing, the modern term for mail order, allows the manufacturer (or trader) to sell directly to the customer. He can sell 'off the page' through press advertising, by direct mail using offers and catalogues, and even off the television screen through either commericals or teletext pages. These are sophistications not beyond possibility in industrialising countries, and throughout such countries correspondence courses have been sold in this way for decades. The final sophistication is to permit payment by credit or charge card. The main consideration is usually the customer's faith in committing money through the post, or of actually receiving the goods. This calls for the customer's faith in the postal service, and his confidence in the supplier. In the industrial world 'shopping without shops' or 'armchair shopping' is the biggest growth area in marketing.

Distribution will also require warehousing and perhaps regional depots, and will depend on available physical communications such as ports, rivers, roads, railways and possibly air cargo routes. Can transport be effected, should it be hired or owned? Warehousing and transportation, and the methods adopted for the packing of bulk supplies, provide further cost considerations which will affect price.

8 Sales Force

Salesmanship is an almost natural art in many parts of the industrialising world, and is an example of the initiative which some people can show in order to earn a living. One has only to watch the hawkers and salesmen in the streets and bazaars of towns and even by the country roadside, to see that selling is in the blood of many people. It reaches a peak in the thousands of shops to be found in Hong Kong. In Nigeria the streets are lined with candlelit stalls far into the night. The food stalls of Singapore and Malaysia are a striking feature. Selling is a way of life in these places.

However, this is not quite the same as the planned and organised selling which a businessman needs if he is to achieve distribution and maintain a regular flow of orders so that he obtains continuous and economic production. Moreover, the sales force is not usually selling to final customers but to distributors who have to be convinced that they can sell at a profit the goods offered to them. Members of the sales force need to understand what they are selling and that requires training. They also have to be capable of withstanding the challenge of tough buyers. This kind of salesmanship calls for men who are both highly skilled and well-trained in selling techniques. They are not itinerant salesmen, living cheaply and selling if and when they can. They will have to work very hard to meet sales targets set by their sales manager, who is committed to reaching the overall sales target which is a primary part of the marketing strategy. Production will be based on the sales forecast. The salemen are the worker ants or bees, feeding the hive of operations. Without their success in the field the whole marketing scheme fails, and that includes winning *adequate distribution* so that customers who respond to advertising are able to find the product in the shops.

The selling of the product or service to distributors, but sometimes direct to customers (as with office equipment), requires the following:

i) A sales manager, supported by a sales office, who is capable of planning the sales campaign, allocating sales territories and directing the sales effort in order to bring in the planned volume of sales. He is the captain of the team.

ii) Recruitment of the right calibre of people to comprise the field sales force.

iii) Remuneration, and other incentives, which will inspire salesmen to perform effectively. Salesmen may be remunerated by commission only, salary only, or by a blend of salary and commission. Bonuses may be paid for extra sales.

iv) Training which will educate salesmen about what they have to sell, and train them in effective selling techniques. Training can be a continuous process.

v) Control so that the sales manager is fully informed about the efforts made by each separate salesman — performance against plan — and about the sales situation in each territory. This control also imposes a discipline on individual salesmen regarding their calls, order taking and regular reporting to the sales manager.

vi) Journey cycle This is the time between regular calls on customers, and it will be determined by the frequency of re-ordering, the distance between customers, and the number of customers. To service customers efficiently the journey cycle should be as short as is necessary, otherwise regular customers and sales may be lost. In addition to regular calls, extra visits may have to be made to those who have made enquiries. The salesman will also be expected to use his own initiative to secure new business, either by making appointments with new prospects, or by *cold-calling* without appointment.

A good sales manager should also maintain good staff relations, which is a form of public relations. Salesmen live lonely, isolated lives and are apt to feel forgotten by headquarters. Good lines of communication, apart from orders and call reports, are vital. Some of the methods that may be used are regular sales bulletins and regional or central sales meetings. Contests and incentive schemes are a method of rewarding top salesmen, and of creating a team spirit. If there is a large sales force it is likely that territorial field sales managers will be necessary.

9 Market Education

The education of both the trade and prospective customers can be extremely important in industrialising countries where new products and services are being introduced, especially if they are strange or so modern that they change life styles. With some products it would be wasteful to indulge in advertising before the market had been familiarised with the product. This, again, is a form of public relations and shows how public relations is not something to be included on its own in the marketing mix — like advertising — but is implicit throughout the elements of the mix.

How can the market be prepared for the eventual launch? There may be a few popular consumer products where secrecy is necessary before the launch, but with the more technical and perhaps more expensive ones it will pay to conduct a programme of educational activities to win market acceptance. This could be called a *pre-selling* campaign. It may require the use of a film or video, demonstrations or samples, stories in the media and so on to get prospective buyers interested and looking forward to the arrival of the new product. Hostility, prejudice, apathy and ignorance may have to be broken down.

Much can be learned from failures to use market education, resulting in big financial losses on premature advertising which failed to sell the product because it was met with disinterest or disbelief. Advertising is a powerful sales tool, but it will not sell anything and is not a magic wand, no matter what media owners or advertising agencies may say.

The classic example in Britain was the costly failure to sell 'safe' New Smoking Mixture cigarettes, which were made of a substitute for tobacco and would not cause lung cancer. But no public relations pre-advertising campaign had been carried out so that smokers were encouraged to look forward to the new safe cigarette. Smokers resisted the advertising, refused to buy, and the manufacturers had to collect the packets of cigarettes from the shops and destroy them. It was a monumental multi-million pound blunder which could have been avoided. Public relations, or market education, was ignored in the marketing strategy. This is the sort of folly which follows acceptance of the 4Ps in which public relations is regarded as no more than product publicity, which could be too late.

All kinds of products and services will be new to societies of rising social mobility, urbanisation, improved education, new forms of employment, higher incomes and opportunities to extend their personal possessions and enjoyment of the many new things that money can buy. The spread of public services will make many new purchases possible and desirable. If there are electricity or liquid gas, piped water supplies, new roads, shopping centres, telephones, better transportation, how shall they be enjoyed? The choices cannot just be thrust on people, to be resisted, wasted or misused. The responsibility for educating all these people rests with those who seek to sell to them so many strange new products and services. Customers are not there to be exploited and disenchanted (as some of them have been with foreign imports from powdered baby milk to tape recorders). They represent tomorrow's market, the people who will go on buying what they like and trust.

Ways of employing public relations techniques will be found in the chapter on public relations. Like marketing research, market education is an excellent insurance against unnecessary risk. Familiarity is a buying incentive.

10 Advertising

A complete chapter has been devoted to this subject in relation to the marketing mix but this is the place to insist that the company advertising manager and/or the advertising agency should be involved in giving advice and making preparations as early as possible. Advertising campaigns should not be planned late in the strategy and have the hopeless task of trying to promote a product which is ill-conceived, under-researched, poorly named, wrongly priced, badly packed, not aimed at a well-defined market segment, inadequately distributed and lacking in market education. A skilled advertising manager or agency account executive could offer valuable advice at all these stages. Advertising professionals are not limited to creative and media-buying services. Or put another way, they should be appointed because they have these extra skills.

Similarly, the in-house public relations officer and/or public relations consultancy should be involved at the onset of planning the marketing mix because he or they can give advice at every stage. The wise marketing manager will engage all the allies he can muster.

11 The After-market

Most products which are not immediately consumed require further services after the product has been bought, in order to enjoy its continuous benefits. Spare parts, accessories, replacements (such as bulbs, fuses or batteries), instruction and service manuals, repairs and servicing, and guarantees form the after-market, according to the product. Without these services, costly products become junk.

Imported products are often criticised because of the lack of after-sales service of one kind or another. It may take six months to import a spare part, dealers may be unwilling to tie up money in stores of parts, there may be import restrictions which discourage buying spares, and there may be few, if any, trained service engineers. Some people will allow a product to deteriorate rather than have it repaired, because of ignorance, carelessness or cost. Finally, it is discarded. The industrialising countries are littered with broken-down products for which there are no spare parts, or which people are unwilling to have repaired. This is a tragic waste of valuable goods.

Let us examine a few examples from Nigeria. The air-conditioning system may be out of action in a hotel because of the delay in obtaining parts. The demand for seats on domestic flights exceeds supply, not so much because every passenger wants to fly but because long distances by road are plagued with the problem that if a motor-car breaks down it is doubtful if parts can be obtained quickly. There has also been a black market in motor-car spares. For some years, this led to corrupt practices at airports where names would be put on the manifest only on paying a bribe of 20 niara or more. This abuse was also compounded by the practice of issuing OK tickets for unconfirmed flights. While power-cuts may be partly due to over-demand by users who will not conserve energy — television sets may be left switched on all day — another reason is the lack of maintenance and spares. There are some hotels like the Federal Palace, Lagos, which were beautiful in the '70s but which have deteriorated simply because fittings broke and were never replaced.

Another problem, common in many African countries, is that radios are bought but the cost of replacing batteries is so prohibitive, especially in the rural areas, that thousands of sets are out of use. The power of radio to penetrate distant places has become a myth in countries like Ghana, Nigeria and Zambia.

Behind this problem lies the basic one that the elusive spare parts must be imported and are therefore expensive. They may be delayed because of the need for import licenses and permission to export currency. There could also be shipping delays, and hold-ups at the Customs. No such problems concern a home-produced product, and so after-market conditions can be satisfactory for an indigenous product *provided the requirements are planned and executed as part of the overall marketing strategy*. This is really the most elementary public relations because the company's reputation depends on it.

The alternative is that the product is so reliable that it rarely requires servicing. No doubt, at the product development stage, with rigorous testing and painstaking quality control before delivery, after-sales services can be minimised. Even so, products can be misused, or severe weather and other conditions may impose unfair working conditions on a product, for which the manufacturer cannot be held responsible.

Ability to supply a product which does not suffer the after-market problems of foreign products could be itself an incentive to go into business.

An important aspect of after-sales service is the instruction manual. It may not be sufficient to print the instructions in two or three languages. Not everyone can read, or they may read other languages. If they can read, short words should be used and confusing technical jargon should either be ignored or explained in simple language. If English is used, care must be taken to remember whether buyers are familiar with British or American English which are often quite different. For example, in motor-car jargon automobile is the American for motor-car; shift for gear lever; trunk for boot; and there will be spelling differences like tire for the British tyre.

The best way to make instructions easy for everyone is to illustrate them with photographs, drawings and diagrams, as in the instruction book for a Japanese camera which may be used world-wide.

12 Maintaining Customer Interest and Loyalty

This can apply to almost any product or service. It is rather like the shop assistant who goes on selling the goods even after the customer has paid his money, telling him what a wise purchase he has made and how he is going to enjoy it. How foolish to allow a customer to lose interest and perhaps think of buying a different make or brand next time!

The devices which can be employed to maintain customer interest and eventual re-purchase may include:

i) Advertising which reminds customers continuously.

ii) Short-term sales promotion schemes such as special offers, price reductions, free gifts and prize contests that again remind but which also encourage extra purchase and deflect brand switching by regular customers.

iii) Introduction of accessories or new services which can extend enjoyment of the product or service.

iv) News items in the media to maintain interest.

v) Feature articles in the media which describe product use.

vi) Documentary films and videos which do likewise, or extend knowledge of the company, its activities and full range of products and services.

vii) Reminder cards or letters, either direct or from the retailer or agent, when servicing may be recommended.

viii) Helpful publications such as calendars, diaries, recipe leaflets and books, maps, guides, advisory leaflets and brochures. Most of these publications may be supplied free, others (especially books and annuals) may be on public sale or advertised on packs.

ix) Invitations to see demonstrations of new models.

x) Discount privileges for previous buyers.

xi) Distribution to customers of an external house magazine.

It will be seen that these methods of maintaining customer interest and loyalty range over advertising, sales promotion, selling and public relations, emphasising their differences yet showing how they complement each other in the marketing strategy. They support the philosphy of 'once a customer, always a customer'. They revolve around that basis of successful marketing, *goodwill*, and goodwill encourages the greatest aid to marketing, *recommendation*, which costs nothing. One of the most successful growth companies in the world is Rentokil which claims that 60 per cent of its business comes from recommendations. That may explain why it spends very little on advertising, but is heavily committed to all forms of public relations.

NEW MARKETING OPPORTUNITIES

Traditional businessmen, used to a quick sale and a quick profit, may be reluctant to invest in advertising, or to adopt the more extended discipline and forecasting of marketing. However, changes are occurring which may be irresistible to the astute businessman that at heart he really is. He may be a sun-loving happy-go-lucky West Indian, a proud African conscious of the merit of making bread, an awakening, self-reliant Malaysian, a shrewd Arab with Islamic principles, a Chinese with his worship of wealth, or an Indian with his merchant's sense. Throughout more than 70 industrialising nations, a new economic era is being thrust upon them.

First, there was the imperialist colonial era when these countries were bled of their primary products so that Europe and the New World were able to industrialise. Second, came the uneasy period of independence when infrastructures were built and new nations became the victims of the economic imperialism of foreign imports and loans leading to fantastic debts. The first claw back was the raising of oil prices in 1973 by the Arabs, shaking the industrial countries which had based their energy supplies on cheap oil. This recession set in and mass unemployment hit the industrial nations. This was not the end of the industrial nations, but it coincided with the death of the industrial era and was the prelude to a new technological micro-chip age with new attitudes to work and leisure.

Meanwhile, the former colonial countries have been moving into *their* industrial age. This liquid situation provides two solutions to the financial and economic dilemmas faced by the new nations. The first is to develop independent home production and reduce, or even eliminate, dependence on many imported goods. The second is to develop trade between industrialising countries, supplying each other with the raw materials one has and another needs. Both situations call for sound marketing strategies, such as identifying, anticipating and satisfying each other's requirements. The opportunities are certainly exciting.

TRADE DEVELOPMENT

The old policy, carried on from colonial days to independence, of exporting primary products cheaply and importing manufactured goods dearly was financially ruinous for the former colonies. It hampered their development. Moreover, it tended to put undue value on the material goods of the industrial countries. The people of the industrialising countries do not necessarily have to copy the life-styles of the richer nations; they can create and develop riches more appropriate to themselves. One effort in this direction is to create their own television drama to replace American films which inevitably depict a totally alien culture.

One of the results of the recession in the industrialised countries in the first half of the 1980s, and the fearful overseas debts of the industrialising countries, has been that 'it is imperative that the South promote greater South-South co-operation', as Datuk Seric Dr.Mathathir Mohammad has said. According to the Malaysian Prime Minister, industrialising countries must adopt stringent methods to stabilise their domestic economies without expecting help from the industrialised world. It has already closed the door on the flight of currency and the intake of some imports, but those are negative actions to prevent the situation from getting worse. How do you make it better?

A country may be lucky like India and have a bumper wheat crop, but it could be a cattle rearing country like Botswana and have no rain for two years. It could also be one of the sub-Sahara countries bedevilled by long-standing drought and famine. Or it could be an oil country like Trinidad or Indonesia, faced with a world oil glut and with China arriving on the oil-producing scene.

Encouraging signs are the trade agreements between Pakistan and Korea, Burma and Malaysia, and Malaysia and Mali. Each has, or can develop, products which can benefit other industrialising nations. They are mostly agricultural and extractive produce. One of the problems confronting a number of these countries was that they were limited to certain major primary products such as cocoa (Ghana) and copper (Zambia), but trade between these countries, instead of only with the former colonial powers, is helping them to become more self sufficient. Examples are that Pakistan wants palm oil and Malaysia has it, while Malaysia wants rice and Burma can produce it.

There is nothing novel about trade between industrialising countries, but it certainly has a new meaning today. The islands of the Caribbean have been linked economically by the Caribbean Community (CARICOM); West Africa has its Economic Community of West African States (ECOWAS); and the nine Southern African states north of South Africa have their South African Development Co-ordination Committee (SADCC). The fourteen Muslim countries of the Middle East and certain parts of Asia have their Organisation of Islamic Conference (OIC) which is devoted to furthering sports and economic co-operation. The Association of South East Asian Nations (ASEAN) brings Malaysia, Singapore, Thailand, Indonesia and the Philippines together on economic and other issues. These common market groupings can enhance trade relations, usually among neighbouring nations in a particular part of the world.

There can also be some regional trading prejudices and influences, such as the Buy British Last versus Look East — mainly Japan — import policies of Malaysia, which Mrs Thatcher sought to contest during her visit to Malaysia in April 1985. Or new influences may appear, such as China which has engaged in railway building in Zambia and has rivalled Indonesia as an oil exporter.

The policy of insisting on *transfers of technology* has advantages for both the foreign manufacturer and the industrialising country to which the technology is transferred, although it may not satisfy local national pride in home products. It cuts imports, retains the reputation of the foreign product, and utilises the labour, raw materials and other resources of the country where the plant is set up. Thus, one may buy ICI, Goodyear, Lever or Johnson products 'made in' whatever the country may be. This satisfies both sides provided the expatriate company is permitted to remit profits to its overseas parent company. There may be a system of indigenisation (as in Nigeria), whereby a majority of shares are owned by the public, employees and institutions in the industrialising country. The Danish toy company LEGO has overcome Korea's ban on toy imports by setting up a factory in the environs of Seoul.

INDIGENOUS INDUSTRY

Imports can be cut if home industries are developed. The production of building products is a good example. The growth of towns and the general infrastructure requires an assortment of raw materials and finished products, many of which can be produced locally instead of being imported. Lifts may have to be brought in from specialist foreign engineering firms, but other items such as ceramics can be home produced.

In fact, there are cases where a tile making industry exists and is actually under-utilised due to imports. The ceramics industry (like the glass industry) can produce a huge range of industrial and domestic products, provided they are distributed and marketed systematically. In the past it has been easy to accept ready-made expensive foreign goods, carrying as they do world-wide reputations which have helped import agents to sell them easily and profitably.

Reputations can be earned. The British motor-car once had the best reputation in Commonwealth countries, yet during the past 15 years the Japanese motor-car has arrived, usurped the British reputation, and established its own. That is a remarkable achievement in a very short time. Once the taxi cab fleets in Nigeria used Morris 1000s but for years they have been replaced by Datsun. Japanese cars are now assembled where British cars were shipped. In Zimbabwe, the British Leyland plant is obliged to build Japanese cars for political reasons. In Malaysia Ford cars have Japanese engines. As familiar as the red London bus is the red Hong Kong Datsun 2-litre taxi.

Some countries try to encourage the purchase of locally produced goods, as with the 'made in Malaysia' campaign. This has been encouraged, for instance, by annual awards for food products made by the Malaysian Institute of Food Technology since 1983. The award is made to recognise and honour local food processors and manufacturers for the time and effort they put in towards producing an outstanding food product. Similarly, the local manufacture of motor-car accessories has been developed in Malaysia, although Mitsubishi, one third partner in the Proton Saga motor-car venture, found that Malaysian-made accessories failed their stringent tests. The Japanese are perfectionists and are capable of faulting a Rolls-Royce so their daunting demands may yet prove to be a blessing to the willing Malaysians.'

But the economic imperialism from Europe and America has often been replaced by an even more dominating economic invasion, especially in the largely agricultural countries of South East and Southern Asia. Japan is succeeding economically where it failed militarily. In desperation Thailand announced a 'made in Thailand' campaign to offset its US$ 1,311.6 million trade deficit with Japan, but Thailand's efforts at self-sufficiency are thwarted by the sheer weight of Japanese influence. There are 137 Japanese companies operating in Thailand, and the homes, streets, shops, offices, factories and farms are choked with Japanese products, both domestic and industrial. Nevertheless, Thailand is seeking ways of converting its raw materials into finished products, and to a transfer of technology to enable this to be done.

Supriya Singh has put the situation in a nutshell[8] by writing: 'The idea is simple. We earn more if we sell curry than raw chicken. Similarly we earn more if we export tyres and furniture than if we sell rubber and logs . . . We have to set up shop, attract customers, present it in the most appealing manner . . . We have to market it'.

Certain countries are more developed than others and in Singapore much technology has been transferred over a number of years. To quote the Minister For Communications and Information, Yeo Ning Hong, when he addressed a meeting[9] to mark World Telecommunications Day in Singapore on May 17, 1985: 'Technology transfer may be expedited if the process and techniques are passed not directly but from an intermediate location where the technology has been transferred already. We believe Singapore is such a location'.

The day is surely past when the jigs of an obsolete British motor-car could be sent to India so that the old motor-car could have a new life in a poor overseas market. Today the latest model is assembled in the poor country, like the Fiat in Zambia and the Peugeot in Nigeria. And now countries like Malaysia and Korea are going further and establishing their own vehicles, with the help of foreign know-how, and exporting them to Britain!

Coupled with better education and training, greater upward mobility of the socio-economic group can provide labour and wages for the production and consumption of goods made by home industries. As one Nigerian businessman told the author concerning the poor in his country, the trouble was not that the people were unemployed but that they were unemployable. That was some years ago, and since then there has been the innovation of Universal Primary Education. The problem is to avoid lost literacy through lack of jobs requiring educated people. Economic circumstances have now imposed on Nigeria the opportunity to exploit what it has.

PRIVATISATION

One of the handicaps experienced in industrialising countries has been state ownership of so many enterprises, which has created civil services rather than profit-seeking commercial enterprises. An answer to this, as undertaken in Singapore and Malaysia, is privatisation. The argument runs that inefficient services like telecommunications, will become more efficient if they are run as private sector businesses. Management will be better and people will work harder when they are not cushioned by the red tape of bureaucracy and the security of government service.

This is a real challenge to industries which are the lifeblood of the nation. It invites the application of marketing principles which may never have been considered in the past by politicians and civil servants who, after all, cannot be expected to be marketing-oriented businessmen. It is a revolutionary prospect, especially where state corporations and parastatals were created, not for socialist reasons, but in order to establish them at all.

For obvious reasons, privatisation may not be favoured in every country. In Britain, a Conservative government which favoured private enterprise and was hostile to nationalisation introduced privatisation mainly to raise money by selling shares to the public. The opposite is likely to be the case in industrialising countries where privatisation is seen as a way of creating greater efficiency. The more socialist inclined countries believe that the state should own the means of production. Different philosophies may suit different countries, but however these giant enterprises and utilities are owned and controlled their efficiency could be improved by the adoption of marketing principles, for even a monopoly can benefit from them.

130 *The Role of Marketing*

References

1 *New Sunday Times*, Kuala Lumpur, Malaysia, editorial, May 5, 1985.
2 *New Straits Times*, Kuala Lumpur, Malaysia, advertisement, May 2, 1985.
3 Jefkins, Frank, *Introduction to Marketing, Advertising and Public Relations*, 2nd Ed, Macmillan, London, 1985.
4 Adeyamju, Banjil, 'Building a Nigerian Car', *Sunday Concord*, Ikeja, Nigeria, August 28, 1985.
5 Kotler, Philip, *Marketing Management*, 3rd Ed, Prentice-Hall, London, 1976.
6 Jefkins, Frank, *Public Relations For Marketing Management*, 2nd Ed, Macmillan, London, 1985.
7 Nwokoye, Nonyelu G, *Modern Marketing in Nigeria*, Macmillan, London, 1981.
8 Singh, Supriya, article, 'Getting the Feel of Industry in Malaysia', *New Straits Times*, Kuala Lumpur, Malaysia, May 18, 1985.
9 *Star, The*, Kuala Lumpur, Malaysia, May 18, 1985.

7
The Use and Role of Marketing Research

INTRODUCTION

Marketing research has been used in the industrialised world for some 50 years, and among its American pioneers were Nielsen and Gallup. Mass observation studies were published in Britain in the late '30s, and A.C. Nielsen set up in Britain just before the Second World War. But the war intervened and, while marketing research persevered in the USA, it came to a standstill in Britain and did not become properly established as a marketing aid until the post-war years. The post-war period also saw a new development, motivational research, of which the most notable exponent has been Dr. Ernst Dichter. Today, marketing research in a great variety of forms is practised world-wide, but to a lesser or greater degree according to local conditions, especially the availability of reliable statistics such as census figures or electoral registers of voters.

Studies can be conducted on many phases of the marketing mix such as product development, naming and branding, packaging, pricing, test marketing and advertising. It can also be applied to the planning and evaluation of public relations programmes.

In general, it is a form of insurance to reduce risk. It is not infallible, although the degree of error can be calculated with some of the research techniques, but it should be used intelligently as a guide to tendencies rather than to irrefutable facts. The accuracy of surveys is usually very high, but there can be errors of bias, human weaknesses in answering questions, and mistakes can be made in interpretation of results. For a simple example of variation in interpretation, if 50 per cent of the people questioned were in favour of a subject under study that could suggest strong support, but equally it means that 50 per cent were not in favour. The result could be read either way. Or, to take a political example, in a democratic election in which the most votes wins the seat, and a government is elected on that basis with a majority of votes, this could actually mean that only 40 per cent voted for the government and 60 per cent (in spite of lost seats) voted against the government, as happened with the election of the second Thatcher government in Britain.

'It all depends what you mean', and figures can be read in different ways. The cynic will say there are lies, damned lies and statistics, but marketing research is nevertheless a very valuable marketing aid. It is marketing's intelligence system. But there are many 'schools' of research, and it is necessary to know what information one is seeking and the best methods of research to discover the most accurate answers.

The example is quoted by Vance Packard, in his book[1], of the airline which used a conventional field study in an attempt to learn why more businessmen were not using an American airline. The survey produced the answer that American businessmen thought flying was dangerous and preferred to travel by road or rail. An advertising campaign appeared, demonstrating how well the aircraft were serviced and how safe was the airline. It failed to convince business travellers. So motivational research was commissioned, and a rather different answer resulted because this form of research went beyond questions and answers and probed deeper to reveal hidden motives. The new answer showed that businessmen thought flying was dangerous, not for personal reasons, but because of obligations to their families. With this revelation, advertising was given a very different slant. Advertisements were aimed at the businessmen's wives, saying their husbands would be away from home for shorter trips if they flew. This advertising was so successful that it led to the promotion of family holidays by air.

This true story helps to demonstrate the possible pitfalls of marketing research, but also its successful use of particular techniques.

Sometimes research can be quite simple, and yet can be valuable when information about markets does not exist. In his fascinating book about the great trading families of the Middle East, Michael Field[2] tells the story of the coming of electricity to Saudi Arabia. The Juffalis won the agency for GEC, the British electronics company, in 1940, and subsequently the concession to supply electricity to Taif in 1946. But they had no idea of the likely consumption of electricity, and there were no population figures. An estimate of potential demand was essential so they resorted to a very clever, if crude, form of marketing research which showed good marketing sense. They visited the local bakeries and took a count of the number of loaves baked daily. From this they were able to calculate roughly the number of people in Taif! Eventually, this basic research led to the Juffalis gaining further concessions for supply of electricity to Mecca and other places.

DEFINITIONS

The two terms 'market research' and 'marketing research' are often used loosely, and may be confused to mean the same thing. They are quite different. *Market research* consists of research which is limited to studies of the market only. *Marketing research* includes studies into not only the market but other subjects related to marketing, such as packaging research and media research into circulations and reader-ships of the press and audience figures for posters, radio and television.

Marketing research may be defined as *the systematic study of data, including the use of scientific methods, to obtain information relevant to the marketing of products or services.*

There is also *social research* to conduct studies such as those made by government, of which a population census is a good example.

SPECIAL AREAS OF RESEARCH

There are many forms of marketing research, but the three main objectives are:

1 to measure opinions, awareness and attitudes;
2 to discover preferences; and
3 to reveal motives.

Research can also be divided into two kinds:

1 *primary* research consisting of research conducted for the first time; and
2 *secondary* research which uses existing data such as studies already undertaken, and statistics and other information which exists in the organisation's records or in published form. Secondary research may also be termed *desk research*.

In addition, there are *ad hoc* surveys which are once-only studies, and *continuous* research conducted periodically that records trends over time which can be shown in the form of graphs or bar charts.

Another contrasting pair comprises *quantitative* and *qualitative* research. In quantitative research, the results are expressed in percentages such as 50 per cent said 'Yes', 30 per cent said 'No' and 20 per cent said 'Don't know'. These results are usually produced by questionnaires. But when the research takes the form of discussions or in-depth interviews, the answers will be summaries of replies and will be reported descriptively so that the quality of the response can be interpreted.

These are refinements which show that different sorts of research can be used according to the specific information required. Because special techniques are employed, it is best to commission experts in them, rather than dabble in amateur do-it-yourself surveys. The sales force of a company should never be asked to carry out a research survey, if only because their bias towards the subject could produce disastrous results.

THE LANGUAGE OF RESEARCH

The jargon of marketing research needs to be understood before we proceed to a description of some of the types of research, and then go on to analyse the problems that may beset surveys in industrialising countries, concluding with consideration of the kinds that are possible and are undertaken. This short glossary of terms will be helpful because some of the words have other meanings in ordinary language.

Marketing research does not require that everyone be questioned, and the section of the community chosen for the study is called the *population*, although it is not the total number of people as recorded in a census. It could consist of all teachers, farmers, motorists or housewives. Another word for population is *universe*.

But we do not question every member of this defined population, any more than the tea or wine taster drinks the whole pot or bottle. We take a *sample*, like the merchant examining a handful of grain from the farmer's sack. A little represents the whole. This is the principle of marketing research sampling. A certain proportion of the population is questioned to obtain the opinions, preferences or motives of the total number of teachers, farmers, motorists or housewives.

The number of people questioned, the sample, depends on the degree of accuracy required, the budget which may decide the degree of accuracy, the kind of sample, and the *characteristics* of the population. The characteristics are the different kinds of people (such as various kinds of motorist) who make up the population.

There are two kinds of sample, a *quota* and a *random*. A quota sample requires the interviewer to find agreed percentages (or quotas) of different kinds or classes of people. The random sample means that an agreed number of people are selected from a list (or street) at certain intervals, say every tenth person. There is nothing really random about this. If every person has an equal chance of being selected we have the probability of achieving a cross-section of the population. In the quota sample people, or *respondents*, have to be found by the interviewer who could select wrongly, but with the random sample the interviewer is given the names and addresses of those to be questioned. We shall return to this when discussing a way of overcoming the problem of not having a list from which to take names at regular intervals.

The *questionnaire* consists of a set of questions to which answers are required, and those questions may follow different styles. A dichotomous question calls for 'Yes' or 'No' answers, with perhaps the opportunity to say 'Don't know'. Multiple choice questions invite the respondent to state, for example, which newspaper he reads, which beer he drinks, or which make of motor-car he drives, from a given list. Order of merit questions ask the respondent to rank in numerical order of preference a list of items. With the semantic differential question, respondents are asked to rate the subjects, say, 'Very Good, Good, Fairly Good, Fair, Poor, Very Poor'. The first three score plus points 3, 2 and 1, and the second three score minus points -1, -2 and -3. Yet another kind of question is the recall, when the respondent will be shown examples (like titles of newspapers) and asked when they last used or bought these examples. Finally, there is the open-ended question, when the respondent is asked to comment freely, and a summary of this reply is entered on the questionnaire.

Usually, an interviewer uses a prepared or structured questionnaire containing a mixture of questions designed as described above, asks the questions and fills in the answers. However, questionnaires may be posted or delivered to members of the sample, handed to passengers, or placed in hotel rooms, but there is, of course, little if any control over their return. Unreliable though this may be, useful information may still be gleaned from the returns.

This description of the design and writing of the questionnaire emphasises why it is wise to commission experts. Questions must not be leading, and they must be carefully worded to be fully understood by respondents, and to obtain accurate answers. An oil company may be conducting a survey among motorists but a question like 'do you own a motor-car'? and 'do you drive a motor-car'? could produce very different results. Those who were buying a car on hire purchase, and those who drove a company car or someone else's car, could say 'No' to the first question and 'Yes' to the second.

In group discussions and motivational research the questionnaire method is not used.

DIFFERENT KINDS OF RESEARCH

Let us now consider some of the different kinds of research which have proved successful in industrialised countries. Some may be unsuitable for the industrialising world, others can be adapted to suit the situations in certain countries, while quite different tactics may have to be adopted in others. Marketing research may have its difficulties, but it is not impossible in countries with comparatively small urban populations. For many years Lever have maintained research units in African countries, even in smaller ones like Malawi. There have been media surveys in Kenya and Zambia. In Nigeria, surveys have been conducted by universities, local research companies and by research firms from London. The groundwork has been done for considerable development of research techniques.

Understanding the nature of the market is often an important starting point. Each country, and each ethnic group, has its conventions, prejudices and peculiarities. Special problems occur in Gulf countries where the Arabs are a minority in their own lands. Kuwait is a case in point where some 160 nationalities live and work in a tiny country. There are people from all over the Middle East, from all over Asia, and from Europe and North America, plus some Africans like Sudanese. A hotel staff may comprise 120 nationalities, as in the Meridien Hotel. Research in Kuwait has to recognise the buying habits of immigrants (who may buy to take goods back to their home countries) and those of the Kuwaitis themselves.

To quote from Michael Field's book again,[3] 'A dominant theme of Alghanim's market research has been the difference in buying habits between Kuwaitis and the various categories of immigrants . . . . Several years ago the staff of the YAAS division marketing household goods, mostly non-Kuwaiti Arabs freshly graduated in the United States, seriously over-estimated demand when they began selling dishwashers . . . the Kuwaitis did not (buy them) because they do not use Western-style dishes. Instead they cook much of their food in a large pot and eat it by hand from a big dish — neither of which fitted into dishwashers. Meanwhile the small tea and coffee cups used in the Arab world would not stack properly or fell through the gaps between the racks inside the dishwashers. The final mistake was in forgetting that any Kuwaiti wife who is sophisticated enough to be interested in dishwashers is rich enough to have servants to wash the dishes for her'.

The following, then, are the main types of research:

1 Field research This consists of sending out a team of researchers, supplied with questionnaires, and using a random or quota sample for interviewing. It could be either an *ad hoc* or a continuous survey. Field studies are usually applied to marketing studies to discover people's likes and dislikes or preferences, such as when testing the popularity of flavours for food and drink products, or why people prefer one kind of motor-car to another. Field studies are also used to assess the readerships of different newspapers and magazines. These surveys will also discover what kind of people have particular preferences.

2 *Opinion polls* (sometimes called awareness or shift research) which seek to learn the opinions or attitudes of various classes or grades of people on a certain issue. The best known examples are probably political polls which rate the popularity or otherwise of parties or leaders. However, this is the kind of research which can be used first to assess the situation before planning a public relations campaign and later to evaluate the effects of the campaign in achieving a shift of awareness, attitudes or opinions.

3 *Image studies* aim to establish the current image of an organisation by comparing it with similar or rival organisations. Respondents are asked to rate the performance of the various organisations (one of which is the undisclosed sponsor) over a range of topics such as price, quality, service, delivery and so on. The results can be shown on a graph so that they can be compared, and the sponsor can see how he rates in relation to the others. This can be very revealing and surprising. He may learn for the first time that people rate his price fairer than that of his rivals but think his service is poorer. This type of research can help in the planning of both advertising and public relations campaigns.

4 *Product pre-testing* seeks opinions of either prototypes or finished products before they are launched on the market. Before a new motor-car went on sale, a number were given to doctors, salesmen and others who drove high mileages. After a few weeks they were asked to report on the car's performance. As a result of this pre-testing, under rigorous but normal conditions, modifications were made to the clutch.

5 *Consumer panels* consist of a carefully selected number of people who are recruited as permanent respondents. They may test products, answer regularly supplied questionnaires, or complete and submit diaries in which they record what, when and where they bought products. Panels may consist of housewives in the case of fast moving consumer goods (FMCGs), but there can be special interest panels of people such as doctors. They are not paid for their services (which might cause bias), but usually receive some token reward such as a chance to win a prize in a competition, or a shopping voucher. If the panel is representative of different kinds of buyers (e.g. social grades, kinds of doctor) the monthly returns will give a picture of what kind of people are buying what brands, in which quantities, how frequently and from which shops or suppliers. Being a continuous study, graphs can be drawn showing movements and trends over time. The effect of

an advertising campaign, rival promotions or the introduction of new products should be shown by the rises and falls of curves (or percentage market share) month by month.

Two variations on this are the *brand barometer* or *pantry check* method whereby a researcher visits a panel of homes and records the brands found in larders and cupboards, and the *dustbin check* which requires members of the panel to place empty bottles, cartons, wrappers and other packages in a plastic sack so that the reseacher can record purchases. Obviously, the diary method gives more information, provided the panelist co-operates responsibly and makes accurate entries.

6 Dealer, retailer or shop audits are popular in industrialised countries, but may be more difficult to operate in industrialising countries where there are numerous small shops and traders. With this technique, a panel of shopkeepers of different size is recruited. They are visited by a researcher who uses a card for each brand and, by checking invoices and stocks, is able to calculate sales. The total figures record the shares of the market over time for each brand and, like the consumer panel, the continous study will record how these market shares move up and down over time. Again, this can show the effects of advertising, promotions and the entry of new products.

7 Motivational research is a totally different kind of research made famous by Dr Ernst Dichter. It applies psychological tests to a small group of respondents to discover their hidden motives. They are rather like intelligence tests, and they test both the characteristics of the respondents and their motives. Two well-known tests are the *ink blot* and the *thematic apperception*. In the first, respondents are asked to state what they think different 'ink blot' shapes resemble or mean to them. One person may say a shape looks like a yam, another person will think it is a cloud. The second test consists of cartoon drawings of people performing various activities, and respondents have to fill in balloons on the drawings to suggest what the characters are saying.

The whole study may take days, and there will be many tests, such as the 'eye blink' test, to show the response to advertisements or packages. A criticism is that the group of respondents is small, say 24 people, and may be unrepresentative, and yet the method probes much deeper and the results can be spectacular, as in the already quoted example of the American airline.

8 Discussion groups are in inexpensive development of the motivation technique. A group of suitable people is assembled with a chairman who asks questions. After a free discussion which sparks off all kinds of responses (like 'brain storming') the chairman writes a consensus of the views or answers given, and passes on to the next question. Discussion groups can be applied to advertising, marketing or public relations enquiries.

9 Media studies can produce figures on the readership of newspapers and magazines, and on poster, radio and television audiences. Field survey methods can be applied to measuring readership and poster audiences, the diary method can be used in radio/television research, and television audiences can also be measured by recruiting a sample of viewers to whose receivers a set meter is attached which records when the set is switched on and to which station.

Media studies have been conducted in many industrialising countries, and are a great asset in planning advertising campaigns. For instance, counts can be made of audiences attending mobile film or video shows. In Kenya, a media study produced an interesting statistic on the number of people who 'listen to newspapers', that is, have newspapers read to them. Radio audience studies have shown preferences for music programmes to the extent of listening to foreign programmes, while people in remote regions are disinterested in news from distant cities which deal with topics outside their experience. Research has also shown the weakness of radio penetration due to broken sets or the prohibitive cost of replacing batteries.

10 Advertisement research This consists mainly of pre-tests to learn the strengths and weaknesses of proposed advertisements and commercials before the final version is printed or broadcast. The *folder technique* can be used to pre-test press advertisements. A selection of layouts is inserted in the plastic sleeves of an album, and they are studied by respondents who are afterwards asked what they remembered about the copy and illustrations. Scores are given for each part of the advertisement remembered correctly. After this, the advertisement may be modified according to the scores attained.

The *hall testing* method may be used to measure audience response to commercials which may be interspersed with short films. One way of measuring responses is to test which of the products advertised members of the audience say they would buy. Another form of advertisement testing is the *recall* test. This is made after an advertisement has appeared in the press, or on posters, radio or television. The advertisement may have been printed or broadcast simply to test it, but advertisements can be tested during the run of the campaign.

11 Test marketing This is a test of the marketing strategy before the launch. A test town is chosen which is a miniature of the national market, and it should have typical shops, customers and media. There are three stages to test marketing: (a) The pre-test to assess what people are buying, say, which existing rival brands. This forms a base for (b) the actual test when the product is put on sale in typical shops and supported by typical advertising. The promotion must not be overdone otherwise the result will be falsified and misleading. A target is set to achieve a certain percentage of sales of that kind of product. Then (c) a post-test, some weeks or months later, is conducted to see what percentage of the market has been won when people have had the chance to make a repeat purchase and sales have settled down. The last figure may be slightly less than the first when the novelty has worn off and customers decide whether they wish to continue buying the product. If the desired share of the market is not obtained it may be decided to modify the marketing strategy or abandon the product. This could save wasting a fortune on a loser, or give confidence in supporting a winner. A dealer audit survey can be used to check the share of the market obtained during the test marketing.

RESEARCH PROBLEMS IN INDUSTRIALISING COUNTRIES

The following are some of the difficulties which may be encountered when carrying out research, and they may differ from one country to another, or from one part of the world to another.

1 Unlike the industrialised world, where marketing and social research studies are commonplace, and people have been conditioned for 30 or more years to being questioned by market research interviewers, people in industrialising countries are unlikely to be used to being confronted in the street or in their homes by researchers with questionnaires. Consequently, they may resent or misunderstand the questioning, and possibly fear it is some enquiry which could be to their disadvantage. They may think it has something to do with tax collecting!

2 Being unfamiliar with the process, people may evade questions, or give untrue or exaggerated answers. They may even try to please the interviewer.

3 It may not be easy to get people to understand the questions, especially in a multi-language society. Care must be taken to use words with exact meanings. There could be local meanings. 'Tea' can mean any soft drink in the Caribbean. There could be problems over whether people are more familiar with British or American English. To the British a yard is a concrete area behind a house, but to an American it is

a back garden, while a tub is a wooden water butt to the British but a bath to Americans. Even the word marketing has its different meanings: a British housewife goes shopping but an American housewife goes marketing. A British research team operating in the Caribbean (with its American and Canadian influences) could run into trouble. The same thing could happen in Singapore.

Some brand names have come to have generic meanings, simply because they were the first products to be introduced to the market. While this has its obvious problems when new brands come along, misunderstandings could occur if a local name was regarded as an ordinary noun. In the Middle East it is not just a case of calling a vacuum cleaner a hoover and speaking of hoovering a carpet. All sewing machines may be called Sing-gers, powdered milk Nido and toothpastes Kolynos. Again, Arabian husbands and wives do not go out together window shopping, and their knowledge of brand names is more likely to derive from watching television commercials. Or a brand may be better known by the name of the local agent, an example being Ali bin Alis instead of Rothmans king-size cigarettes. These examples are again borrowed from Michael Field's book[4].

4 There could be ethnic taboos, customs or behaviour which may affect the answers given. In Muslim countries it is often impossible to interview women, or at best to do a hand count when a census is taken. In Eastern Nigeria, Ibos believe that to count children is to condemn them to death. But if asked how many children he has, an African may exaggerate their number in order to prove virility.

5 Sampling is likely to be the biggest problem. It could be very hard to find quota samples, while lack of census figures and published lists could make normal random sampling impossible. Malaysia and Singapore have carried out careful censuses in recent years, but Nigerian censuses have been disastrous since figures were falsified in order that states could claim oil revenues. Even the registration of votes prior to the last civil government elections produced protests and doubts about their veracity. Statistics are chaotic in a country which may have 80 to 100 million people, give or take 20 million!

6 Because surveys may have to be restricted to urban areas, the results will not be representative of the country as a whole, when the majority of the population lives in rural areas. The product may well be on sale in hundreds of small country towns and villages, where response to enquiries could be quite different. An example of this might be a detergent which is effective in towns where hot water is used for washing clothes but not in villages where clothes are washed in cold

water. On the other hand, the cash economy could be mainly in the large cities so that the survey would be reasonably representative of the majority of people able to afford the product.

7 Also to be considered is the quality, suitability and experience of the interviewers. They need to be mature people, free of bias, and capable of questioning all kinds of people in a firm but tolerant manner. In Britain, married women often make good interviewers. They also receive training before conducting surveys, and they are supervised and their returns checked to see that they are obeying instructions. In most parts of the industrialising world it would either not be permissible for women to undertake this work, or they would not be acceptable to respondents. Either way, male domination would prevail, except in those countries where women were emancipated. From what sort of men can interviewers be recruited? Some are expatriates or foreigners brought in to conduct surveys. Several British research companies operate internationally.

Where local male interviewers are recruited the choice is among the educated, but it is seldom a well-paid job, and usually the work is on a part-time basis as surveys are not conducted frequently. This is one reason why British housewives are recruited. The most likely available reservoir of part-time interviewers consists of university students during their vacations. Educated they may be, but mature they are not, and the standard of interviewing, including the credibility of such youthful interviewers, is bound to be low.

8 Another factor is the kind of population triangle which exists in an industrialising country. It is usually the reverse of that found in Europe. The American population triangle is changing with the growth of the Hispanic population, and the increase in the young black population. But the contrast between European population triangles and those in the countries under discussion is largely one of age. Fifty per cent of the people in industrialising countries are under the age of 15. There are large families and a fairly small expectation of survival to very old age, whereas families are small and populations are ageing with several million pensioners in European countries. The population triangles contrast as shown in Chapter 6. This has the effect of reducing the size of the total population of people who can be interviewed, since such a large number are outside the cash economy unless they are the children of middle class and upper class parents.

9 The foregoing also brings us to a comparison of social grades or classes, or socio-economic groups. The following three tables show the comparisons between the social grades (based on jobs, not income) in

Britain, and the social groups in the industrialising and the less developed countries, These are borrowed from another book by the author[5].

SOCIAL GRADES IN BRITAIN

	Grade	Members	Percentage of population
A	Upper middle class	Top businessmen, other leaders	3
B	Middle class	Senior executives, managers	13
C¹	Lower middle class	White-collar, white-blouse office workers	22
C²	Skilled working class	Blue-collar factory workers	32
D	Working class	Semi- and unskilled manual workers	20
E	Lowest level of subsistence	Poor pensioners, disabled casual workers	9

TYPICAL SOCIO-ECONOMIC GROUPS IN DEVELOPING COUNTRIES

	Socio-economic group	Members	Percentage of population
A	Upper Class	Royal and well-to-do families	2
B	Middle class	Educated people in business, education and health services, civil service, professions, officers in Armed Forces	23
C	Lower class	The majority, mostly farmers, factory workers	70
D	Subsistence level	Beggars, disabled, unemployed	5

SOCIAL CLASSES IN VERY POOR COUNTRIES

Social class	Level of education	Members	Percentage of population
A	University graduate	Teachers, lawyers, doctors, etc.	1
B	Secondary school	Office workers	5
C	Partly literate	Unskilled workers	14
D	Illiterate	Farmers, miners, fishermen	80

POSSIBLE RESEARCH IN INDUSTRIALISING COUNTRIES

In spite of all these drawbacks, marketing research is possible and does take place, and some feasible examples are as follows:

1 *Foreign research teams* with overseas experience can be hired. Some foreign research organisations have offices in industrialising countries and employ nationals who have been well-trained in research techniques.

2 *The random walk or random location* is a successful variation on the random sample, and can be applied in urban areas, calls being made on houses at pre-determined intervals, such as every fifth house in a street. Housing areas are usually easily classified for this purpose.

3 *Street interviews* can be conducted at places where people congregate, or where certain types of people are to be found, such as at petrol stations, shopping streets or outside supermarkets or schools.

4 *Quantitative surveys* based on in-depth interviews lasting from one to three hours, have found favour when qualitative interviews based on large samples and structured questionnaires have proved impracticable. The method has been used in Nigeria to research domestic insecticides, and to position the proliferation of brands of beer which have appeared from breweries in most of the 19 Nigerian states. This is done quite thoroughly to include the major ethnic groups, and has not relied on a cosmopolitan city like Lagos where many of them may be found. Thus, surveys are conducted in, say, Yoruba, Ibo and Hausa cities, and in the local language. The results of the interviews are than translated into English for assessment and the final report.

In spite of what has been said about the immaturity of university students as interviewers, there are universities which specialise in sociology and statistics which have conducted valuable surveys. They collaborate with organisations in both the private and public sector to provide research services. These studies are of course mounted, directed and supervised by teaching and research staff at the universities. One such study was conducted by the Department of Mass Communications, University of Lagos, into communications at village level, featuring, for instance, the famous gong-man or town crier of West African villages[6].

The difficulties facing the researcher in countries such as Nigeria is brought out in the following extracts from an editorial, 'The need for national statistics', which appeared in *The National Concord*[7].

'... how do you import enough rice, sugar and milk or plan a water scheme without an idea of the number of consumers? How do you plan an education scheme without knowing the number of pupils and teachers? How do you plan an agricultural scheme without ascertaining the approximate number of farmers and their distribution in the country? Indeed, how do you expel illegal aliens when there is no evidence by which a Nigerian can be identified?

'The inability of successive governments to answer these questions has automatically reduced the process of planning to a nightmarish ordeal and leaders have had to go by guess and by God. And if God has not solved all our problems, it is only because heaven only helps those who help themselves'.

References

1 Packard, Vance, *The Hidden Persuaders*, Penguin, Harmondsworth, 1975.
2 Field, Michael, *The Merchants*, John Murray, London, 1984.
3 Ibid.
4 Ibid.
5 Jefkins, Frank, *Modern Marketing*, (2nd Ed), Pitman, London, 1986.
6 Ugboajah, Frank, *Conceptual Models and Research Methodologies for Communication in African Traditional Societies*, The International Broadcast Institute Regional Seminar, Ibadan, June, 1974.
7 *National Concord*, editorial, 'The need for national statistics', Ikeja, September 27, 1985.

8

Communication Strategies for Rural Third World Development

INTRODUCTION

We started out in this book by being very cautious of what we regard as industrialising countries. In the main, these are what is commonly regarded as the Third World. Here we are also dealing with an abstraction. The diversity of the countries known as the Third World is so great that it is difficult, sometimes embarassingly so, to make a meaningful classification that would be applicable to all, or even most, of the countries. We must therefore know what we are talking about, and to whom, in order to think usefully about the problems of communications which confront the so-called Third World. A specialist in Third World problems and at one time a most trusted strategist of President Ronald Reagan, Ambassador Jean Kirkpatrick[1], has confessed her difficulty in identifying 'one generalisation that applies to all the countries in the developing world'. For one thing not all of the Third World is poor.

Among United Nations' members, for instance, the Oil and Petroleum Exporting Countries are usually referred to as the Third World. Sometimes, Third World refers to new nations even though, of course, some of them have a distinguished ancient history. Nor are all of them technologically backward. Such technologically sophisticated entities as the Association of South East Asian Nations, or countries such as Argentina, are regularly classified as developing nations. More and more, particularly after the Falklands War, Argentina has identified herself as a Third World nation in spite of her high levels of technology. Despite these distinctions, however, the Third World countries are still to be regarded as the most impoverished, most colonised, most retarded economically if the most culturally rich part of our globe. These are regions with very high rural urban population ratios. Our introductory chapter is clear about this.

Because many Third World countries were colonised, they have no

146

cultural or natural boundaries and are therefore beset by problems of multilingualism and cultural identity. These problems are most serious in South Asia and in Africa. Colonialism often imposed its language as the *lingua franca* in these countries, although since colonial times administrative units have continued to change. Such a trend, as is apparent in post-colonial Nigeria, for example, accentuates an increasing number of ethnolinguistic centres while greatly improved communications by road and rail, and the subsequent flow of urban migration, has improved and increased contact between ethnic groups. This also implies language contact.

Under current administrative arrangements in Nigeria which constitutionally delineate a three-tier structure — local, state and federal administrative levels — three socio-linguistic classes have emerged. These can be called language of the soil (local), language of the region (state) and language of the nation (federal). These languages have quite distinct uses. For example, the language of the region is used for educational, administrative and mass communication purposes, sometimes also for legislation and the judiciary at the state level. These dynamic linguistic changes and adaptations are important political features of most colonised Third World countries.

PIDGIN

Where slave trading and coastal slave activities have been part of their history, the Third World has tended to develop another peculiar trend of language contact. This is popularly called pidginisation. Pidgin, in the words of Dadzie[2], is a stage in language acquisition, particularly second language acquisition, which functions as an auxiliary language for communication between speakers of mutually unintelligible languages. Pidgin is the product of contact in which a prestigious language exists side by side with another, and in which the need to communicate between speakers of the two distinct languages imposes the need to find a common language which is usually a pidgin.

Pidginisation is a natural process of the simplification of a code with the grammar of one language forming the basic substratum and with the vocabulary of the other imposed on it as superstratum. The word *pidgin* may have been first coined for Chinese pidgin English which evolved because of the need to do business. The word itself may have sprung from a Chinese mispronunciation of the English word, 'business.' Some scholars, however, insist that pidgin evolved after the arrival of returned slaves or their resettlement from slavery.

This view seems plausible for the Caribbean islands, Mauritius and still more plausible in West Africa considering that several words, particularly from Twi and Yoruba and, of course, cultural manifestations mix freely with an English base to result in pidgin. In other words, the heterogenous crowd became homogenised as a result of contact, and the need of people to identify with one another in their plight resulted in the growth of pidgin English in West Africa. Krio, a major language spoken in Sierra Leone, is a result of pidginisation.

Pidgin also functions as an auxilliary language for communication between speakers of mutually unintelligible languages. An example is Juba spoken in Southern Sudan. Juba borrows words from various indigenous languages. It has very simple phonology with few, if any, morphophonemic processes. In Juba grammar is governed by word order, by separate inflected pronouns or auxilliaries which may not even be there.

A pidgin language is relatively easy to learn. It can spread rapidly when a need for interlingual communication arises. It is pertinent to note that, since it is not bound up with cultural aspirations of any particular group in a multilingual situation, it spreads quite easily and is acceptable as an alternative language and a welcome medium of communication. Hence, the Yoruba, the Igbo, the Efik and the Hausa of Nigeria meet on common ground when speaking pidgin, and this tends to dispel such ethnic animosities and suspicions as are bound to arise if any of the indigenous languages is the medium of communication. It is thus reasonable to suggest that in such a situation, the adoption of pidgin as a *lingua franca* for Nigeria, and for other countries of the Third World with problems of multilingualism and cultural diversity, would result in the cohesion so vital for these countries.

The colonialists ignored this possible advantage of pidgin and discouraged it by selling the idea that it is unsophisticated and thus not worthy to be spoken by the civilised. However, pidgin grew stubbornly by interaction among the low uneducated class. The language has great potential, and will continue to acquire a wide currency, provided it serves the simple needs of people who need to communicate in the language, and it should be left alone. If pidgin could not one day attain the status of an official language, it certainly has the potential to serve as the language of development and should consequently be allowed and, indeed, encouraged in the interests of the socio-economic development of its speakers.

Pidgin easily integrates with locally existing culture and folk ways. As a communication vehicle it could be used horizontally to reach a wider spectrum of Third World populations especially those in the slum or semi-urban sector. Pidgin could thus be used as the medium through which to address the endemic problem of environmental sanitation found in urban and slum areas of the Third World.

The following sanitary attitudes still beleaguer Third World and particularly African cities: spitting, anywhere; dumping refuse into drains and gutters; defaecating in open spaces, gutters and rivers; urinating in corners, gutters and elsewhere; building houses without toilet facilities, even though these important elements have been included in the approved plan; throwing rubbish, for example, leaves, pieces of paper, rags, fruit peelings all over the place; and abandoning old vehicles and other forms of scrap anywhere.

The cause of the preponderance of these habits is the lack of sustained education using effective vehicles and methods which pidgin can readily provide. There is also the lamentable void of peer group and official disapproval of these habits. The Third World should develop strong corporate environmental sanitation programmes using the medium of environmental education.

COMMERCE

Developmental strategies have been slow in application to the Third World, even in the sphere of commercial activities. Of course, industrialising economies are often treated as the sellers' market. British colonial policy in Africa, for example, though planned to benefit Africans in some token respect (land ownership was not exclusive to Europeans, save in Eastern and Southern Africa, investments from outside were encouraged, grants-in-aid were extended, and contracts were facilitated) was nevertheless primarily administered to foster British interests. Records show specific and frequent willingness to subordinate economic advantage of the African to the interests of British producers and consumers (preferential duties, import quotas, maximum prices and currency restrictions were established for the benefit of the British rather than the African). Private monopoly groups, dealing with or trading in Africa were permitted to operate without effective restraint. The enterprises which extracted minerals were controlled by Europeans and were permitted to enjoy high earnings, while the flow of money from the mines into the African economy was conspicuously thin.

There are few areas of the world today in which social, economic, political, anthropological and historical factors are fused as complexly with commercialism as in Africa. Yet international or rather transnational marketers in Africa have not taken pains to study this situation in order to develop a workable sense of market behaviour to guide the formulation of appropriate commercial objectives. Casually, it is taken that life in Africa is carried on according to social and superficial cultural premises which are the antithesis of those in the Western world and can be reduced to a few basic units of which the most obvious is the tribe.

Commercial promotion in Africa is still carried out *unstrategically* by word-of-mouth and circulatory rumour, save in some urban markets. Large foreign import firms use unselected newspapers, television, cinema and radio, in short, the mass media, where they aim to appeal to the more literate metropolitan Africans. Advertisements of foreign concepts and origins predominate. Commercial strategies have little to do with geography, content, appeal, intended effect, intended audience, sponsor and demand influences.

The channels of distribution are scarce or non-existant, import-oriented and backward moving, lacking functional specialisation, not working as a chain linking intermediaries and completely unsuitable for the domestic distribution of locally manufactured goods because of its import-oriented nature. There is nothing in the ethics of marketing that can be differentiated from the general ethical norms of society.

The price mechanism and contractual obligation do exist but unethical market practices by Asian distributors, in collusion with unscrupulous Europeans and their African agents, dominate the big-store retailing business. Most consumers are illiterate and under-informed. Methods have yet to be devised to make them aware and well-informed about the products they buy and the nature of the market.

THE CULTURAL ARGUMENT

In dealing with the cultural argument about life in the United States of America, Professor George Gerbner[3], of the University of Pennsylvania, and his colleague designed what they called cultural indicators. This is a 'message systems analysis' which is an annual monitoring of samples of prime-time and weekend day-time television network drama series. Professor Gerbner holds that 'the industrial revolution reveals itself in the domain of the production of message,' and, as a result, mass communication, particularly television, produces a short-circuit in the other fields of social communication and reality. America and the industrialised world develop their ideology mainly with the consequences of the mass-media, and cultivate themselves through mass communication. Heavy viewers of television in the Western World, according to the cultivation theory, have internalised a certain view of society and a sense of values and norms coupled with it. For example, such viewers would have ideas about the risks in life and the price to be paid for breaking the law.

In the Third World, cultural factors in communication have merited little attention from scholars as economic issues. And it cannot be denied that no thorough-going economic questions can be answered without the consideration of the cultural component. This is because, as Professor Constantino[4] of the Philippines reminds us, culture is a pervasive, if subtle force which helps to determine the acceptance or rejection of economic development policies in the Third World. The people of industrialising nations must have to restore in their consciousness the link between economics and culture to understand how culture is being used to deepen their economic underdevelopment, or to deliver them from it.

Culture may be defined as *the organisation of shared experience which includes values and standards of perceiving, judging and acting within a specific social milieu at a definite historical state.* In other words, culture is the complex of material and spiritual goods and values created by human activity in the process of social development. Hamelink[5] describes a national culture as a system of values and techniques that enables a people to adapt better to its particular physical, psychological and socio-historical environment. If a country allows an invasion of its communication systems by a foreign culture, adapted perhaps to another context but not to that of the country, the adaptive capability of that country is reduced or might even vanish, as is becoming the case in Kenya which has an open door policy to tourism. Commenting on the 'wild-life craze', Norman Miller[6] speaks of 'the culture conflict' inherent in wild life management in Kenya. African rural values, he points out, are in conflict with a set of Western values which are 'alien, irrelevant, and contrary to prevailing ethics of most African farmers.' He further observes that while very few whites remain in official government positions, the broader conservation movement is heavily influenced by whites.

Both culture as patterns of behaviour and thought, concepts, standards and values, and culture as aesthetics arise from and are shaped by material life. Many material developments, e.g., technology, the organisation of the labour force, and so on, define, limit and modify cultural forms. Reciprocally, culture, by shaping human consciousness and defining the self-view of a people and their view of that world, also influences the development of material conditions. A 'Cultural Charter' adopted by the Organisation of African Unity (OAU) in Port Louis, Mauritius in 1976, took note of the above concepts of culture and underlined the importance of 'traditions, languages, ways of life and thought which reflect distinctive character and personality'.

Despite the solid impact of colonialism and westernisation which have functioned as culture killers in Third World countries, inspirational cultural symbolism is being consciously applied as part of the trend of political policies of many post-colonial countries in the Southern Hemisphere. For instance, some of the new states of Africa — Ghana, Guinea, Mali, Benin, Bourkina Fasso, Zimbabwe, Zambia, Malawi, Tanzania, Zaire and Togo — have drawn new names from Africa's glorious past and conducted successful campaigns to replace foreign personal names with indigenous ones.

In dress, there is evidence of a cultural renaissance. In West Africa, where cultural continuity is much stronger than in the rest of Black Africa, this renaissance is much more pronounced. Because of the absence of a dominant non-African immigrant settler population in West Africa, many Africans in this region did not have to use the small European ruling class as a reference status symbol in matters like dress or decorum, as in the case of Kenya, Zimbabwe and South Africa.

In some sectors of African urban life, there is a continual adaptation of purely cultural or traditional organisations. This feature of African development will be explored fully later in this chapter. However, a study by Sandra T. Barnes[7] of the suburban political community within greater metropolitan Lagos, revealed that the most important transition taking place was the proliferation of purely African political culture at the grassroots level. The increasing Africanisation of the polity is seen, for example, in the spread of traditional authority figures who adapt their roles as chiefs or patrons to the modern urban market place, assisting residents to fulfil personal and political needs.

There also exists a number of invisible or secondary organisations and networks, such as land-owners' associations, secret societies, herbalists' associations, town unions, religious sects and groups, and dispute settlement committees which must be considered as a strong, functioning part of the political process. The extent to which these bodies complement rather than contradict formal governmental institutions should be of cultural significance. There is, however, evidence of the adaptation of old political models to the new settings. Today in Nigeria, many businessmen, public officials, newspaper editors, international civil servants and religious functionaries see the acquisition of chieftaincy titles as a way of establishing their credibility and boosting their political and societal positions.

Despite the impact of the modern mass media, such as radio, which has now been acquired by nearly all countries, in Africa, for example, for people who are at the grassroots rural level where emotional attachment to traditional patterns of life continues to have meaning and influence, the chief's gongman's calls in the streets continue to bring them out to hear what they can only ignore at their own peril. The call-drum still commands assembly of the courtiers and war companies in times of national crisis, say to organise a search for a marauding wild animal, or for the rescue of a fishing boat in difficulty at sea. Traditional fashions of exchanging greetings at different times of the day, and their conventional responses, continue to be the sign of belonging in every African society.

Nothing could be more inspiring than the sounds of call-drums, and the flourish of horns, to urge people on to the task of a communal assignment. There are many traditional songs that, more than anything else, perpetuate the native *esprit de corps* that has been handed down from generation to generation and continues to hold the people together. The 'Tesitos,' the 'Harambees' and the 'Tsooboo' are as potent now as they were in the not very distant past when nationalism was the continental password that indentified the new African personality emerging from bondage.

Broadcasting, particularly radio, has begun to respond to the Cultural Charter of the OAU in varying ways. Nigeria, the most populated black nation of the world and a centre of black cultural activities (e.g. FESTAC), is manifestly revolutionising its music to be Africa-relevant. Michael Real[8] compared tapes of medium-wave broadcasting in Lagos and Ibadan and found that music of Western origin occupied 46 per cent of the time while indigenous music claimed 74 per cent. Music of Western origin was exclusively American, made up of a mixture of soul, reggae, middle of the road, gospel and classical.

Most of the music of African origin was from Nigeria itself. These included the juju sound of Chief Ebenezer Obey and Sunny Ade as successors of the 'highlife' tradition, apala music, sakara sound of Southern Nigeria, music influenced by the Afro-beat of Fela Anikulapo Kuti, the 'resistance' musician (whose own music is seldom heard on air due to various political controversies), and a wide range of other popular styles. Nigeria, by the early 1970s, boasted of record racks thriving with a healthy output from the indigenous music industry. There were 24 recording companies and labels and 14 radio stations, with a substantial output of indigenous as well as international music.

The number of radio stations in Nigeria, in the '80s, has escalated to over 30.

Compare the situation in Nigeria with that of Liberia and a vivid picture of dependency in media and culture becomes apparent. Liberia has such close historical and cultural ties with America that it uses the US dollar for its currency. Only a small proportion of Liberian and other African music is played by the radio stations of Liberia. However, alongside the domineering American soul and gospel music, one can hear, in Monrovia, some African highlife and similar music from Kenya and elsewhere. Several popular 'national integration' songs can be heard on Liberian radio, especially around Independence Day.

Drama has also gradually grown in popularity in West Africa. Again, in Nigeria, it is a strong element of the mass media. Television drama occupies a prominent position in this development. It has a wide urban audience and has often provoked constant comments in reviews, which mirror both the tastes and the expectations of viewers. One healthy development, noticeable in the past few years in television programming in Nigeria, is an increase in the number of locally generated and deliberately tailored indigenous drama programmes. These are fast replacing the previously imported Western classics and fillers. More is still to be said on this development, later in this chapter.

ORAMEDIA STRATEGIES

To define oramedia, we shall be guided by Frank Ugboajah's theoretical formulation. Oramedia, most often called folk media or traditional media, are based on indigenous culture produced and consumed by members of a group. Unlike the mass media which reach many people at a time but have only cognitive influence (knowledge, awareness and interest), oramedia can only reach few people at a time, but can be an effective relay chain to the mass media.

Oramedia have visible cultural features, often quite conventional, by which social relationships and a world view are maintained and defined. They take on many forms and are rich in symbolism. Oramedia cannot be separated from folk cultures in whose context they are significant. One can see oramedia as group media but it is better to regard them as interpersonal media speaking to the common man in his language, in his idiom, and dealing with problems of direct relevance to his situation. African and Asian intellectuals of oral tradition hold that the field of oral literature is co-extensive with all domains of human life and action. At that level, oral tradition is more complete than the modern written Afro-Asian literature.

We have dwelt on the question of language in our beginning paragraphs. Here we return again. A.J.A. Esen[10], a Nigerian educationist, has pointed out in his discussion of the Ibibio language that 'no language is basically inferior to any other'. This statement seems to be supported by the following poetic observation from Rev. Sister Marlene Scholz[11] on the African language:

'Sounds, sights, tastes and smells age-old and ever-new
experience of joy and grief, of hunger and war, of harvest and
festivity give that language its own quality. It is a natural
audio-visual language, which can teach us something about
communication in Africa. It is the medium that communicates
the totality of experiences of a person or of a community,
rather than just ideas and thoughts. It expresses the whole
person. It is the quality we are after in the communication of
faith.'

One of the greatest beauties of the Ibibio language of Nigeria is the large number, variety, expressiveness and sheer wisdom of its proverbs. Speaking in Ibibio is an art, for what can be more artistic than the use of spicy proverbs to ardorn and decorate a discourse, turning it, in effect, to a beautiful canvass of word pictures.

The Ibibio word for proverb is *nke*. This is a statement or a saying which has both a literal meaning and an inner and hidden meaning. The literal meaning is relatively unimportant. No one uses a proverb if all he wants to say is contained in the literal meaning, since that meaning is often quite obvious. It is rather the inner or hidden meaning of the proverb that is its essence. It is this that requires some wisdom or experience to distil the raw material of its literal connotations. As an art, the effectiveness of the proverb lies in its appropriateness to the level of discourse and of the audience. Proverbs are truly the gems of the African language.

To native speakers, the *nke* is the spice of discourse, such as one hears in the meetings of elders in the villages. No one may claim a real knowledge of an African language, such as Ibibio, or the ability to use it effectively, if he does not know a good many of the *nke* of the language.

Proverbs have been proved to relate closely to the economic, social, psychological and other concerns of the African people. Just like the *nke* of the Ibibio, the content of traditional knowledge communicated within the Chagga community in Tanzania is primarily compressed wisdom of life. It relates to all aspects of human existence: physical, social, economic and spiritual. It has a supernatural and religious dimension, and is mediated, not through words but also through audio-visual means. The Chagga express themselves with song, the tally-stick and symbolisms. It is a sign of mastery of the Ibibio language to be able to throw in one *nke* after the other during a discourse or argument, and to do so where the *nke* is apt and appropriate. Examples are as follows:

1 'Mkpat eka unen iwot-to ndito',

translates, 'Chickens do not die from the trampling of their mother'. The meaning is that people learn to adjust to their environments.

2 'Enyon ese — ayaan ebok',

translates, 'Even a monkey can fall off the tree' which means that experts can also make mistakes.

The domain of oramedia is the rural sectors or village environments of Third World countries, where more than two-thirds of the population live and interact. Oramedia have had little impact in official communication development in the Third World, simply because they are unassuming, and like those who use them for socialisation, they are politically weak except during cultural protests or revolts, and make little demand on the national resources. The ponderous mass media of the urbanites receive all the attention, all the budget for communication development and all the expansion, yet oramedia are the real media at the grassroots level.

Indeed, oramedia relate to Africans in a divine way as Lutzen Kooistra,[12] a Christian artist from Tanzania, notes:

'The God of Africa is the God of space, of open country, the God of blue skies. He is also *the God of dance, play and song*. The churches of the West have retreated into their buildings of heavy stone walls. Their spiritual leaders are not among the people in the field or the community; they sit in offices, behind a desk.'

Not only for Africa can this observation be made. Sylvia Moore[13] has uncovered in her ethnomusical studies in Latin America, among the Indians of South America, that ceremonial socialising penetrates the rural — urban continuum. In these communities, socialising has implications for the entire social and *religious process*. Through ceremonial socialising, common bonds and common ancestry are manifested. In the case of Indians and peasants living near Lake La

Cocha, according to Moore, a common myth of orgin is also manifested at specific festivals.

Ceremonial socialising in the Third World strengthens supportive economic, social and family networks which operate all the year round, and they are occasions for interpersonal and intervillage exchange. The cultural products engaged are metaphors signifying social values. They are microcosms of the community, carriers of myth, history, social and cultural dimensions of their view of the world.

The African world makes a stronger case for oramedia. The most significant thing about oramedia is not their esotericity, which is borne out of the ignorance of the observer, but the fact that the village audience has learnt to attach great significance to them. Oramedia have force; oramedia have credibility and prestige. They inject stability into African's social systems and indigenous institutions.

Rumour (which terrifies most tottering governments and institutions), *oratory* and *poetry* are very important modes of oramedia. Rumour among the Amharam of Ethiopia is a veritable communication channel. The Tiv and the Yoruba of Nigeria are, respectively, orators and poets. The Yoruba is distinctive for his artistry in greeting personalities with appropriate songs in masterful quality of tone, produced by mere voice.

Music infuses all the activities of the African, from the cradle to the grave. Ashanti music of Ghana, as has been documented by Sylvia Moore[14], demonstrates that 'music is history because it is memory; it is value because it is knowledge of social custom; it is participation, because it tunes in to nature, to the living and the spirit world; it is spiritual and economic because it demonstrates the non-material in the material; it is the prime transmitter of diverse and widespread messages because all are givers and receivers; it is a healer and consoler because of its therapeutic powers; it is a source of change from within because it is the meeting place of traditional values — and factors of change; it is a synthesis of artistic experience, creativity, expression, spiritualism, and function'.

At the University of Zaire, a series of studies to establish the role and impact of music as a force in the national integration of Zaire has been launched by the Department of Journalism at the University of Zaire.

Singing accompanies the normal work activity of the African, improving team spirit and promoting the co-ordination of tasks.

Africa's indigenous communication systems cannot be said to be all orally mediated. It is not well known that the Vai and Mum of West Africa communicated among themselves by *written scripts*. The Bantus were equally interacted through *symbols* and *cult inscriptions*.

Permanent records were kept also in *people's memories or on mnemonic or mechanical devices*. Most anthropologists agree that they have learnt to trust 'men in the bush' more than most American tabloids.

The drum takes on yet another important oramedial function in the African context. It is an extending, vibrant and unmuffled medium which communicates either by 'signatures', by 'pitch' , or simply by 'talking' in tongues. African languages are tonal and full of *nke* so the drums are made to 'speak' tonal proverbs through pitch, timbre and volume. Thus, we speak of the talking drum, a familiar phenomenon in Zambia.

The linguists of rural Africa are expert disseminators and interpreters of messages. The linguist acts as a messenger among the Amhara of Ethiopia. He is taught secret musical notes in order to establish his identity and the authenticity of the written notes. Among the Mossi of Mali, the linguist acts as an intermediary between an audience and an oracle. He also plays a patrimonial role in courtships.

Ornaments, charms and insignia serve social, aesthetical and communication functions, providing influence and information about the wearer. A Mende who wears a leopard's tooth is from a royal family. *Masks* portray the mythical being of the wearer. For the Igbo of Nigeria, masks are revered as mediums of communication with the dead. To the Dan of Ivory Coast, masks symbolise the spirit of benign ancestors. Masquerades appear in important ceremonies such as funerals, yam festivals, chiefs' installations and cult ceremonies.

Market places throughout Africa and Asia, in themselves, are communication forums. Market place gossip is a form of folk media. They are not institutions for stock-brokers or investor relations, though they might well be, in a very small and insignificant way. In Ghana, the 'Queen Mothers' are custodians of the market place. They celebrate the 'Hamowo' Festivals annually in this forum. This is purely an interactional ceremony to give thanks to the market gods who provide happiness and livelihood to the people.

Essentially market places are not just where people go to purchase or sell but are diffusion forums of social interactions and exchange. In the villages of Eastern Nigeria, a case of incest is given social disapproval by parading the offender, adorned with a necklace of shells and live millipedes, in the forum of the market place. An unmarried pregnant woman still living with her parents is scorned at by her peers with songs and dances demonstrated in the market place. Stealing any commodity from the village earns instant punishment by disgrace in the market place.

No wonder a 'Seminar on Motivation, Information and Communication for Development in African and Asian Countries', sponsored by the London-based International Broadcast Institute, in Nigeria, drew attention to the fact that the market place 'remains effective at all times because of the tremendous amount of interaction it generates'. It serves various purposes to the village — economic, social, political, cultural, religious and psychological.

As a news centre, the market place attracts personal as well as public information on subjects such as public affairs, family affairs, educational matters and religious concerns mostly at the rural or village level. Communication in this oramedial sector goes on in both verbal and non-verbal forms but mostly symbolically. Market place associations serve as sub-forums for economic co-operation and social communication.

Festivals as oramedia are reminders of the past, and therefore serve a historical and solidarity purpose. The 'Tuk Ham' Festival, celebrated by the Nok each year in Nigeria, recalls the glory of Nok, an ancient civilisation which flourished in Nigeria for more than 2,000 years. Tuk Ham is commemorated in a small village in Northern Nigeria called Kwoi. It has been established that Nok was in the iron age when most of Europe was still in the stone age!

This ancient civilisation came to light in the early 20th century, when tin mining started there. In the process, several moulded clay heads (terracotta figurines) were discovered. When archaeological research was applied, it was found that they were made by an ancient group of people who were the ancestors of the present Nok people. The figurines discovered varied so much in style and sophistication that they were seen as products of a highly complex society. The Nok were creative artists. Their exquisite designs on their pots were also reflected on the figurines. Some of their figures wore bracelets and ornaments around their waists and legs, while others had necklaces of beads. The Nok had great skill in the use of iron and were able to produce weapons of war which lent them military power and superiority. They lay claim to the name 'Fu Nyow Why', which means 'People Waging War Or Starting War'.

Traditional festivals are strong reminders of the historical past. In Ethiopia, festivals are celebrated with the gathering of people in major public centres and they sing songs orchestrated by drums (keberd), flute (washint) and string instruments (kirar and masinkko).

A casual bird's eye-view of oramedia inventory in rural Sudan would run like this:

1 Visual symbols and colours

2 Talking drums
3 Town/village crier
4 Drama, mime and dance
5 Story teller
6 The travelling lorry driver
7 Poets and singers
8 Traditional chiefs and leaders
9 Traditional midwife (daya)
10 Village barber
11 Traditional hairdresser (mashata)
12 Religious men and preachers (Imam)
13 Traditional saleswoman (dallallia)
14 Witch-doctor (koujour — faki)
15 Oramedial structures:
   i) Chief's court
   ii) Market place
   iii) Wedding forums
   iv) Funeral processions
   v) Mosque
   vi) Church
   vii) Voodoo (zar)
   viii) Festivals
   ix) Qoranic schools (khalwa)
   x) Religious occasions (Ramadan, Korban Biram)
   xi) Schools
   xii) Clinics

In the traditional Third World setting, therefore, communication is so integrated and person-centred that it would be unfair to analyse oramedia simply in terms of carriers and processors. Communication plays a very significant role in the cohesiveness and stability of rural people and such communication is oramedial in outlook. This is evident in the grassroots political and economic institutions which foster considerable informal and interpersonal communication through a group system of village social structure, title and secret societies, exogamous marriage structure and oracles (see Fig. 8.1). For the typical Third World rural village society, the law cannot be differentiated from the custom. The rule of law is therefore guided by sanctions made up of a body of communicative rules regulating rights and imposing correlative duties. Social disapproval means a withdrawal of communication or using communication to punish.

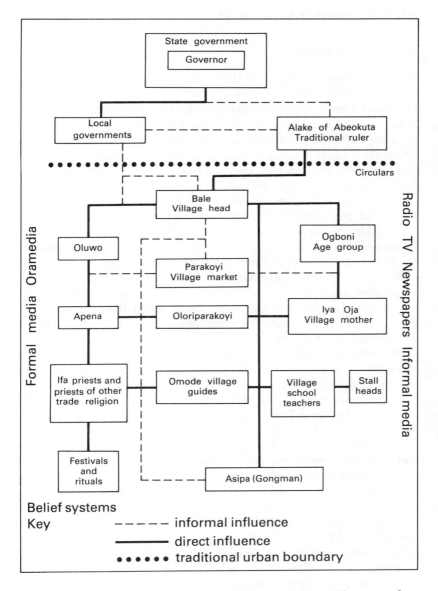

Fig. 8.1 Flow of influence in an African society (The case of Yorubaland)

AN INTEGRATED APPROACH

A Cultural Perspective

The case cannot be overstated that oramedia constitute the communication environments of the rural sector of Third World countries. Oramedia, though legitimisingly effective, are relatively slow and small. And we must not ignore the fact that most parts of the world are currently living in a communication age where information is the key resource. And without information, social development is impossible and virtually unattainable. Information is also crucial for decision-making because it makes alternatives and implications known.

While we speak about oramedia in the Third World, the industrialised and post-industrialised countries of the world, such as Britain and the United States, are adapting communications into every field of human endeavour and rapidly transforming the economic, political, social and cultural lives of the world at large. What is happening is that millions of persons in Britain and the US have moved into what economists call the service sector and the information sector – jobs which provide services or work with *words* rather than jobs in which *things* are made by hand. The information sector currently occupies just about half of the total US work force.

Perhaps the crucial point, when stressing the importance of oramedia, is to underline a cultural perspective and effectiveness in the communication or information development and planning in Third World villages *per se*. Recommending a 'traditional urban media model' for African development, Ugboajah[15] advanced a 'Mass Media Africana' which should be a fusion of oramedia and relevant modern mass media towards an equilibrium, resulting in a balanced communication development for rural reformation.

The communication effort should be to reconcile the total media environments of Africa so as to exploit those of the rural, the slum and the urban sectors in order to make communication audience-relevant. The aim would be to add speed to oramedial credibility in information diffusion in the villages, where the populace suffers from information underuse. It is known that in a developed industrialised country, the majority of the people live in urban or metropolitan settings. In a developing industralising country, the great majority of the people live in rural settings. In both countries the electronic media, print media and television are urban-based. Such mass media in an industrialising country concentrate on minorities while information drops off rapidly between the city and the village (see Fig. 8.2).

A media equilibrium will remove the umbrella and reconcile the conditions which shade off the rural non-participant sectors of society from mass communication (see Fig. 8.3). A balance would result in:

1 mass media being coupled with group discussions in media forums;

2 oramedia being utilised along with modern electronic media;

3 interpersonal channels being used in a special way to reduce the heterophylly gap between extensions or outreach workers and their clients; and

4 mass media content being audience-relevant, enjoining messages about motivational progress in the total society.

Explanation   **A** (5%)

Bulk of society's elite: white collar jobbers, managers and sinecure holders (politicians, academics, civil servants, bench and bar, police/military brass, business executives, orthodox clergy, etc.). Major benefactors from the national resource.

B (25%)

Bulk of semi-skilled and unskilled labour, unemployables (those needed for production and city management, factory workers, janitors, chauffeurs, househelps, mineworkers, jail inmates etc.). Itinerants between town and village.

C (75%)

Bulk of contributors to the national resource and receivers of the least national benefits (farmers, owners of lands where mines are located, tax payers for the maintenance of the largest part of national administration, community developers and cultural repositors, etc.).

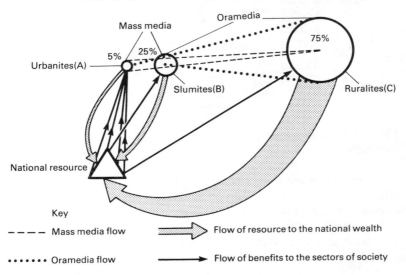

Fig. 8.2 The structure of an African society

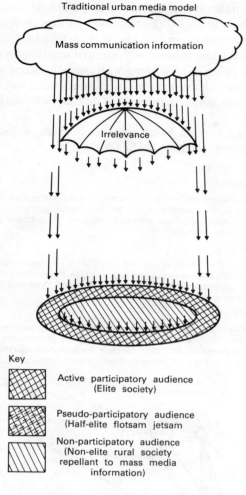

Key

Active participatory audience
(Elite society)

Pseudo-participatory audience
(Half-elite flotsam jetsam

Non-participatory audience
(Non-elite rural society
repellant to mass media
information)

Fig. 8.3 Mass message receptivity in an African environment (The umbrella paradigm)

Two questions are always being raised. Why do we speak in generalities about oramedia? How do we integrate them with the mass media to retain their credibility and increase their effectiveness?

The answer to these questions is provided by an important communication seminar, which was held in India in 1974, on the integrated use of folk media and mass media in family planning communication, reported by Malik[16]. This was part of UNESCO's drive for the integration and legitimisation of oramedia in communication planning.

Specialists on folk media from 21 countries were assembled in New Delhi to participate in the seminar, and to observe the way oramedia are used for motivational purposes in India.

The experts were unanimous in their opinion in a joint report that oramedia are often suitable for carrying modern messages in industrialising countries, and could be satisfactorily adapted for the mass media, provided care and caution are exercised at the fundamental stages, such as:

1 the identification of the flexible elements in folk forms;

2 the treatment of development messages to suit the forms used;

3 the skilful integration of folk forms with mass media; and

4 the presentation of communication packages with adequate pre-testing and evaluation.

These are research questions, which means that the integration of oramedia with the mass media should be a carefully programmed research policy put in the charge of expert communication researchers.

All these sound very plausible, but are hampered by four major problems which plague communication studies in the Third World. The *first* is the lack of trained and locally socialised indigenous researchers. The *second* is the absence of developments in the area of innovative and adaptable research methodologies for local communication problems. The *third* is the lack of awareness and response by policy-makers and research institutes to the need for communication and social research in the process of development planning. The *fourth* is the inability of interested researchers to attract financial and moral support, either nationally or internationally.

COMMUNICATION FOR SOCIAL DEVELOPMENT

Oramedia can be categorised into various classes depending on their contexts. In India, for example, they could be grouped into five classes of oral forms: folk theatre, folk songs, predominantly narrative forms, including ballads, folk tales and other story telling forms, religious discourses and puppet shows.

Folk songs, such as the 'Burrakatha' of Andhra Pradesh, can also double as folk theatre. 'Ramlila' is performed all over northern India in both the rural and urban areas in October, during the festival of 'Dushera.' 'Ramlila' allows considerable flexibility and improvisation. The folk theatre, 'Yakshagana', in South India, is almost 300 years old. Its emphasis is on battle scenes and tales of valour with themes coming from bountiful Indian epics. It also has a lot of flexibility.

Puppets are very popular all over India and Malaysia. There are generally four types of puppets: the string puppet, the shadow puppet, the rod puppet and the glove puppet. Puppet performance is accompanied by singing, music and humour. In Indonesia, 'Wayang Pancasila' was initiated by the Ministry of Information to communicate the ideological pillars of the nation. In Thailand, the folk-art form most successfully adapted to radio and television had been the Mau Lum, a folk opera or folk story drawn from the pool of North Eastern Thai tales and myth.

Once their flexibility is established, oramedia are easily adaptable to the mass media, particularly television. The Indian Satellite Instructional Television Experiment (SITE) can be rated as successful by its effective adaptation of oramedia for mass literacy.

Nigeria's most successful television serial drama, 'Village Headmaster', is criticised for what has been generally regarded as the decline in quality of production, caused partly by a perception that has gone askew, and the disappearance of certain key characters. As a serial which meticulously exploits life in an imaginary rural area, 'Village Headmaster' has tremendous cultural, educational and entertainment value. The earlier portion of the serial, which centred around the school headmaster who was a symbol and prominent personality in all local communities at a particular period in the history of Nigeria, contains some of the best things that have been shown on Nigerian television. The metamorphosis of this venerable and archetypal character into a psychedelic headmaster was not successful. This fate of the 'Headmaster' is a clear demonstration of the strengths and weaknesses of television serial drama adaptability.

Another success on Nigerian television is 'The Masquerade', a hilarious slapstick comic serial. According to its producer, Iroha, who himself is an actor in the play, 'after the Nigerian Civil War (1967 – 1970), I thought our people had had enough emotional crisis. They needed some kind of fillip, some sort of humour to lessen tension and anxiety. I also thought our society has been infested with people who tended to hide their shady identities, people with dual personalities. I saw my idea as a means of drawing attention to the evils and pretensions of our society. I therefore created 'Masquerade'. In 'Masquerade' the actors seem to be saying: 'If you take away the mask (which makes us masqueraders) you will see the real us'. But the masquerade (*mmuo*: deity, in Igbo) is an authority that cannot be challenged in Nigerian tradition, according to Oreh[17].

The popularity of 'The Masquerade' may stem from the fact that people not likely to laugh occasionally could at least laugh heartily at themselves. The story has it that the Nigerian Head of State and his cabinet, along with other leaders in the country, never missed 'The Masquerade', but took it seriously. The play's chief character, an old man, Chief Zebrudiah, whom tradition accorded great freedom of speech, berated not only his household and his irredeemable house-helps, but fearlessly chastised the government and society for their lapses.

The success or popularity of the plays stems from the following:

1 There is the dynamic attraction of the local or indigenous appeal of the spectator's mother tongue. All the plays, inject indigenous languages and dialects, including pidgin, into the dialogues of the play. This common denominator, rather than the content of the play, makes them classless in the sense that they are neither highbrow, for the few educated elite, nor popular only for the mass audience.

2 Next to this mixture of English pidgin and indigenous languages, which produces a seemingly mother-tongue effect, is the audience's natural fondness for familiar scenes and ways of life.

3 Most television audiences watch television for its entertainment value. Nigerian television drama producers are aware of this and strive to adapt the light entertainment attraction these comics represent.

4 Many of the plays afford the audience opportunity to laugh at their political leaders and their propaganda while at the same time identifying with some of their successes.

The traditional urban approach of oramedia has a strong advocate in the area of health delivery services. The move towards the integration of traditional medicine with modern medicine is taking place in China, Zaire, North Africa and parts of East Africa. China's Peking Institute of Indigenous Medicine has made great advances in this direction through innovative research and development. In India, the creativity of Delhi New Centre For Ayurredic Medicine has resulted in serious efforts to what is currently known as 'symbolic traditionalism', a trend towards introducing and injecting new outlooks into traditional medicine. In Vietnam, traditional healing men number in their hundreds because the average Vietnamese places very high confidence in traditional medicine.

In Nigeria, an innovative and famous psychiatrist, Professor Thomas Lambo, who is currently Deputy Director-General of the World Health Organisation, has succeeded in blending traditional psychiatry with modern psychiatry in his Aro Mental Hospital, Abeokuta. His research in indigenous psychiatry has resulted in a most effective diagnosis which he calls 'village treatment'. Remarked Professor Lambo, in a radio interview, 'There is nothing you can mention in the Western sophisticated management of the patient that we did not find in the way the traditionalists do their own'.

Igbo herbalists in Nigeria are also famous in bone surgery. Where the cause of the ailment is magic, sorcery, breaking of taboos or act of malevolent spirits, the healing process may well be spiritual. The Igbo medicine men, as well as their counterparts in other parts of Africa and the Third World, believe that ill health is sometimes caused by malevolent spirits as well as by ordinary mishaps. When established that the sickness is caused by spirits, it requires spiritual treatment by experts who are capable of encountering the forces of the mystical evil. *The Guardian*,[18] a prestigeous Nigerian newspaper, gave prominence to a traditional priest who offered to be chief rain-maker for the Nigerian government:

'A priest and leader of the Order of the Morning Star, claiming that rainfall is the antidote to Nigeria's economic travails, has offered his services as chief rain-maker to the country. In separate letters to the Head of State and the Chief of Staff, the priest, Peter Sydney Mwaneri Nathaniel De Madufor, has undertaken to come out with yearly weather reports in obedience to the call to help the Federal Government in its policies and programmes in the light of changing circumstances and the requirements of the nation . . . '

Indeed in Tanzania, Indonesia and the Philippines, agricultural science is turning to the study of traditional farming systems. This must be explained by the inhibitions caused by the prohibitive cost of imported fertilisers, insecticides and equipment. In Botswana, India, Indonesia, and many other Third World countries, the adaptation of oramedia for education and community development is also being encouraged because of their cultural values and inexpensiveness.

However, attempts to introduce more indigenous elements into journalism and broadcasting formats have been too slow because formats come complete with hardware and professional training, which unfortunately tend to lead towards cultural and economic imperialism. There have been, however, some success stories, as indicated above.

Students of drama at Ahmadu Bello University in Nigeria have produced effective drama for farmers, based on the realisation that the real media for the dissemination of scientific information necessary for agricultural development are oramedia, such as masquerades, drumming and dancing, story-telling and songs which make rural development messages so immediate, effective and pertinent. These place emphasis on basic goals of participation and self-reliance.

Oramedia can play very significant roles in mobilisation for community development. This is demonstrated in the building of Ikono Ibom Comprehensive Secondary School in Ikono Ibom Village in Nigeria, as investigated by Rita Nkanga[19]. Oramedia were found to have played the most important role in the mobilisation of the villagers in contributing their quota to the building of the school.

The ranking of the folk media forms, according to the role they played, were as follows: the elder's council, the village council, the gongman or village crier, the village Church, drums and drumming, age-grades association, friends and relatives grassroots societies, the market place, songs and praises. The big media, such as newspapers and the radio, played negligible roles in this community effort.

BUSINESS COMMUNICATIONS

Business and commercial communications in Third World societies must recognise that they are a part of an innovative and cultural communication for development. Cornelius Pratt[20] is unmistakable in reminding corporate communicators to demonstrate enthusiasm and 'adapt to the host country's value systems'. Even on the surface of theory, nothing brings about the hostility of Third World citizens more than a display of a holier-than-thou attitude. People of the industrialising world, like people elsewhere, place a premium on their culture, but welcome new practices that treat their cultural system as a basis, rather than a stumbling block for development and change.

A few things corporate and commercial communicators should understand about industrialising countries, particularly those with similar rural configurations to Africa, are that cultural music is very motivating in commercial communication, and that a socio-cultural approach can be successful in the presentation of messages, The successful television series in Nigeria, 'Village Headmaster' and 'Masquerade', can be an illuminating guidepost. Humour and eloquence of language, be it pidgin or an indigenous language, are major strategies used by innovative commercial communicators to arouse consumer interest. The injection of humour into a communication enhances persuasion. The popularity of 'Masquerade' is expressed in B.N.Adiele's[21] letter, which appeared in the *Daily Concord* on September 25, 1985:

Make 'Masquerade' last longer

'May I seize this opportunity to thank the Nigeria Television Authority, Victoria Island, Lagos, for placing the play "The New Masquerade" in their programme and wish to remind the authority that the 30 minutes allowed for the play is not adequate compared with its educative outlook.

'This play is, in no small measure, helping the present administration in their campaign on war against indiscipline to reach the grassroots; hence many Nigerians are gradually becoming aware of self-discipline, self dependence and better management of the scarce resources at their disposal.

'Furthermore, I hope it will continue to instil unprecedented moral discipline among Nigerians if given the assistance it requires.

'I therefore plead with the authority concerned to extend the present 30 minutes allowed for the play up to 1 hour so that the play will be starting by 8.00 pm and last till 9.00 pm.'

B.N. Adiele
Kano

The choice of colour, in the presentation of products, packages or pieces of commercial communication, is culturally and psychologically important. The African has a multi-colour tendency but also has a colour choice. Commercial messages for rural Africa should underline the following cultural guidelines in concepts and presentation:

1 respect for tradition (e.g. elders, married women);

2 eating (not openly, mostly vegetables and starch, heavy feeding);

3 sex (preference for fat women, strong and muscular men, lighter complexion, spite for nudity, conservative attitude on open romance and dating, unkind to kissing, recognise and appreciate male superiority over female);

4 family system (large family size, extended family and relations, gregarious, preference for sons to daughters).

Regrettably it is known that in many countries of the Third World in the last three decades, transnational corporations have become potent agents for cultural change. The presence of transnational corporations in the manufacturing sectors of developing countries facilitates the transmission of their 'business culture,' their management concepts and operational techniques, to Third World partners and to local entrepreneurs. No one would have quarrelled with this, except their managers are copied by local executives, while suppliers and sub-contractors must adjust their production concepts and styles to transnational corporation priorities and standards. Their sales campaigns have resulted, for example, in increasing consumption of white bread, confections and soft drinks among the poorest people of the world by convincing people that status, convenience, and sweet taste are more important than nutrition. Among the rural dwellers, these new foods may appear more nutritious, given the tendency, common among the colonised, to regard foreign foods as superior. As Constantino[22] has observed, in the case of the rural Philippino, it is sad to see mothers selling fresh coconuts and giving part of the proceeds to their children to buy a bottle of Coke!

Commercial communications can be educative, receptive and effective when they are *socio-cultural* and relevant to the host country. The following pertinent observations have been made in a few of the advertisements that appear on Nigerian television or radio.

'Omo' detergent is advertised in English and in Nigerian languages. The concept of 'Omo' is that it 'washes brighter and it shows'. The commercial setting is Nigerian – two housewives, clad in traditional costumes with braided hairstyles, doing their laundry the way they do it in Nigeria. One of them carries a raffia bag and both have their two children in school uniforms that are ready to be washed. The setting of this advertisement can be said to be pertinent and socio-cultural and therefore well-integrated with the product and the consumer.

Another socio-culturally effective advertisement is 'Elephant Blue Detergent'. The setting is completely African. The actors are the popular television comedian, Chief Zebrudiah of 'Masquerade' fame and another popular actor, Samaraja. The costumes are Nigerian, the Yoruba agbada sewn in 'Mala' style. The women in the advertisement are depicted as typical Nigerian housewives washing their clothes in a stream, Nigerian style. Both the personality and cultural appeal are an excellent piece of commercial creativity. The language is pidgin, so it cuts across all market segments and linguistic groups.

'Scheweppes,' a soft drink, is also competing on Nigerian television. The language is English. The setting is completely European. The scene is an English wedding. Except for two people, a black lady and an African waiter, the actors are white. You would immediately begin to see a master-servant relationship between the African and the main actors. The costume is European. The whole package has no Nigerian reference at all, and it becomes difficult to see to what target the appeal is being directed. This is a good example of an inflexible and snobbish communication in market development.

'Vitalo' is a beverage. The concept of the radio advertisement is that 'Vitalo is good for health'. The message is in Yoruba, a major Nigerian language. Although the language is indigenous, the background music is foreign, rendering the cultural factor distorted and bringing a feeling of anti-climax. It appears that the advertisement was produced in English for a foreign audience, and had the Nigerian language dubbed on it. Here is an example of corporate irresponsibility, where research, development and cultural realism are sacrificed for convenience.

RELIGIOUS COMMUNICATION

It has been observed that Christian evangelism in Africa, in particular, and the Third World, in general, especially that by the more established churches through the mass media, has often been presented in an orthodox and 'hell-fire' way. Presenters are usually Europeans or Westerners such as those on 'Eternal Love Winning Africa' (ELWA) radio of Liberia, who speak as though they were addressing people on the hills of Tennessee or in Hyde Park. Only the media, *not* the communication of the orthodox churches which serves the Lord's purposes, have changed. Recently we have witnessed an enormous proliferation of churches in Africa, breaking away from the orthodox Christian churches. Many reasons have been advanced for this:

1 Africans took charge of evangelism from Westerners in the orthodox churches, leading to a new touch and sudden growth in the number of sects and orders.

2 The fusion of African traditional values with the Christian religion led to modifications and diversifications into marginal religions. What happened was that the new leaders selected some European patterns and values to add to or substitute for some of their own, where they found the former particularly effective in dealing with the perennial problems of their congregations. At the same time, they kept those elements of their own religions which are still satisfactory, and Africanised those borrowed from the outside.

3 All Europeans, whether merchants or civil servants or missionaries, were lumped together as Christians and their colonial roles were resented and interpreted collectively as exploitative. When changes came the Christian churches were not spared. They came under the crucible of nationalism.

4 The Christian missionaries were also seen as founders and directors of the press, an agency that played a double role. It did so much for the dissemination of colonial policies, and at the same time powered nationalist resistance against the colonial oppressors. The reliability of the missionaries, and that of their institutions, could therefore no longer be assured.

5 Spiritual dissatisfaction, engendered by the atmosphere of worship alien to Africans, led to large breakaways from the Western established churches by people in quest for fulfilment of their spiritual being in the African milieu.

The old churches, including the most orthodox and doctrinaire of them all, the Catholic Church, are beginning in hindsight to see their original folly of having not respected or recognised and applied African belief systems, which they had dismissed as 'pagan' and 'fetish', into their liturgy. They lament the loss of their congregations, which move in large numbers to marginal religions. A preamble in the ecumenical *Christian Communication Directory, Africa*[23] confesses that the listing is deliberately called a 'Christian Communication Directory' and not a 'Christian Media Directory'. This is because we are convinced that in Africa the centuries old traditional means of communication are as important as modern media.

> 'The Churches are becoming increasingly aware of this fact,
> and acknowledge that Christian communication refers not only
> to modern mass media and techniques but also to the
> communication dimension of local culture and society.'[24]

Theologians are now recommending African oral literature to be used as Bible stories in the same way Jesus or Mohamed made up their parables. Interpretation and application of these stories can be made in allegorical, symbolical and realistic terms. Proverbs or *nke* are good starters for group religious discussions. They are also good summaries in arguments simplifying and making the points effective and clear.

Observations in marginal or new churches of Africa have found the adaptation and usage of a large number of cultural artefacts and symbolisms for motivational purposes. The Emmanuel Church of Christ and the Starlight Emmanuel Church of Christ in the slums of Lagos use a great deal of non-verbal cultural motivators for religious purposes – items of clothing, bands, staff to indicate hierarchies, colour, incense, crucifixes, holy water, bells, drums, gestures, palm fronds and intrapersonal composure, such as transcendental meditations. The leaders of these churches strive to give spiritual and temporal direction and comfort to their members, while they, as an act of reciprocation, contribute effectively to the support of their clergy and church. Prophecies and testimonies give all of them a real sense of belonging and participation. In keeping with African cultural tradition, marrying of many wives is endorsed and encouraged. This becomes a real incentive devoid of any stigma. Such an act would have merited condemnation, even excommunication in the orthodox churches.

Holy water is given freely to members of the Lord (Aladura) and God Mission Church (Idhosa), also located in the same part of Lagos. The significance of holy water is that it brings about spiritual sterilisation and healing. In instances of headache or stomach ache, or even serious illness, holy water is advised to be taken and bathed in. There is also the strong belief that it has the power to wipe out witchcraft. Families bring containers for holy water which is given free to the congregation. Some even take it home to sell to those needing spiritual help.

Other motivational strategies used by these new churches are revival services, when people with problems are asked to assemble for special prayers and miracles. The Catholic Church copied this evangelical strategy during the 43rd International Eucharist Congress held in Nairobi, Kenya in 1985. The mass media, such as radio and television, are also skilfully used by the marginal religions to show spiritual drumming, hymns, dancing and visions. Music cassettes and records are recorded with evangelical songs and preachings and widely distributed. Some of the churches conduct marriage ceremonies in the local way.

A sect called Jesu Oyibo Church, also in Lagos, operates large business concerns such as restaurants, food canteens, poultry farms, hair salons and healing clubs, thus providing not only spiritual care but also economic opportunity and jobs for its congregations. Religious communication has fully recognised the power, effectiveness, cohesiveness and motivational character of oramedia. All churches in Africa are now investing in it. True African religion is finally converging with oramedia. The same is happening in Asia.

CONCLUSIONS

Oramedia are courageously moving also into the policy domain. The Indian government agencies have frequently resorted to folk media as a means of popularising and spreading the word about official projects and five-year development programmes. In Tamil Nadu, the state government has attempted to use 'Yakshagana' for family planning project implementation. The Song and Drama Division of the government of India has used 'Bhavai' to propagate fertility themes in plays such as 'Aram Rajya', produced in collaboration with Darpana. 'Tamasha' has also been used by the Song and Drama Division for the last 20 years to disseminate five-year development plan messages. 'Ek Tamasha Achha Sa', written in Hindi but based on 'Tamasha', was produced in Delhi. It has proved to be extremely popular.

Already we have mentioned 'Wayang Pancasilla', initiated by the Ministry of Information of Indonesia, for the propagation of the national ideology. Historically, Indonesia has used art drama forms successfully to promote social and political transformation.

In Kenya, 'Panga Uzazi' is a radio adaptation for the promotion of family health in the official implementation of the 'rural focus'. And in Nigeria the national mobilisation and moral rehabilitation programme, 'war against indiscipline', has recognised the usefulness of oramedia (songs, proverbs, pidgin, drums, etc.) in the planning of the nation-wide campaigns, especially those beamed to the rural areas. Many such cases can be cited for nearly every country in Asia and Africa and parts of Latin America. Oramedia seem to be moving into the policy domain of Third World countries simply because the expectations of the big, very expensive media have been rather frustrating and largely disappointing for development.

It would appear that the Third World is finally returning to its roots for cultural inspiration. It is interesting to note that the 'signature tune' of a regional broadcasting station, Imo Broadcasting Corporation (IBC) in Nigeria, should draw the blazing wrath of a keen listener because of an unwary cultural mistake, as reported in the *Nigerian Statesman*[25]. 'Now quite recently,' he began, 'the IBC was born, and with it emerged a new signature tune ... For those who do not know, the beat is recognisably the drums of "Eshe" which, in parts of Mbaise, is a funeral drumbeat rolled out on the death of a deserving man.'

The writer, George Ibecheozor, queried what a funeral beat was doing on a broadcast channel 'in heralding the news.' 'Is the news broadcast about the dead?' he asked. Stretching his cultural argument further, Ibecheozor criticised even the proverbial song accompanying the broadcast drumming: 'Onye akpala nwa agu aka na odu', which translates 'Let no one touch the tail of a leopard's cub, whether it is dead or alive, let no one'. He notes that the song is belligerent and the message bewildering, 'The song is a serious warning, a war cry. Every Igbo person knows that'. He felt that the emergency insinuation of the signature tune was out of place because its funeral and marshal con-notations 'combine to create a beat that is sad, forlorn and aggressive'. He suggested that the tune be changed for audience relevance.

This illustrates the need for careful pre-testing before oramedia are grafted onto the big mass media. Imo Broadcasting Corporation was inadvertently busy putting its general audience into a situation of insecurity while feeling that it was doing them a cultural service.

Adaptation of oramedia for successful development programming needs a great deal of carefulness, which underlines the need for research and evaluation. But oramedia are very basic for the developmental motivation and participation of the Third World, which by definition means regions which had suffered colonialism, are economically retarded, are impoverished with very high rural — urban population ratios, but are most culturally rich if spared cultural imperialism. Such areas are inhabited by men such as the Nuer of Ethiopia, who made such an impression upon two western travellers, Graham Hancock and Richard Pankhurst[26], that they have this tribute to pay:

'For the urbanised visitor, a day spent among the Nuer constitutes an unforgettable experience. Modern western man, with his extreme sophistication, his technological knowhow and, let it be said, his cares and worries engendered by the frenetic pace of late 20th century life, here finds his exact polar opposite – a people whose mode of existence is as slow, timeless and unchanging as the river that flows through their land. Bright-eyed, intelligent and endlessly curious, the Nuer are very far from meriting that ill-judged epithet "primitive", but theirs, undoubtedly, is a simple culture, uncomplicated by the need to adapt to rapid changes and uncluttered by the pressures, phobias and anxieties of the modern world. It is a mistake either to scorn or to idealise such a culture – better just to accept it for what it is, and to be glad that our world is still wide enough to accomodate such "simplicity". '

We agree; please handle with care.

References

1 Kirkpatrick, Ambassador Jean, *Center Magazine*, March/April 1985.

2 Dadzie, 'Pidgin in Ghana: A Theoretical Consideration of its Origin and Development', in *Mass Communication, Culture and Society in West Africa*, ed. Frank Okwu Ugboajah, Hans Zell, Oxford, 1985.

3 Gerbner, George and Gross, Larry, 'The "Mainstreaming" of America, Violence Profile No.11', *Journal of Communication*, Vol 30, 1980, Philadelphia: Annenberg School of Communication, University of Pennsylvania.

4 Constantino, Renato, *Mass Culture and Development*, paper presented in a conference on Culture and Development, Centrum Kontakt der Kontinenten, Soesterberg, The Netherlands, May 10, 1985.

5 Hamelink, Cees J., *Cultural Autonomy in Global Communication: Planning National Information Policy*, Longman, New York, 1982.

6 Miller, Norman, *Swara*, May/June, 1983, Kenya: East African Wildlife Society.

7 Barnes, Sandra T., 'Political Transition in Urban Africa', *The*

Annals, Volume 432, July, 1977, Philadelphia: American Academy of Political and Social Science.

8 Real, Michael R., 'Broadcast Music in Nigeria and Liberia: A Comparative Note', in *Mass Communication, Culture and Society in West Africa*, ed. Frank Okwu Ugboajah, Hans Zell, Oxford, 1985.

9 Ugboajah, Frank Okwu, 'Oramedia or Traditional Media As Effective Communication Options For Rural Development in Africa', *Communicatio Socialis Yearbook*, Rome, Vol 11, 1982–83.

10 Esen, A.J.A., *Ibibio Profile*, Lagos, Press and Books Ltd, 1982.

11 Scholz, Rev. Sister Marlene, *Exchange*, Leiden, Vol. XII, No 36, 1984.

12 Kooistra, Lutzen, *Njau Champions the Gods of Africa, Action*, No. 85 London; 1983.

13 Moore, Sylvia, *Participatory Communication In The Developing Process*, background paper for experts meeting of the UN Commission For Human Settlement, The Hague, The Netherlands, September, 1983.

14 Moore, Sylvia, Ibid.

15 Ugboajah, Frank Okwu, Ibid.

16 Malik, Madhu, 'Traditional Forms of Communication and the Mass Media in India', *Communication and Society*, No. 13, UNESCO, Paris.

17 Oreh, O.O., 'Masquerade and Other Plays on Nigerian Television', in *Mass Communication Culture and Society in West Africa*, ed. Frank Okwu Ugboajah, Hans Zell, Oxford, 1985.

18 *Guardian, The*, Lagos, Nigeria, June 25, 1985.

19 Nkanga, Rita, 'Use of Traditional Media in Community Development Programmes: Case Study of Ikono Ibom Comprehensive Secondary School', BSc (Hons) thesis, University of Lagos, 1984.

20 Pratt, Cornelius, 'Public Relations in the Third World: The African Context', *Public Relations Journal*, New York, Vol 41, No. 2, 1985.

21 Adiele, B.N., 'Make "Masquerade" last longer', letter, *National Concord*, Ikeja, Nigeria, September 25, 1985.

22 Constantino, Renato, Ibid.

23 *Christian Communication Directory Africa*, Ferdinand Schoniagh, Aachen, 1980.

24 *Exchange*, Vol XII, No 36, Leiden, December, 1984.

25 *Nigerian Statesman*, Owerri, March 11, 1985.

26 Hancock, Graham and Pankhurst, Richard, *Selamta*, Vol 1, No 4, in-flight magazine of Ethiopian Airlines.

9
Communication Challenges in the Third World

INTRODUCTION

It is impossible to divorce communication issues from the issues of society. There is no theory of communication. Instead, there is a theory of society within which we can deal with communication problems and issues in their cultural setting. To deal comprehensively with the role of the Third World press in relation to its Euro-American counterpart, a look must first be taken into the social context in which both operate.

Within social contexts, there are systematic differences between social groups in their stock of knowledge. There are differences which result from variations of experience, social position, life cycle and future expectations. The term, 'social distribution of knowledge', refers to this basic fact, and serves to remind us of the provisional, diverse and changing character of human society.

The boundaries of social interactions become apparent when we encounter members of other cultures and societies or social groups who do not share our basic assumptions and meanings. We do not perceive or interpret even the physical world in the same way as members of other cultures or other epochs.

A church sermon preached in St. Paul, USA, on Sunday, August 28th, 1983, would have caused consternation if it had been given in Lagos. The pastor in all seriousness has asked his congregation this question: '. . . Who is to care for the mentally handicapped, the people on East Franklin Avenue (black community), the refugees, the Africans and Jamaicans who are without Christ, our own lost neighbours and work associates?' You can see the picture in the head of the pastor in his categorisation of those needing God's redemption. He was quite accurate within his own images and his congregation's perception of people who are outside their culture.

Just like the sermon, the mass media or communication structures cannot be universal. They are under constant pressure from the demands of the society within which they operate. Science itself is not neutral or value free. It is influenced by its cultural, political and economic context, that is, by contextual values. The directions of scientific research are determined by the goals of scientific institutions which support them.

The construction of concepts and theories is often influenced by cultural assumptions and ideas and the determination of objective, value free facts is more difficult. What is called the value-neutrality of science is itself a set of methodological or institutional norms (objectivity and universatility, freedom of enquiry and open communication) which often conflict with other interests and values.

THE VITAL DIFFERENCE

The vital difference between the industrial world and the industrialising world is mirrored by contribution and capability in the share of modern science and technology. Whereas the Third World is credited with just five per cent of the effort in developments in science and technology, the industrial world contributes 95 per cent in both the appropriation and the expenditure, as well as the development of scientific and technological knowledge. Economic indices show that manufacturing and production per capita is almost insignificant in the industrialising world.

In the USA, for example, the arms race of the past 30 years has had a secondary effect, by spawning research and development for the essentials of the information age – computers, micro-electronics, lasers, microwave radio, rocketry and communications satellites and the complex techniques to manipulate masses of data called 'software.' In the 1960's, however, the trend of research and development appeared to be shifting towards non-military goods.

No less important have been the recreational devices made available to the mass market by the application of micro-circuitry. Almost unknown in 1970, citizens' band radios in the USA now dominate the total number of two-way transmitters used in mobile services. Citizens' band radio is also commonplace in Europe. Hand-held computer games compete with simple calculators as novelty toys. Videotapes and videodisc units add new dimensions to television as an entertainment and perhaps an educational medium. Thirty-six million hand calculators were produced in the USA in 1977 and between 1950 and 1975 $12 billion worth of US-made mainframe computers and about $2 billion worth of mini-computers were shipped to foreign markets.[1]

Philips in Europe and the Japanese have made all kinds of domestic and commercial electronic equipment widely available on a world basis.

Currently, American banks are finding themselves competing with telephone carriers. Chain retail establishments are competing with banks. Printers are vying with information service industries. The evolution of cheap microprocessors and the complexity of computer programmes are reversing the time-honoured trend of increased specialisation.

The scientific scenario in the USA, Europe, Australia, Japan and other industrialised areas has also had an impact on books in selected fields. In the USA in the 1950's, books on science and technology numbered about 1,400 titles, ranking third among all classes of books published. Fiction took the leading position with about 2,000 titles published. Books on sociology and economics came second with about 1,600 titles, while books on sports and recreation trailed behind with only 300 titles on the shelves.

By 1975 a remarkable turn around in readership and publication had taken place. Over 7,000 titles appeared on sociology and economics. Science and technology took a second place with 5,000 titles published. Fiction took a third place and declined absolutely with only 3,000 titles on the shelves. Sports and recreation, although trailing behind, showed an encouraging increase in absolute numbers with about 1,000 titles published, an increase of 233 per cent from the '50's. Books on literature, which originally took the fourth place in 1950, still held on to this position but declined absolutely. Less than 2,500 titles appeared in 1975. The popularity of science and technology was not unconnected with the technological marvels which took place in the USA in the 1970's, particularly in the field of information. Similar changes occurred elsewhere. In Britain a whole new press developed of magazines devoted to computers, even at home computer level. In 1986 there were over 100 computer magazines, according to *Benn's Media Directory*.

THIRD WORLD SCENARIO

The 1984 World Development Report, an authoritative document of the World Bank, underscores the fact that industrial countries provide a market for almost 65 per cent of the exports of developing countries. These exports are based on raw materials. The buoyancy of the industrial world and the amount of trade protection they choose to employ have had a most critical effect on the foreign exchange earnings of the Third World. These earnings are indeed crucial for technology acquisition and socio-economic development. Because of the predominance and pre-eminence of the industrial countries, and the tie-in colonial heritages, the manipulation of industrial strangleholds, based on selfish prestige and power, have weighted negatively on industrialising nations.

The Third World has ineffective infrastructure. Primary producers or farmers in the industrial countries like Australia, Britain, Canada, France, USA and West Germany, have few problems, such as poor roads, canals or railways, to divert their attention from their main occupations. Most of the amenities, which the Third World scarcely have even in urban areas, are more than available to the prairie or rural farmer. He has easy communications with the sources of his inputs and equipment, such as excellent postal and telephone services. He has liberal arrangements for credit with sophisticated banking services, state subsidies and guaranteed prices. His domestic life is as good as anyone would expect in any of the urban cities. The poorest small holder has television in his cottage, and the modest fisherman can radio his wife while at sea.

The African rural primary producer on the other hand, be he a subsistence peasant farmer or large scale commerical farmer, has, in addition to problems relating to his enterprise, a whole host of domestic and environmental problems. Some of these require the full-scale consideration of the government. Others more closely related to his own rural or immediate community require local and personal considerations. The Third World represents a situation where the essential infrastructures, such as electricity and the telephone, are luxurious commodities. In such situations, other costs besides the primary charges enter into their use.

Transport and communication overlaps are more obvious in our industrialising societies. One often spends more to travel to a public telephone than on the cost of the call itself! In the African experience, the mail delivery system has currently collapsed and is virtually out of existence. Indeed the black world seems to suffer most in the Third World context. Compare this with the way mail-order firms in Chicago were able to supply goods to the distant Mid-West farmer, thanks to the USA mail and railway services, *more than 100 years ago*!

Current world-wide economic problems are now the major issues. These have hit the industrialising world most. We have scores of countries now referred to as 'the least developed nations,' which are also 'the most affected' in the present economic crises. Such countries include large nations, such as India, and politically important ones, such as Egypt, but particularly very poor countries, like Bangladesh. These countries cannot afford to join the information age while they are battling with hunger, sickness, population explosions and the rape of the environment.

We witness in the industrialising world, that of half of its countries, the income share for the lowest 40 per cent of households averages 12 per cent. Of the other half, the share is only 9 per cent of the total national income. And, surprisingly, developing countries have much greater relative inequality than the developed. Although the average per capita income of the Third World has increased by about 50 per cent since 1960, the growth has been unequally distributed among countries, regions within countries, and socio-economic groups. Moreover, once the psychological needs of the bulk of the population for food, clothing and shelter have been satisfied, many supplementary needs or goals will arise — for cultural growth through education and community life, for creativity and dignity through job satisfaction and a greater sense of participation, and for freedom of mobility, association and expression.

An economy of poverty is an apt description of the Third World. This poverty is evident in the fact that for most African countries which constitutes its bulk, there is an inability to fully utilise labour resources. There is shortage of working capital. There is a dearth of cash earning activities other than farming. There is inability, through lack of money, to make full use of cash earnings. There is increased dependence on high-cost imports. There are social and technical costs of marketing cash crops. Subsistence farmers preoccupy themselves with satisfying minimum survival needs and providing protection against crisis periods.

Such is the lack of initiative that a Zambian farmer, unwilling to produce more and so contribute to the economy will say what do I need money for? It is a depressingly negative attitude.

Infant mortality per thousand in these under-industrialised countries, is high. Adult literacy is about 48 per cent compared with 97 per cent for the industrial nations. Indeed the economic, social and political claims specific to the Third World, especially in the arena of international organisations, tend to displace international politics from its exclusive East-West axis. What we see is a North-South structure, the industrial world pitched against the raw material world. As Willy Brandt pointed out in 1979 in his call for a 'North-South dialogue', we cannot afford to wait a hundred years to solve the conflict between the North and the South which constitutes the major social issue of the second half of the 20th century.

With rich forest resources and abundant precious mineral wealth, it would appear ironic that the Third World should allow itself to be so impoverished. Development cannot take place without the co-operation and involvement of the political leadership. General Olusegun Obasanjo, who ruled Nigeria, the once richest black African country, for five years, admitted in 1977 that 'the merchant adventurers of Western Europe' made our shores trading posts where primary products were exchanged for processed goods. He observed that we saw ourselves, from the beginning, as importers of foreign consumable goods and exporters of raw materials. Obasanjo declared that the modifications and complications of modern economic organisation and exchange apart, Nigeria's uneven partnership with Europe and North America had remained basically the same, unaffected and unchanged. Nigeria continues to be a trading post which supplies primary products in exchange for processed goods. The existence of import substitution industries does not detract from this fact.

Obasanjo noted that these trading posts are *currently run and maintained by our citizens.* He categorised the trading post agents into four groups.

1 'Intellectual trading-post agents,' comprising individuals and intellectual institutions such as the mass media.

2 'Commercial trading-post agents, transnational agents, currency traffickers and smugglers.

3 'Politico-bureaucratic trading post agents' in the government ministries and the uniformed forces, politicians of convenience and planners who cherish kickbacks and enjoy making guilt-laden technological assessments and recommendations. (A clear example being an aerostat balloon system recommendation that cost Nigeria ₦140 million and yet left her without a communications technology.)

4 'Technical trading post-agents' in the engineering and economic fields, whose role has slowed industrial take-off resulting in obsolete machines and rising frustrations.

These trading-post agents have their counterparts in other parts of the Third World. Their role is to play the middle-men for transnational corporations and to render attempts at development ineffective. Perhaps, in terms of their poisonous effect on development, the most tragic of the four groups are the intellectual trading-post agents of which the mass media are most guilty. One doubts if there is indeed any thin line of operational independence among Obasanjo's four groups of agents.

In some industrialising countries, the poverty syndrome is never acknowledged. African political leaders, either civilian or military, find the poverty of their environment and citizens embarrassing, a situation that communicates a sense of shame. Rather than be accepted, poverty is deliberately hidden or blatantly overlooked. Beggars are better forcibly carried away from the streets, especially before the visit of foreign dignitaries, a tour by the Head of State, or the staging of international jamborees. A wall of polished corrugated iron-sheets is often built in a hurry to circumvent the filth of the shanties. Also it is felt expedient to keep from view hawkers and roadside mechanics who give the country away as a sample of technological crudeness.

As Reverend Adeolu Adegbola observed in a presentation to the African Council on Communication Education (ACCE), in Lome, in November 1984, in most countries of the Third World, 'we have reached the point where honest admission of national poverty might be taken as subversive.'[2]

The African political philosopher and leader, Dr. Julius Nyerere of Tanzania, reflected the fact that the end and objective of wealth would be the banishment of poverty, because, as he theorised, wealth would be to poverty what light is to darkness. But this had not been so in some Third World countries that inadvertently came in contact with wealth.

Nigeria is an eloquent example of such a disappointment. 'Trading-post agents' of greedy individuals and voracious groups have found power and prestige in the misappropriation of the public wealth of the country. They have lacked the political will and have used wealth, even to the point of abandoning patriotism, not for the satisfaction of the people's basic needs but for the purpose of acquiring power in the pursuit of neocolonialistic, nepotistic, ethnocentric and petty life styles and policies. Wealth, ironically, has become a fashion for the tolerance of poverty, not its banishment. There are some who are able to contemplate Swiss bank accounts they could not spend in many lifetimes, while millions of their compatriots live in squalor.

The problems that beset Africa today can be summed up under six major headings:

1 how to select national inspirational symbols that promote time-honoured traditions;

2 how to resolve the conflict between national cultural identity and growing cultural convergence;

3 how to go about unloading the cultural burdens of departing colonial masters;

4 how to tackle the problems of nation-building and the challenge of economic development and modernisation;

5 how to resolve the unknown cultural consequences of development in the process of the above;

6 how to end, once and for all, the socio-political struggle for independence in the south of the region.

Added to the above are the internal problems of leadership – the lack of a sound guiding philosophy for development, the absence of a leadership code of ethics, the hysteria of leadership insecurity which results in suspicion and hostility against local talents, the tendency towards public perception and personification of the leaders' idiosyncracies and life styles, giving rise, in most cases to corrupt citizens. Perhaps these syndromes are applicable to industrialising countries all over the world. They call for a sound cultural policy which would, ideally, integrate all the above concerns.

It would, however, be wrong to suggest that such a policy was entirely absent in the minds of pioneer African leadership. The trend of cultural consciousness began with the independence movements of the 1950's and 1960's, led by visionary statesmen such as the late Kwame Nkrumah of Ghana, the late Sekou Touré of Guinea, the late Jomo Kenyatta of Kenya, Julius Nyerere of Tanzania, Kenneth Kaunda of Zambia, Milton Obote of Uganda, Leopold Senghor of Senegal and Dr. Nnamdi Azikiwe of Nigeria. These movements had roots that can be traced to the 19th century, and were marked by what could be described as cultural management. Great men of such dimension in other Third World countries include the late Mahatma Gandhi of India, Sukarno of Indonesia and Gamal Abdel Nasser of Egypt. In Zambia, Kenneth Kaunda has a Leadership Code which applies to any manager, and in poster form it is displayed in offices.

THE CULTURAL CHALLENGE

A reawakening of this cultural consciousness arrived in the '70s with the world movement to bring about a new international economic order (NIEO) and the new world information and communication order (NWICO). The latter would enable the Third World countries to speak for themselves in international communication channels and to converse equally with other countries. The NIEO would bring about an equitable sharing of the world's economic resources between the industrialising and the industrial world, to remove poverty, to slow the arms race and make it impossible for 'trading post agents' to flourish. These arrangements would provide a basis for healthy cultural exchange, self-determination, eliminating one-sided dominance.

Within this climate of opinion on international relations, an inter-governmental conference on cultural policies in Africa was held in Accra, Ghana, in 1975, under the auspices of the OAU and UNESCO.

The conference took note of the world-wide spread of technologically-based culture that confronts African cultures, 'it being all too likely that levelling forces at work in the world may be more powerful than the forces of differentiation and may thus wear away the specificity of the African personality.'

A conference of Heads of State and Government in the OAU which met in Port Louis, Mauritius, in July 1976, also signed a 'cultural charter' for Africa. The aims and objectives of this charter were as follows:

1 To liberate the African peoples from socio-cultural conditions which impede their development, in order to recreate and maintain the sense and will for progress and the sense and will for development.

2 The rehabilitation, restoration, preservation and promotion of the African cultural heritage.

3 The assertion of the dignity of the African and the popular foundations of his culture.

4 The combating and elimination of all forms of alienation and cultural suppression and oppression everywhere in Africa, especially in countries still under colonial and racist domination including apartheid.

5 The encouragement of cultural co-operation among the states with a view to the strengthening of African unity.

6 The encouragement of international cultural co-operation for a better understanding among peoples, within which Africa will make its original and appropriate contribution to human culture.

7 Promotion in each country of popular knowledge of science and technology; a necessary condition for the control of nature.

8 Development of all dynamic values in the African cultural heritage and rejection of any element which is an impediment to progress.

The Heads of State agreed that, in order to fulfill the above objectives, the following principles are necessary:

1 Access of all citizens to education and to culture.

2 Respect of the freedom to create and the liberation of the creative genius of the people.

3 Respect for national authenticities and specialities in the field of culture.

4 Selective integration of science and modern technology into the cultural life of the African people.

5 Exchange and dissemination of cultural experience between African countries, in the field of cultural decolonisation.

The African stand constitutes the vanguard to the general outcry against cultural domination. The danger of being written off culturally from the world's surface is now the central concern of Third World countries. As a result, critical evaluations are being vigorously made in every aspect of international relations. Technological assessments are becoming vital in development programming. Prudent questions are being asked as to whether the technology available locally is adequate both in qualitative and quantitative terms for the specific goals of development involved.

It is no longer wise for any Third World country to import technology wholesale without taking local conditions into consideration. Nigeria is currently emphasising Made-in-Nigeria goods and internal origins of raw materials for local industries. Similarly, Malaysia operates the same system, with competitions for excellence. Malawi has a policy which aims at raising the living standards of the ordinary people in the villages by building up basic economic institutions, modernising agriculture, industrialising the economy and developing mineral resources. It is significant that the leadership has imbued in the people a sense of self-confidence, and this mental attitude contributes greatly to the country's development. In Malawi people do indeed 'walk high'. One can even see it in the way people walk about the streets.

The challenge facing the Third World countries is to become more self-reliant and turn the tables against neo-colonialism. These are efforts to detach themselves from colonial dependence culturally and economically. To do this effectively in the area of the mobilisation and motivation of the populace, the mass media will have to be identified as crucial agents. But one can perhaps go too far by adopting a Face East campaign, for example in Malaysia, turning backs on Europe and encouraging the newer economic imperialism or colonisation of the Japanese!

The mass media are crucial simply because, in the act of producing media content, a society is also producing culture. And in using the media, the nation celebrates its own existence. The media are thus an integral part of the attempt to build a national culture. Culture, in its broadest terms, must then be seen as an area of conscious planning, as another mode of intervention in a country's social and economic life. Culture shapes human consciousness and defines the self-view of a people and their view of the world and so influences the development of material conditions. But this is not helped if the media, in its quest for popular and commercial gain, merely ape the more sensational Western press. Sadly, we have seen this in Nigeria.

THE MEDIA

We have so far been attempting to map out structurally the vital difference between the industrial world and the new industrialising world. We have argued that a theory of society is vital for a critical analysis of the mass media. We shall now offer a 'media proposition'.

It is evident that the media, in exercising their information as well as diversionary functions, gain increasing influence over the process by which men arrive at those immediate decisions that govern the social contract. Upon these media may rest the responsibility of change, and perhaps upheaval, in both the policy and organisation of our basic social institutions – in government, in education, in our law courts, and in all those agencies and systems by which social stability is perpetuated and progress assured. A party-tied media system will strive to have one-sided political content. Politics can never be far removed from those media which in any country enable few to speak to many. The more subordinate the media system is to the political system, the greater access the political spokesman will have to communication outlets. It will then appear that the greater the media autonomy, the greater the tendency to balance political information. In Malaysia, for instance, there are first class newspapers which, in production quality, excel those of Fleet Street, but their independence is sometimes undermined by political party ownership.

Political interference in the process of mass communication can be explained much more succinctly by explaining what politics means to the Third World person, particularly the African. A plausible explanation is that, in the absence of any meaningful industrial activity, politics is the biggest industry in black Africa and a major source of power, social mobility and prestige. Politics is practically conterminous with African society, rather than being a part of it. The dominance of every aspect of Africa's socio-cultural life by politics, and particularly the extreme reliance on political solutions for every socio-economic problem in the society, has tended to *increase* cultural and social strain. The African media would thus preoccupy themselves in celebrating politics as a matter of routine because of manifest and widespread political agenda.

Given the codes of conduct drawn undiluted from the Western concepts of media professionalism, however, most Third World journalists are sometimes unaware or ignorant of the cultural contexts in which they practise or the communications goals which must be aimed at. Jeremy Tunstall, the renowned British media sociologist, has pointed out, in his book, *The Media Are American*, that American professional orientation has ironically been the most influential among communicators world-wide, to the extent that editors and reporters look up to New York and Los Angeles for leadership and ideas, which means that even Third World countries import their media ideas. He went on to identify the mode of media systems transferred to Africa.

1 A heavy stress on daily newspapers based in cities and modelled on the prestige papers of the West, including sizeable proportions of foreign news.

2 A low emphasis on rural media, in general, and rural or weekly newspapers in particular.

3 Heavy emphasis on the cinema, which is also a primary urban medium.

4 A tendency to introduce television to the major cities before radio has reached most of the rural population.

5 A substantial element of government influence or control in the media.

6 A tacit (or formal) bargain struck between the national government and the transnational (especially Anglo-American) purveyors of media products by which substantial media imports are allowed to enter.

Tunstall's observation is corroborated in the media systems of India and Nigeria, where the management of the media, despite strong local cultural values, contrives to follow the American model.

However, Tunstall's reference to foreign news has interesting contradictions. Some African newspapers have little foreign news and isolate their readers from the outside world. On the other hand, Caribbean newspapers are rich in foreign news for two reasons. There is insufficient local news to fill a daily such as the Trinidad *Guardian*, but Trinidadians have great interest in the USA, Canada, India or other places which they have visited or where they have friends or relations. There are also English-language newspapers published in Third World capitals (e.g. Jakarta) which are read mostly be expatriates and they rely heavily on syndicated material from overseas.

Professer William Hachten, of the University of Wisconsin, (see *Rand Daily Mail* of 2nd March, 1981) would argue the American viewpoint that:

1 Western media and their concepts do not propagate 'cultural imperialism', which can be regarded simply as a myth;

2 Western movies and television programmes are not imposed but are sought and paid for by willing governments;

3 Western systems of newsgathering are the only independent means the world now has to inform itself;

4 The new world information order 'would give an international stamp of approval, through UN and UNESCO declarations, to restrictions on foreign journalists gathering news in the Third World and socialist countries;

5 Communication (cultural) policies mean government control of news.

THE LIBERTARIAN TRADITION

Hachten's concepts are advanced to underline the libertarian theory of the mass media as propagated in Western democracies, particularly the United States. It unfortunately goes to further the apt observation of Tunstall that the media are American and are expected to be American all over the world. Nkereuwem Udoakah, in an M.A. thesis written for the City of London Polytechnic in 1984, debates the whole concept of the libertarian theory which subsumes strongly the conditions under which the press is said to be free. Such conditions must be dictated by the cultural and social practices from which they are drawn.

There is always the tendency, in discussing the Third World media, especially those of Africa, for a considerable emphasis to be placed on the problems of censorship controls conceived largely in terms of the free flow of information and the freedom of the journalist. But some writers, like Hachten, easily forget that those concepts have their origin, very largely, in the philosophical tradition of the West. Difficulties of the freedom of expression do indeed exist in Africa, but one notes that writers who discuss the issue struggle to express adequately in concepts which have a non-African origin the social, economic and political context of communication in Africa.

Certainly, the most essential task in discussing controls and constraints in communication is to engage in a critical assessment of the role of information and communication in the society they serve. This implies a careful analysis of how people of that society typically communicate in carrying out the tasks of economic, political, religious and others institutions. Another stage is to reflect on the values of the cultures which are assumed in choosing a particular pattern or model of communication. Out of this is likely to develop a theory of the press or broadcasting; in short, a public philosophy of communication comparable to that which John Stuart Mills developed in 19th century England but consistent with the local demands of social and political development.

At present, one observes a series of paradoxical situations in which

Third World journalists attempt to guide the proper development of communication, within political forms that were inherited from Europe and America. Journalists in the Third World must understand the policies of national leadership in terms of the most elusive element of their political life, namely, national integration and mobilisation. There is also the need to understand the role of the mass media in the formation and expression of public opinion – a central function of any form of journalism.

How, for example, is opinion formed and expressed in the African context? The answer to this question would demand more ethno-cultural rather than socio-psychological considerations. This cultural contradiction often underlies the difficulty confronting journalists and officials in organising acceptable opinion polls in Africa, whether this be a census or an election. When public opinion has been monitored using methods borrowed from the USA or Europe, what are its socio-cultural significance and political implications?

We might go a step further to say that even in Western democracies, the concept of press freedom is not uniform. The British, the French and the Americans operate press freedoms under different contexts. As Tunstall in his *Media Sociology* (1974), has pointed out, 'American understanding of the British media – and probably even more so the media of most other countries – has often been rather imperfect'. One society's better form of press control may be another's worse form. For instance, British observers of their mass media constantly debate whether private ownership is preferable to state intervention as a mechanism for guaranteeing a greater degree of media freedom. Some American theoreticians of the press state that to look at the difference between press systems in full perspective, one must look at the social systems in which the press functions. And to see the social systems in their true relationship to the press, one has to look at certain beliefs and assumptions.

The argument that the press in the so-called libertarian systems could serve a particular interest becomes glaring with the evidence of newspapers with alarming financial losses being kept in business by massive subsidies from multinational corporations. A ready example are the losses made by Fleet Street newspapers generally in the 1970's. The *Times* and the *Sunday Times* lost £8.5 million in the first half of 1983, and that after losing a total of £23 million in 1981–1982. The *Rand Daily Mail* of Johannesburg, South Africa, would not have folded up in April 1985, if it had toed the steps of the apartheid system. Western advocates of free flow of information and the freedom of journalism capitalise heavily on the experience and emotions of Third

World people and people freshly liberated from fascist-occupied and war-ravaged continents. But accompanying the rhetoric of press freedom are powerful economic forces employing skilful political and semantic strategy.

But we also have to consider *why* newspapers lose money or fold in the West. In the first place, a privately owned, as distinct from a state-owned (and usually subsidised) newspaper is a commercial business, even in the USA where the newspaper follows the 'Fourth Estate' concept more than it does in Britain. A newspaper can make money only if it succeeds in three respects:

1 It is produced economically.

2 It attracts a large number of readers (or a significant penetration of its class of reader).

3 It sells advertisement space.

A major reason for the financial losses of Fleet Street newspapers has been the power of trade unions to impose restrictive practices, which have prevented proprietors from introducing single stroke keying direct input which replaces composing rooms, and from moving from letterpress to offset-litho. In many parts of the world, including the Third World, newspapers have already adopted the new technology. While this is apparent in Kuala Lumpur and Nairobi, it is incredible that in Nigeria the *Daily Times* is still badly produced, although modern equipment was installed a few years ago.

The battle for circulation and readership, and the sale of advertisement space, exists in a very competitive situation, especially in Britain where there are 12,000 newspapers, magazines and other publications. Although the London *Times* may be regarded as a great newspaper, it has to be remembered that the *Sun* captures more than 4m sales daily, compared with the *Times*' mere 400,000 which is no more than the *Daily Times* in Nigeria.

Newspapers tend to succeed if they print what people want to read, which is evident by the phenomenal sale of the sensational German daily, *Bild*, which is read by 20 per cent of Germans. The *Times* has a small circulation, but only a small number of people want to read political, financial, legal or foreign news. Most people want to be entertained so they read the *Sun* or the *Mirror*, and those in between read the *Express* and the *Mail*, while executives read the *Telegraph* and intellectuals read the *Guardian* or the *Independent*.

The media situation is therefore very different in the industrialising world where only a small proportion of the population is literate or able to afford to buy newspapers; where the number of advertisers is small and income from advertising is low; and when production may be hindered by the cost of imported newsprint, poor printing workmanship, or breakdown of equipment and inability to obtain foreign currency for replacement parts.

The question of official news leaks that probably lead to obnoxious press laws and regulations in Africa, such as the highly volatile Decree No. 4 of Nigeria, is not only the preoccupation of Third World political leadership. In the USA, attempts are being made by the Reagan administration to plug official leaks. There are attempts at the rewriting of the Classification Order, passing a broad version of the Agents Identities Act, rewriting the Freedom of Information Act, implementing a programme of lie-detector tests, requiring pre-publication review of material written by government officials with access to sensitive information and barring the press in Granada. The Reagan administration is indeed hypersensitive to unofficial leaks of government information and believes that leaks are everywhere and must be stopped. In Britain there have been court cases over the leaking of information by civil servants who objected to the Thatcher regime.

GREATNESS OF THE WESTERN MEDIA

What makes a newspaper great? Merrill and Fisher[3] list the following characteristics of an elite or a great newspaper:

1 Completeness of coverage of foreign and internal affairs, business, the arts, science and education.

2 Concern with interpretative pieces, background articles and in depth news articles.

3 Typographical and general editorial dignity.

4 Lack of sensationalism. The authors hold that a mere chronicling of negative aspects of reality, a steady diet of sensation (war, crime, sex, rioting, etc) may satiate the mass appetite for vicarious and effortless adventure but it does little to create a homogeneity of thought or thoughtful people.

5 Depth and analytical perception of stories.

6 Absence of hysteria and cultural tone.

7 Thorough and impartial news coverage and serious-minded moral approach to news.

8 Imagination, decency, interest in democratic problems and humanity.

9 Excellent editorial page.

10 Orientation that rises above provincialism and sensationalism.

11 Emphasis on political, economic and cultural news and views.

12 Financial stability, integrity, social concern, good writing and editing.

13 Determination to serve and help expand a well-educated, intellectual readership at home and abroad.

14 Desire to appeal to and influence opinion leaders everywhere.

The following newspapers have been nominated by the authors as the very best in the world of journalism, regardless of ideological context.

ABC (Spain), *Aftenposten* (Norway), *The Age* (Australia), *Al Ahram* (Egypt), *Asahi Shimbun* (Japan). *Atlanta Constitution* (USA), *Berlingske Tidende* (Denmark), *Borba* (Yugoslavia), *Christian Science Monitor* (USA), *Corriere della Sera* (Italy), *The Daily Telegraph* (England), *O Estado de Sau Paulo* (Brazil), *Le Figaro* (France), *Frankfurter Allgemeine* (West Germany), *The Globe and Mail* (Canada), *The Guardian* (England), *Haaretz* (Israel), *Helsingin Sanomat* (Finland), *The Hindu* (India), *Isvestia* (Soviet Union), *Journal do Brasil* (Brazil), *Los Angeles Times* (USA), *Le Monde* (France), *Neue Zurcher Zeitung* (Switzerland), *The New York Times* (USA), *Osservators Romano* (The Vatican), *El Paid* (Spain), *Pravda* (Soviet Union), *Die Presse* (Austria), *Rand Daily Mail* (recently defunct, South Africa), *Renmin Ribao* (People's Republic of China), *The Scotsman* (Scotland), *La Stampa* (Italy), *St. Louis Post Dispatch* (USA), *The Statesman* (India), *Suddeutsche Zeitung* (West Germany), *The Straits Times* (Singapore), *Svenska Dagbladet* (Sweden), *Sunday Morning Herald* (Australia), *The Times* (England), *The Times of India* (India), *La Vanduardia Espanola* (Spain), *The Wall Street Journal* (USA), *Die Welt* (West Germany), *Winnipeg Free Press* (Canada) and *The Yorkshire Post* (England).

An important observation is that the majority of these newspapers are from the Western world, notably the United States. The greatness and elitism which they enjoy, according to the criteria listed, is linked to their cultural base which is economically, technologically and scientifically far better endowed than what obtains in the Third World.

Backed by most modern telecommunications and skilful international broadcasting (VOA, BBC, OFTR, Deutchewelle, etc.) and powerful news agencies, notably, Reuters, Agence France Presse, United Press International, Associated Press and New York Times Wire Service, the above Western newspapers have succeeded in culturally conquering the world, particularly the industrialising world, showing them the way they should think about themselves, as well as the images they have for themselves.

But this invasion has also created the false impression that these newspapers are the popular ones in these particular countries, and are representative of the views of the people, even of the governments of these countries. In many industrialising countries many people think that the *Times* is the only newspaper that matters in Britain and are astonished when told of its minority readership. More significant are the wire services which supply news to all the newspapers, at home and world-wide.

Not only in the field of the press but also in the area of telecommunications has the industrial world a resounding technological advantage over the Third World. The late President of the International Institute of Communication, Jean D'Arcy, in a speech to a symposium on the cultural role of broadcasting organised by Hoso-Bunka Foundation of Japan in Tokyo in October 1978, identified *three* trends in the information explosion and communication challenge in the industrial nations:

1 *Abundance*, for example, the capacity of satellites has increased in 15 years from 240 to 24,000 telephone circuits, and fibre optics have capacities nearer 100,000 circuits. The potential of communication available but not yet in use is probably as great as the volume of neurons in the human brain which, for reasons which may one day emerge but are still unknown, we appear not to use.

2 *Planetarisation* No point on the surface of the earth is now out of range of satellite consortia of Intelsat, Molnya and stationary systems. NASA has ordered a study of the science-fiction dream wrist radio telephone that will enable anyone anywhere to communicate with anyone of his choice. It is expected that this will be possible during the 1990's.

3 *Individuation* This trend seems to be the clearest and most important. It is embodied most strongly in teledata processing, wide-band interactive telecommunications networks, teletext, video cassettes and video discs, all products of the technology of miniaturisation and microprocessing. They are having the effect of de-massifying the media so that there are now 100-channel television sets to receive scores of cable and satellite programmes. The mass audiences for the conventional monopoly programmes of the BBC, ITV companies and state or private systems elsewhere will diminish because of the greater choice available to viewers.

In the post-industrial countries of the world, it appears that the age of mass communication is almost over. Such technological feats and trends were not anticipated some 30 years ago. They are leading the Euro-American societies irresistably in the direction of a single electronic system of expression. Newspaper publication by teleprinting, television displays and teletext and cinema by video transmission, broadcasting and telephone communications by means of teletext along the lines of Viewdata and Antiope are striking examples of the communication revolution. The educational and informational import of these discoveries is immense.

The technological trend is one towards the restructuring of mass communication. The present vertical mode of the organisation of the mass media (press, radio, cinema, television, data processing, etc) is being replaced by a horizontal structure divided into the functions of gathering, production, transmission and circulation of information. The laws and regulations set up for vertical media structures will have to change. There is at present in the West, little distinction between the press and broadcasting. High technology has almost converged the two.

THE CENTRE-PERIPHERY RELATIONSHIP

International relations between the industrialised world and the industrialising world have now been likened to those between the centre of a circle and its periphery, between an orbital planet and its satellites. This is not only in the sphere of economics and politics, but also in the sphere of mass communication and information.

Consumer spending on mass communication between 1968 and 1977 rose phenomenally in the US from about $15 billion to nearly $40 billion. In the ownership of radio sets, television sets, telephones and automobiles throughout the world, the United States would claim ownership of 40 per cent. Africa's share is insignificant, not even up to one per cent and Asia and Latin America, although much better blessed in this direction, can hardly be compared with the favourable conditions in the West.

Africa receives only 0.8 per cent attention in the American media, 1.9 per cent in West European media and surprisingly, just 5 per cent in Third World media, as against 26 per cent Third World coverage for Euro-American countries. This shows how little the Third World is forced to know about itself. The low proportion of correspondents in Africa, for instance, and the dominance of the international wire services on the African news market result in quantitatively inadequate reporting on Africa, both in the Western press and the African media themselves. It is amazing how little Third World top flight journalists and editors know about their various continents. This is sadly discovered in job interviews.

Press scholars refer to Africa, for example, as an expanding continent with a shrinking press. Some social theories hazard the guess that the 'take-off point' for press development in the Third World would come at a time when the particular country had attained 20 per cent literacy and 10 per cent urbanisation. This notion seems to have crashed in the case of Africa, where the character of the press more than two decades after independence has struggled to mirror the political and social evolution of the new nations. As one of the 'inherited institutions' from a different culture and system, its role, despite cultural homogenisation, cannot be expected to be the same as in Western democracies.

In the early pioneer days of the USA, the town newspaper was created as a form of democratic expression. In Britain, newspapers began as coffee-house political sheets. The great newspapers were developed to support the Liberal and Tory parties, and the *Times* was Disraeli's famous 'Thunderer'. Today, the political views of newspaper owners seldom match those of their readers. British newspapers tend to represent the various social grades and circulation figures follow the volume of population represented by the social grades. The majority of the population read the popular press. There is virtually complete freedom of expression at all levels.

Western legal traditions have been passed on to Africans, but in the case of the press, the law as it is written and intended has relatively little real meaning in terms of what the press can do or cannot do. The governments of the new nations are concerned with the press as an institution outside the framework of a libertarian constitution. The press is looked upon as an institution of political expediency before it is an institution for democratic expression. Where the press law does not cover a situation unacceptable to the political leadership, an executive order does. As a consequence, the press in Africa is regulated by a method that could be termed 'extra-constitutional' and 'supra-legal'.

In this framework, the powers granted to the government weigh more heavily than the rights granted to the press. The African ruling elite believes that state intervention in mass communication is a necessary factor in economic and social development of the state. Besides, journalists themselves are beset by gross ethical problems and unprofessional unions where 'brown envelopes' thrive and corruption proliferates. Such a climate would not permit professional reputation that would allow real freedom of speech and the press, even according to African morals. In Britain, the brown envelope method of bribing journalists would be held unethical by both the Institute of Public Relations and the National Union of Journalists.

The pre-eminence of extra-legal controls of the press was not strictly an African trait. Colonial civil servants originated the 'scandal'. Lord

Lugard, probably the greatest figure in Britain's colonial history and the architect of the policy of Indirect Rule, was very wary of news-papers. As governor of Nigeria in 1917, he framed a law which gave him power to appoint a censor of the press whenever an emergency arose or he thought was about to arise. Lugard wrote in his decree the power to seize the printing presses, confiscate any newspaper printed and impose a bond of 250 British pounds on publishers. His view of an African journalist was that of 'a mission-educated young man who lives in the village, interfering with native councils and acting as a correspondent for a mendacious native press'.

There has never been a Western-type press freedom in Africa and there will never be even with current journalism practice. Not many of Nigeria's journalists have heard about or read the Seditious Offence Ordinance of 1909, enacted by the British Colonial Governor, Egerton. This dealt with the issue of *bringing government into contempt*, causing disaffection among the ruled or bringing about feelings of enmity between different classes or *causing any official to disregard his duties or fail in his duties*. This Ordinance was codified under Sections 50 to 52 of the Nigerian Criminal Code and amended by the Adaptation of Laws (Miscellaneous Provisions) Order 1964.

This law continued to be enforced after the period of colonisation. As Chude Okonkwor of the University of Nigeria, in a recent scholarly article in *Journalism Quarterly*, Vol. 60, No. 1, (1983), in reference to this law, which would be described as the historical root of Decree No. 4, aptly remarked: 'The Seditious Act of 1909 was, in fact, used to repress expression of opinions deemed inimical to the status quo' and 'the Federal Republic of Nigeria not only inherited the colonial technique of maintaining social stability but also was *enthusiastic to use it at the slightest excuse*' and 'the Federal Supreme Court, invested with the powers of judicial review over legislative and administrative action, acquiesced in letting the laws remain immutable, thereby divesting Section 25 of the Constitution of all protective ability'. Nigeria has lived since independence with Decree No. 4. It is purely a matter of semantics, a rose by another name.

African politicians, without exception, see the function of the mass media as a significant factor working quite directly to create a new political order in a pluralistic and ethnic society. Close control of the press is seen as essential in the process of governing. The key to understanding press law and press freedom in post-independence Africa should be understood as the problems of nationals emerging from colonial influence.

One glaring characteristic of the media scene in the post-independence era is their linkage to state security. State security is defined to include all the necessary means at a government's disposal for securing or protecting the nation or state from danger of subjugation, either by an external power or through internal insurrection. African governments take it as their responsibility to regulate the distribution of information.

In nearly all countries of Africa, the most important newspapers are owned by the state or the political parties. Expatriate papers were bought up or taken over by the state immediately after independence otherwise they were tightly controlled, as was the case in Kenya and in Francophone and Lusophone countries.

Because of tight government intervention in the ownership and management of the press, newspapers in Africa do not grow. They rather diminish in most cases. Africa accounts for eight per cent of the world population and only one per cent of her newspaper circulation. Compared to the rest of the world, Africa is the least developed, including the matter of mass communication generation and use. This can be seen by studying the situation in the Caribbean and Asia.

Taking a most imaginative look, governments usually *seem* to be the only capable institutions that can own and operate newspapers successfully in Africa. This is because only government can possess the needed capital required to operate successfully a newspaper establishment. The government would make maximum use of the newspaper for directing development, especially in the area of literacy and development campaigns. Neither advertising revenue nor subscription incomes would deter the government from operating the newspapers which can be produced and distributed freely as a social service, as is the case in Botswana.

Government import controls and taxes would not hamper production as they would in the case of private ownership. The government can fuse the newspaper into the overall information apparatus to draw from press releases and national news agency sources. This would bring in some cost-effectiveness which would not be possible in the case of private ownership. There is wide-spread lack of purchasing power by readers, which could limit private ownership. In many African countries the price of subscription is 20 per cent higher than the average income, whereas in some Western countries it is less than one per cent. Nevertheless, the economic and psychological situation in a few nations like Nigeria is such that, unlike most African countries, privately-owned newspapers can co-exist and compete with government newspapers.

Despite these factors, the growth in total circulation of daily newspapers in selected African countries (Cameroon, Ethiopia, Ghana, Guinea, Ivory Coast, Kenya, Liberia, Nigeria, Senegal, Somalia, Sudan, Tanzania, Togo, Uganda and Zambia) has risen considerably from 751,150 copies in 1959 to 2,470,000 in 1980, an increase of 229 per cent.[4] This rise would indicate little progress, or even retardation, if compared with the trend outside Africa, or if compared on a country by country basis within the continent itself. It would probably reflect the trend in Nigeria, but hardly the picture in Togo or Uganda.

To serve 22.4 per cent of the earth's surface with a population of 410 million (by the 1975 census), and largely agricultural population living in villages and speaking about 2,500 different languages, the following are the currently circulating national newspapers and magazines of Africa:

Algeria	*An Nasr*, *El Moudijihad*
Angola	*A Journal de Angola*
Benin	*Ehuzu*, *L'Action Populaire*
Botswana	*Botswana Daily News*
Burkina Faso	*L'Observateur Carrefour Africaine*
Burundi	Unite et Revolution
Cameroon	*Cameroon Times*, *Cameroon Tribune*
Cape Verde Islands	*Voz di Povo*
Central African Republic	*Centrafrique Presse*
Chad	*Info-Tchad*
The Comoros	No newspaper
Congo	*Le Courrier d'Afrique*,
	Le Semaine Africaine
Djibouti	*Le Reveil de Djibouti*
Egypt	*Al-Ahram*, *Al-Akhbar*,
	Al-Gomhouriya, *Al-Misaa*,
	Egyptian Gazette, *Le Journal d'Egypte*,
	Le Progress Egyptien,
	L'Economiste Egyptien,
	Akhbar al-Yom

(Note: Egypt's recorded history dates back more than 6,000 years to the Pharaohs)

Equatorial Guinea	*Elabo*
Ethiopia	*Addis Zemen*, *Ethiopien Herald*
Gabon	*L'Union*
The Gambia	*The Gambian*, *The Sun*, *The Nation*
Ghana	*Ashanti Pioneer*, *Daily Graphics*,
	Ghanaian Times, *Sunday Mirror*,
	Christian Messenger

Guinea	*Horoya*
Guinea-Bissau	*No Pintcha*
Ivory Coast	*Fraternite Matin, Ivoire Dimanche*
Kenya	*Daily Nation, The Standard, Weekly Review, Kenyan Times, Taifa Weekly*
Lesotho	*Mochochonono*
Liberia	*Daily Liberian Star*
Libya	*Arraid, El Balag*
Madagascar	*Le Courier de Madagascar, Madagascar-Matin*
Malawi	*The Daily Times*
Mali	*L'Essor-la Voix du Peuple, Bulletin Quotidien*
Mauritania	*Le Peuple*
Mauritius	*Le Cernee, Le Dimanche, Le Mauricien, Mauritius Times, L'Express, Advance*
Morocco	*Al-Alan, Maroc Soir, Le Matin*
Mozambique	*Noticias, Tempo*
Namibia	*Allgemeine Zeitung, Windhoek Adviser, Windhoek Observer*
Niger	*La Sahel, Le Niger*
Nigeria	*Daily Times, Sunday Times, New Nigerian, Daily Sketch, Nigerian Standard, Daily Star, Nigerian Observer, Nigerian Herald, Nigerian Tribune, Sunday Sketch, Sunday Observer, Nigerian Tide, Lagos Weekend, Nigerian Chronicle, Evening Times, Sunday Star, Irohin Yoruba, Gaskiya Ta Fi Kwabo, Gboungboun, Punch, Sunday Punch, Vanguard, Newswatch, Sunday Sketch, Udoka, Nigerian Statesman, New Times, National Concord, Sunday Concord, Business Concord, Concord Weekly, Business Times, Financial Punch, Times International, Women's World, Soja, The President, The Guardian, The African Guardian, Drum, Spear Magazine, Development Outlook*
Reunion	*Le Journal de L'Ile de la Reunion*
Rwanda	*Hobe*

Sahrawi Republic	*SADR News*
São Tomé and Principe	*Revolucao*
Senegal	*Le Soleil, Afrique Nouvelle*
Seychelles	*Nation, Le Seychelles*
Sierra Leone	*Daily Mail, Sunday We Yone, Tablet*
South Africa	*The Argus, Beeld, Cape Times, The Daily News, Die Burger, Die Transvaler, Die Vaderland, Die Volksblad, East London Daily Despatch, Eastern Province Herald, The Evening Star, Hoofstad, Imuo Zabantasundu, The Natal Mercury, Pretoria News, Rand Daily Mail* (recently defunct), *The Star, Sunday Express, Sunday Times, Sunday Tribune, The Weekend Argus, The Sowetan, Sechaba Azania Combat*
Sudan	*El-Ayam, El-Sahafa, Sudanow*
Swaziland	*Times of Swaziland*
Tanzania	*Daily News, Ngurumo, Sunday News, Uhuru*
Togo	*Togo-Presse*
Tunisia	*L'Action, al-Amal, Assabah, Le Presse do Tunisie, Biladi, Dialogue*
Uganda	*Uganda Times*
Zaire	*Elima, Salongo, Zaire Afrique*
Zambia	*The Times of Zambia, Zambia Daily Mail, Sunday Times of Zambia, Weekend Mail*
Zimbabwe	*The Herald, The Chronicle, Sunday Mail, Sunday News*

The observation is that Africa is an expanding continent with a shrinking press. The enthusiasm for founding newspapers is present, but the frustration in operating them is formidable. So many newspapers die at birth and few struggle to survive.

MEDIA NEWS SOURCES IN THE INDUSTRIALISING WORLD

What sources do African newspapers depend on for gathering news? This question is critical in the face of accusations of media imperialism charged against foreign news sources.

Many governments of Africa, in their efforts to supervise and control the contents of their media, have founded their own national news agencies. The first such news agency was the Middle East News Agency (MENA), founded in Cairo in 1956. This was followed by the Ghana News Agency (GNA), founded by President Kwame Nkrumah in 1957 in the year of Ghana's independence.

According to Professor William Hachten, in his widely-read book, *Muffled Drums*, by 1956 there were more than 27 national news agencies and semi-official news services in operation throughout Africa. These included Camerounaise de Presse (ACAP), Agence Congolaise de Presse (ACP), Agence Dahomeene de Presse (ADP), Agence Gabonaise d'Information (AGI), Agence Guineene de Presse (AGP), Agence Ivoirenne de Presse (AIP), Agence Malgache de Presse (AMP), Agence de Presse Senegalaise (APS), Algerie Presse Service (APS), Agence de Presse Voltaique (APV), Agence Tchadienne de Press (ATP), Ethiopian National News Agency (ENNA), Kenya News Agency (KNA), Libyan News Agency (LNA), Maghreb Arabe Presse (MAP), Somali National News Agency (SNNA), Tunis-Afrique Press (TAP), Shihata of Tanzania and Zambia News Agency (ZANA).

Generally these so-called national news agencies are paper tigers in the face of the formidable international news agencies, such as Reuters, Associated Press, United Press International and Agence France Presse. Indeed the latter provided the technical and financial assistance for setting up the national news agencies in the Francophone countries. Its position as a major news broker has not been dislodged by the appearance of these weak government institutions.

Some national news agencies, particularly those of the Anglophone regions, have become relatively effective. In this class are GNA, KNA and MENA. The recently established News Agency of Nigeria (NAN), which began operation in 1978, is probably the most vigorous and viable of all the news agencies of Africa. According to its assistant editor-in-chief, 'NAN began to have the semblance of a modern news agency in 1979 when it operated with a skeletal network that linked only four state capitals with Lagos. The links it provided were the "one way" type and this served for both news gathering from and news distribution to all states'. Five years after this initial move, 'NAN offices in each of the 19 states of Nigeria and her new capital Abuja have a two-way communication link with one another and Lagos. This has made for speedier, wider and more reliable service.'

NAN has, at present, about 184 subscribers in the country comprising newspapers, radio stations, television stations, government institutions, educational institutions, commerical, financial and industrial houses, Nigerian cultural and information offices abroad and foreign diplomatic missions. This is not a modest achievement for an African national news agency.

The year 1982 saw the launching of the Pan-African News Agency (PANA) with its headquarters in Dakar, Senegal. The reason for this project was to achieve a long-standing dream of encouraging the exchange of news between African nations and with other nations, what has often been referred to as 'a south-south dialogue'. PANA has yet to earn the credibility of its existence. Its main problem is political and this hampers its independence. But there is a dire need to improve its manpower resources, professionalism and general operational efficiency. PANA is still Africa's only hope of replacing or curtailing the activities of the transnational news agencies.

There have been signs that African journalists and reporters are more concerned with vertical dissemination of information than providing horizontal forums for people to discuss vital issues of the day. There is also another complaint that news in Africa is heavily urban in content, whereas a majority of Africans live in the rural areas. If we consider media facilities as a national resource to be distributed, it is obvious that the rural areas are short-changed. In the case of newspapers, it is mainly through the initiative and encouragement of UNESCO that over 50 rural/community newspapers have been founded in 16 sub-Saharan African countries since 1971. Most of these newspapers are published in local languages, for the primary benefits of new literates in rural areas. Because of their limited circulation, printing costs and lack of advertising revenue, these worthy UNESCO experiments fold or experience instant problems as soon as UNESCO money dries up. Now think of 2,500 local languages against 50 rural newspapers. What a colossal information/communication gap!

The largest country in Asia, India, has the largest number of daily newspapers in Asia and ranks fourth in the world. The other major publishers, as we have already mentioned, are the United States, Britain, the Federal Republic of Germany and Japan, and we might add the Republic of China. By the end of 1952, there were already 330 dailies, 1,189 weeklies and 1,733 other periodicals in India. This further points out how dispossessed and deficient Africa is in media ownership, even when compared with a single Third World country outside its orbit.

It is estimated that there are now 1,173 dailies and 15,995 periodicals in India, according to the Report of the Press Registrar of India. Such phenomenal proliferation of the print media, and other attendant expansion in circulation, might not indeed be very significant in real terms when compared with shifts in India's literacy levels.

Another observation is that the marginal increase in print media circulation is almost zero when compared with the expansion rate in the broadcast sector. For instance, the number of licensed radio sets in India increased from 2,142,754 in 1960 to 20,674,113 in 1979, an expansion rate of 864.84 per cent. An unprecedented record growth of 26,609.38 per cent was observed in the number of licensed television sets during the period. The increase in absolute number was from 4,170 sets to 1,157,311 sets. India, it should be remembered, also has an enterprising film industry.

In the context of transitional societies such as those of the Third World, it has been observed that the media have a paralysing effect of creating 'psychological illiteracy' among media consumers who seek self-identification with the elite norms and high-brow culture always propagated by urban-based mass media. The continued reliance on imported and import-engineered news and programmes inevitably results in culture shock and conflicts. Even where indigenous attempts are made, there should be prudence and extreme carefulness.

It is observed, for instance, in Thailand that there is a struggle between traditional and foreign materials. Traditional entertainment in Thailand thrives on variety. Foreign entertainment, with its classical form of beginning, development and conclusion, is not appreciated in Thailand. Giving up the 'jelly fish' form of variety entertainment is the price Thailand has to pay for her media development. In India, indigenous film producers present two conflicting cultures without offering a resolution. Direct educational casting facilitated by the Indian SITE to the villages does not achieve much since it is done in one language, inside a multi-ethnic and pluralistic society. India continues to suffer the Third World's problem of urban-based mass media.

We might look at the African scenario by returning to NAN which carries news which is mainly from the national and state capitals. The vast countryside is shut off from the news flow. The imbalance in the news that the new information order seeks to redress is even more lopsided in the flow of domestic news.

Sylvanus Ekwelie, in an article in *Media Development* (Vol. XXXII, No. 1, 1985), suggested that Third World news gatherers can provide local angles to stories, do their own gate-keeping on Western wire-service despatches, delete offensive references and then interpret distant news for their own nationals by rewriting received features and news to match local needs. The most important Third World journalists' contribution would be, according to Ekwelie, the service they render as a link between the city and the country, thereby giving meaning to local and national policies, the weather, the fauna and flora as well as crop yields, receding water, social relations, capital projects, incidence of diseases, health care, tradition and the impact of these on economic development and social welfare. While these journalists, like leaders of the Third World, address the issue of global information imbalance, it is ironic that their cities and the countryside continue to live in different worlds within each national boundary.

Empirical evidence reveals that the African press carries more news about Africa than elsewhere in its international coverage, but most news reported has to do with urban areas and political actors. NAN uses more news from international news agencies based in the West than from socialist sources. There is a dearth of local language media, and even the few vernacular newspapers and specialised broadcasting programmes are urban-oriented. Only a negligible number of correspondents is stationed outside the urban capitals. Articles and features on women often treat mundane issues such as fashion, cookery, fertility, and hairstyling, which contribute very little towards the total integration or cultural emancipation of women.

There is little dialogue between African journalists and their Third World counter-parts, in comparison with their idealisation of Western media men. Western news agencies, radio broadcasts and Western elite newspapers very significantly dominate the orientation and content of the African media. Colonial linkages, BBC-mentality, semblances in media practices and practitioners' educational orientation make mass communication less effective, inappropriate and accountable for a never-changing colonial *status quo*.

Although this could be regarded as a world phenomenon, there is a greater tendency for Third World news agencies to concentrate on political/military and economic news. Iraqi News Agency, in 1978, for example, transmitted 75 per cent of such news items as a proportion of its total news budget. Qatar News Agency had 75 per cent of such news also. Saudi News Agency, Emirates News Agency, Kuwait News Agency respectively transmitted 67.6 per cent, 52 per cent and 47.2 per cent of such news. A study in 1979 on the coverage of foreign news in the Nigerian media revealed that such issues dominate the news media with such images as Nigeria's economic experience with Britain and her commitment to US-type presidential democracy[5]. Concentration of political bilateral and economic bilateral stories were found in the Turkish press by Phil Harris and his colleagues (see Unesco, *Flow of News in the Gulf*, Unesco: Paris, Order No. 3). AFP is the most important news source of the Turkish press. News coming from a variety of sources is, in most cases, a summary of news transmitted by the three big international agencies – AFP, AP and Reuters.

THE NEW INFORMATION AND COMMUNICATION ORDER (NICO)

The centre-periphery nature of information flow in the international system soon became a heated issue between the developing Third World, principally, and the industrialised Western World. UNESCO in 1978 appointed the International Commission for the Study of Communication Problems, under the distinguished chairmanship of an Irishman, Sean MacBride, a Nobel prize winner and Lenin Laureate. In its report titled *Many Voices One World*, the MacBride Commission, as it later became known, underscored the presence of uneven flow of information from the developed to the developing countries in these words:

'There is no doubt that communication resources are unequally distributed on a world scale. Some countries have a full capacity for collating information regarding their needs; many have little capacity to do so and this constitutes the major handicap in their development . . .'

Western apologists hold that the existing domination of the Western media institutions is a function of advanced technology, and that there is no hard incontrovertible evidence to justify claims of domination and imbalance. They hold that the 'shrill polemic' coming from the Third World on the subject has been unrealistic, while warnings about the rectification of the imbalance without scientific data shows there is little understanding of the problem.

Third World scientists and their supporters argue on the other hand that the problem is even larger than MacBride has identified and that the NICO is atheoretical in approach and could be described as 'mission impossible' because it lacks depth and comprehensiveness. The notion of NICO debate might succumb like the controversy of the new international economic order (NIEO), which was finally relegated to the purgatory of good intentions. Prophetic enough, NICO, because of the fever of American withdrawal from UNESCO, is no longer mentioned or referred to in UN-sponsored forums.

Western advocates attribute the supremacy of their media and the cultural invasion of particularly American media to the American slogan of 'free press' principles, her leadership in media technology, her co-operation with Britain and the use of the English language which has colonial and technical universality. The concept of free press and free flow of information is indeed designed to give America global, military and economic influence. A strategic American outpost for the promotion of the concept of free flow is the United States Information Agency (USIA). This agency distributes tape programmes and scripts to about 5,000 stations throughout the world. These materials are broadcast for 15,000 hours a week. USIA also operates 59 transmitters overseas. Of special interest to the Third World is the fact that USIA prepares regular television series programmes for Nigeria, Thailand, Japan and all of Latin America and that VOA has chartered 'fan clubs' (comprising young people between 18 and 30 years of age) in Nigeria.

Similarly, the British Central Office of Information issues press, radio and television material, including material of commercial export value, world-wide. Likewise, the External Services of the BBC and its World Service broadcast internationally in many languages, and some programmes are technical ones of export interest to commercial suppliers of information. These programmes are often monitored by overseas newspapers. The COI and BBC services provide major public relations outlets for British firms.

America's military interest in the control of communication globally can be detected by her attitude at the World Administrative Radio Conference (WARC). The radio spectrum is a multidimensional resource with international characteristics. Radio frequencies are, in certain ways, as much of a shared global resource as the oceans and sea beds. Under current United States law, at least the spectrum is what the economist would call 'a common property resource': being the property of no one user. Like the air mantle or migratory fish, it becomes the common property of all.

But the United States is opposed to *a priori* spectrum planning abroad. This appears to derive from ethnocentric or implied concerns over economic distortions, technological retardation and military security. The US is against preplanned allocation that holds open shortwave frequencies for latecomer access. This in her view would impair her military communication flexibility. Expanded or rigid band width requirements for television could further reduce her access to VHF and UHF military mobile channels with adverse effect on military requirements. Such potential constraints, she argues, are indeed serious because extra channels are needed to ensure instantaneous contact with far-flung security forces in the event that primary short wave frequencies are jammed or destroyed.

The US also believes that *a priori* reservation of space frequencies and orbital slots will impede optimal development and use of satellites for civilian, as well as for military purposes – navigation assistance, direct broadcasting, data processing, radio astronomy, space research, the monitoring of weather, crop and forest conditions, ocean resources, environmental quality and other forms of remote sensing.

Third World countries are generally the late comers to spectrum allocation. A great majority of these disadvantaged countries are from Africa. They are late to acquire the technologies needed for the exploitation of the common resource of the radio spectrum. Legitimately, as sovereign nations, they would not acquiesce to the high technology nations which are endowed with the capital and know-how for exploiting the spectrum. Increasingly, the latecomers demand their own share, even privileged access (to the lower, congested, but less costly-to-use spectral regions already occupied by advanced nations) to compensate for their long-standing deprivation.

The contrasting approaches to global spectrum management of developing and developed countries were nowhere more vivid than during the deliberations of the WARC in 1979, over specialised planning conferences for geostationary orbit and short wave frequencies and preferential access to unused short wave frequency fixed assignments to Third World applicants. We must underline the basic fact that, in the matter of communications and information, and in spite of the 'free-flow' slogan, the US is always guided by its military, political and economic interests on the globe. Once these interests are at stake the US becomes recalcitrant, sometimes reactionary, and compromises its so called principle of libertarianism.

Through the vigorous promotional activites of commercial attachés, the US private sector floods the Third World with programmes, entertainment and commercials. Foremost among them are the American Broadcasting Company (ABC), Radio Corporation of America (RCA), Columbia Broadcasting System (CBS), and Harris Corporation. The ABC-TV network, Worldvision, reaches 23 million television homes all over the world. Of 500 international companies dealing in broadcast equipment and services mainly exported to Third World countries (*World Broadcast News*, July – August, 1984), 254 or a little over 50 per cent of them are companies based in the USA.

Even for advanced nations, the US media influence is heavily felt. No wonder Jeremy Tunstall, the British media sociologist, has aptly remarked that the media are American. Since more than half of the Canadian population is within the service range of radio and television stations of the US, even considering the more limited range of television stations, there is, of course, ready access for those Canadians.

With the amount of money the US networks have to produce or purchase programmes, with the American skills in light entertainment so highly developed in broadcasting and other media, with the engines of publicity promoting programmes, actors, comedians, pop musicians

and other performers, and with such promotion associated with the sale
of products that are distributed on both sides of the border, there is no
wonder that the average Canadian listener or viewer is more conscious
of American programme series and is therefore a psychological
American. Such a case can be made of American media influence in the
Caribbean too.

In Nigeria, the Voice of America (VOA) fan clubs are being enthu-
siastically formed by youth and actively promoted and chartered by the
USIA. Is it not amazing that the Lagos Chapter of the VOA fan club,
the most vigorous of them all, has as one of its objectives '. . . to
promote and defend the VOA at any time, anywhere, any place'?

It should therefore be agreed upon that the free flow of information
which has been historically pushed out from America is used primarily
for political, military and economic reasons in the Third World.

The push, by the US, for 'free flow of information' in Third World
countries led to global interests among other nations of the industrial
world in assisting the new emerging nations to develop their
communications infrastructure. Most external assistance was co-
ordinated by UNESCO in the form of experimental programmes and
projects. In Africa the best known experiments are the rural radio
forums such as that in Ghana in 1962 and Zambia in the '70s.

Togo also benefited from UNESCO assistance in rural broadcasting
between 1964 and 1970. This was for an educational service for the rural
areas. Senegal, with the help of UNESCO, organised a special
department for educational radio and rural sociology. Listening clubs
were established in key places in the countryside. UNESCO also
supported a pilot project in Upper Volta in the 1970's, where radio was
used as a tool to support women's rights to equality in education. In
1965 the local language, Wolof, became an important vehicle of
broadcasting in Senegal, when television viewing clubs were established
through the assistance of UNESCO to train illiterates and jobless
women. The World Bank, through UNESCO, in the late '60s, assisted
Niger in schools programmes using television. The success of this
experiment prompted Ivory Coast to engage in a comparative
experiment of the same type to achieve the following objectives:

1 To rectify the failure of the educational system to contribute
effectively to development.

2 To redress rural-urban imbalances in education.

3 To correct biases against the rural populace.

4 To introduce new methods of teaching.

5 To provide children with materials pertinent to their own needs
and society and thus engineer a cultural heritage.

Other so-called 'bilateral' assistance to Africa in the area of communication would also include that by USAID and USIA. Assistance given by Studio-Echo de l'Office de Cooperation Radiophonique (OCORA), Berlin Institute for Mass Communication in Developing Countries, Union of Czechoslovak Journalists, and International Organisation of Journalists (IOJ) is often of help to Africa in communication development.

Most often this assistance is suspect, because of its government to government nature. Certainly, the granting government has goals and gains in mind for itself in these so-called bilateral agreements in which Africa, in its weakness, gives cultural subservience in exchange. Aids from the East emphasise socialist philosophies, while those from the West recommend the capitalist viewpoints and approaches, none of which are based on African cultural indigenous systems. For example, in a recent (January 1985) World Bank solicitation for special assistance to aid Africa's food crises and economic recovery, Britain insisted that its aids be tied to the purchase of British goods. The US reincarnated the Reagan preference for bilateral rather than multilateral assistance which makes the US reluctant to give money or aid to countries opposed to its foreign policies. We have seen this with the so called Caribbean Basin initiative too.

A few Western countries are open in their aid policies. Canada, through its International Development Agency (CIDA) awaits an invitation from a host country in specific ways of assistance to communication, before initiating a programme or project. CIDA has aided Nigeria, Niger and Kenya in this way. The German government has also assisted 17 African countries. In these cases, non-governmental, non-profit organisations have contributed help. Such foundations have been mindful of promoting any specific political viewpoint.

The British Broadcasting Corporation (BBC) has been the most influential in broadcasting development in British colonial territories of Africa. The BBC has contributed more to short-term training of Africans than any other foreign organisation, but not without 'professional overkill' which has rendered some of its training counterproductive. By 1972 over 2,000 African broadcasters had gone to London under BBC sponsorship 'for training and experience'. The Thomson Foundation Television College in Glasgow, Scotland, trained well over 200 African television producers, and engineers in the 1970s and is assisting, today, the development of television centres, such as Nigeria's Television College, Jos, Nigeria.

Despite all these aids to uncritical media and communication development in the Third World since the 1960s, and regardless of the huge social and financial costs, what we are witnessing now is an assessment of damages to development. We now speak of revolution, of rising frustration, rather than of rising expectation. We speak of debt-ridden instead of profit-endowed nations. It seems that economic retardation in these countries has been a result of the process of communication itself: that vertical, one-way, non-diversified dissemination of the message which once seemed unavoidable but against whose deadly consequence we must now contend.

Rather than promoting, with heavy national expenditure, the slow construction of terrestrial national broadcasting networks which, step by step, will cover the national territories only by the 1990s, by which time satellites will be available, would it not be better to apply the same effort to the spread of low-pressure local stations, less expensive and not necessarily linked to each other?

This is essentially the reason why the closure, in 1984, of the so-called 'mushroom radio stations' in Nigeria should be condemned. Such stations are capable of reestablishing the horizontal format of communications, linking individuals and families of a small geographical area.

Would frequency modulation really be an unnecessary luxury? Would it not be possible to encourage the manufacture of cheap standardised FM receivers for the poor of the Third World? Nigeria is currently spending about US $67 million on telecommunications in a single state of the 19 states that make up the federal republic. It has reaped no real dividends, so far, in terms of economic development from this prohibitive expense.

UNESCO's communication projects in Africa can be grouped as follows:

1 radio and television equipment assistance and manpower training;
2 news agency development;
3 rural communication (including rural press) development.

The African Council on Communication Education (ACCE) is a virile continental organisation that unites professionals, academics and trainers in the field of communication in Africa. The ACCE benefits from UNESCO funding. Its Institute for Communication Development and Research in Nairobi co-ordinates several inter-institutional activities in communication, including the operation of a documentation centre.

We must agree that the mass media provide much of the material which members of one nation use to form the images of other nations. This is what is called a stereotype. The stereotype of the African among Europeans is that of a poor, famished, bush-bound, sickly-looking person. The Third World leader is always portrayed as a corrupt blood-thirsty demagogue.

The images of mass communication represent those spheres of human society where emotions tend to run high, attitudes are often forcefully expressed and ideology is seldom absent. The nature and quality of the media play a part in the quality of our lives. To say that media issues are value-laden is to understate. The media are saturated with social values of every conceivable kind. No two media from different societies can be the same. Any attempt to force such a situation must result in social conflict. The media must represent and reflect the society in which they operate.

This is true in Britain, as already stated, where the national newspapers represent a breakdown of the social grades A, B, C¹, C², D and E. For instance, the *Times* and *Financial Times* represent Grade A, the *Sun* and *Mirror,* the more numerous and less intellectual Grades C², D and E. In developing countries, similar readerships are likely to follow the spread of education and literacy. At present, newspapers such as those published in Nigeria have broad readerships composed of those who can read and afford to buy.

An argument for the type of journalism suitable for the industrialising world has been put forward by critical scholars. Most agree on what is now called 'development journalism'. This is based on the premise that economic development is essential to assure the well-being of a society and the sovereignty of the state. Effective communication to all sectors of society, particularly the rural sector, is therefore a principal instrument of economic development. Only the government, an effective, responsible government, can perform this function; therefore the government invariably must control the mass media in the name of socio-economic development.

One is hesitant to advocate a complete take over of the media by government in pluralistic heterogenous Third World countries, because of imbedded, very delicate ethnic balances existing in such societies, but the impact of government must be felt and it cannot be over-stated that mass media must come to terms with their environments, simply because the media serve the society. Aping the foreign ideals of a distant medium not only results in social conflict and economic deterioration but also advances cultural imperialism, brings about increased urban heterogeneity, decreased interest in cultural and community life and other forms of frustration and disorientation.

The challenge facing Third World countries will always remain how to use communication to foster cultural development. The big media of the West are not entirely without function, especially when applied skilfuly and within the cultural context. There is evidence that some television stations are becoming vehicles in cultural development. The Nigerian Television Authority (NTA), in Ibadan in Nigeria, according to the findings of Lucas Ojo in an M.A Thesis (1985) for the University of Ibadan, 'has contributed immensely to the revival of Nigerian culture which has been under siege, in response to Nigeria's import-orientation,' by foreign culture. Local programmes on NTA, Ibadan, now account for 86 per cent of the broadcasts. There is a station policy not to broadcast 'Westerns' which previously dominated the screens. Television programmes in Nigeria are reflecting African scenes as producers now 'go to the villages, sometimes to the thick forests to record programmes'.

In the same country, the Kano State Agency for Mass Education, in pursuing its objective for mass literacy in Kano State, is using a successful multi-media approach which includes the broadcast media (newspapers, magazines, posters and books). These media are used for mobilisation, enlightenment, motivation and instruction. After all, it might be said that not all the so-called foreign media or media techniques have cultural bias. Some have indeed contributed to social, economic and educational progress in Third World countries. Yet the point remains that the threat of cultural imperialism by mass communication is real and challenging.

References

1 Solomon, Richard Jay, *World Communications Facts*, Philadelphia: The Annenberg School of Communications, University of Pennsylvania, prepared for the International Conference on World Communications: Decisions for the '80's hosted by The Annenberg School of Communications, 1980.
2 Adegbola, Adeolu, 'Concepts of Development: Trends in Africa', paper presented to the 4th Biennal Conference of the African Council on Communication Education (ACCE) on the theme 'Communication Strategies for Rural Development in Africa: The Challenge of the '80's.' November 11–17, Lome, Togo, 1984.
3 Merrill, John C. and Fisher, Harold A., *The World's Great Dailies*, Hastings House Publishers, New York, 1980.
4 Mytonn, Graham, *Mass Communication in Africa*, Edward Arnold Ltd, London, 1983.
5 Ugboajah, Frank Okwu, 'Foreign News Coverage in Nigerian Media', George Gerbner and Marsha Siefert (eds), *World Communications*, Longman, New York, 1984.

Index

WITHDRAWN
from
STIRLING UNIVERSITY LIBRARY